Walker Percy, Philosopher

Leslie Marsh
Editor

Walker Percy, Philosopher

palgrave
macmillan

Editor
Leslie Marsh
International Academy of Pathology
The University of British Columbia Hospital
Vancouver, BC, Canada

Chapter 7, Section Two, "Peirce and Modern Semiotic," by Walker Percy, is printed with permission of McIntosh & Otis, Inc. Copyright © 2018 by Mary Pratt Lobdell and Ann Percy Moores.

ISBN 978-3-319-77967-6   ISBN 978-3-319-77968-3   (eBook)
https://doi.org/10.1007/978-3-319-77968-3

Library of Congress Control Number: 2018945532

Cover painting: Walker Percy by George Rodrigue (1982). Courtesy of the George Rodrigue Foundation of the Arts.

Printed on acid-free paper

This Palgrave Macmillan imprint is published by the registered company Springer Nature Switzerland AG
The registered company address is: Gewerbestrasse 11, 6330 Cham, Switzerland

For
Dave, Charlie, and Doug

Courtesy of Christopher R. Harris, known as "Walker Percy's photographer" (1982)

Foreword

Percy: The Wondering Physician-Philosopher

A woman lies in a coma, having been admitted to the intensive care unit following a beating by her lead-pipe-wielding boyfriend. She is alive, but her neurologic prognosis is uncertain. The chaplain assigned to the case hovers outside her door, afraid to enter. A man of peace, he anticipates that the moment he steps inside he will be engulfed in the family's rage. Their loved one bruised, swollen, and unconscious, they will want nothing more than vengeance.

Finally, after reciting a prayer, the chaplain takes the plunge. Inside, the family is clustered around the bed. As soon as he introduces himself, the victim's brother approaches him, takes him aside, and whispers a request that he offer a prayer. To the chaplain's surprise, however, the prayer he has in mind is not for the perpetrator to be brought to justice. Instead he asks the chaplain to lead the family in a prayer of forgiveness.

Reactions to such stories differ. Some respond with disbelief that anyone clustered around the bed of a battered loved one could possibly seek mercy for the wrongdoer. Others express a sense of indignation, seeing in forgiveness a failure to respect and protect the interests of a vulnerable person. Still others, and I suspect Walker Percy might have been counted among them, respond to such accounts with a sense of wonder.

Wonder at what? Wonder at the capacity of human beings, at least on rare occasions, to rise above base expectations, to put the needs of others ahead of narrow self-interest, and to respond to fear and anger not with amplification but in a spirit of compassion. While no walk of life enjoys a monopoly on the opportunity to witness unpredictable but ultimately laudable responses, those who practice medicine are presented with more than our share.

The opportunity to witness humanity up close and personal makes Percy's turn away from the practice of medicine to a philosophical calling all the more puzzling. Occasioned at least proximately when he contracted tuberculosis while working as an intern at New York's Bellevue Hospital, Percy's long convalescence provided him with an opportunity to read great works of philosophical literature by Kierkegaard and Dostoyevsky. He would never complete his medical training.

As Leslie Marsh indicates, Percy left behind pathology and its essential questions, "What is the patient's disease?" and "What did the patient die of?" Through his reading and reflection, he arrived at a different set of questions—namely, "Is this person really living?" and if not, "What would it take to bring this person to life?" Despite robust vital signs and productive daily agenda, a human being can be dead inside.

In the popular mind, apocalypse implies the end of everything, but it its original meaning, it refers less to mass destruction than to massive revelation. Brian Smith reminds us that Percy was attracted to destruction precisely because it reveals to us more clearly what is truly at stake. It is only in confronting the ineluctability of our own mortality and the fragility of the human species that we begin truly to grasp all we have to live for.

Why did Percy turn toward philosophy? Perhaps he feared that he might transmit his disease to his patients. Perhaps his illness had taken too great a toll for him to contemplate the rigors of full-time medical practice. Or perhaps his illness and the reading it made possible opened his eyes to new forms of diagnosis and therapy curiously missing from the profession of medicine—above all, a new appreciation for the power of wonder.

In medicine, wonder is typically overlooked, and when it does attract notice, it is often viewed with suspicion. Whether at the laboratory bench or the patient's bedside, medicine's emphasis is on collecting data and formulating and testing hypotheses. Medical students are taught that every good question has an answer. Their mission is to conduct inquiries that lead to conclusions about what ails the patient and take steps to remedy the situation.

The underlying paradigm is this: the ailment lies among the organ systems, organs, tissues, cells, and/or biomolecules of the patient. Afflictions are above all biological phenomena, and if the physician can ask the appropriate questions, perform the appropriate physical examination maneuvers, and collect the appropriate laboratory and imaging data, a definitive diagnosis can be achieved, which will in turn suggest an appropriate course of therapy.

Wonder may have a role to play, but only in a utilitarian sense. As Bacon might have said, the pursuit of wisdom may begin in wonder, but once the investigation has begun, wonder should fade into the background, to be replaced by the elucidation of certain knowledge. As a physician matures, wonder should progressively give way to the appetite for conquering nature and relieving man's estate. Wonder may get things rolling, but no one should aim to sink the ball in wonder's pocket.

When it comes to diagnosing and treating diseases, such an approach can prove highly effective, and we owe many of the triumphs of medicine over the last few centuries to precisely such marching orders. But what works well in the domain of disease does not necessarily suffice in the realm of suffering humanity. When Percy reached Osler's fork in the road—does the disease have a patient or the patient a disease?—he opted for the latter path.

If physicians are not careful, we can become, as Nathan Carson puts it, jaded. What we encounter habitually ceases to astonish us, leading us down David Hume's path in supposing that only extraordinarily rare events could count as miracles. Yet the truly wondrous often lies in the mundane—such seemingly everyday events as birth, death, reconciliation, and forgiveness. Our task is less to venture into uncharted territory than to see, as Patrick Connelly suggests, the place we have inhabited all along.

The scientific method as espoused by the likes of Bacon and Descartes sought to figure things out in terms of universal laws. As applied to medicine, every case represents by definition a particular instance of a universal law—the pathophysiology of a particular disease process. For example, every patient suffering from pulmonary thromboembolism has evidence of blood clots in the branches of the pulmonary arterial system.

Kenneth Ketner points to the danger in a science that recognizes as fish only what it happens to catch in its net. Against the ever-present temptation to define reality in terms of our tools, Percy calls us to recognize the inherent limitations of our own perceptual and cognitive apparatus. When a physician and a patient encounter one another, something far richer and more significant than what is described in medical textbooks is inevitably taking place.

In illuminating the universal, the scientific lens also obscures the particular, providing the observer with an ever more reductive view of the individual. This obscuration of humanity works in two directions—

obscuring not only the humanity of the patient, but that of the physician, as well. Each case of a particular disease process may share features, but suffering as experienced by each patient is always distinctive, and it is in these very differences that we must look to find the human person.

The Percy who found abstraction from the individual so troubling in the middle of the twentieth century would find today's situation truly desperate. The evaluation of medical students relies more than ever on standardized tests that completely overlook their distinctive interests and life experiences, the training of residents is far more deeply grounded in impersonal goals and objectives, and practicing physicians are pressured to work faster and evaluated by conformity to guidelines.

In other words, to know the patient and know oneself as a physician have become even more difficult than they were in the day when Percy turned away from the practice of medicine. The path of science, as Percy came to see it, leads not toward self-discovery and mutual recognition, but toward an alienation from self and humanity. Is it any wonder that, at the very moment when biomedical science has progressed furthest, physicians are suffering an epidemic of burnout?

As Stephen Utz and Carolyn Culbertson remind us, Percy, following Peirce, was acutely aware of both the limitations of language and the powerful role that language plays in shaping our perceptions, ideas, and feelings. And this is precisely why wonder is so important. To experience wonder is to encounter something unexpected, unfamiliar, and perhaps even inexplicable. Our very lack of words enables us to assume the role of witnesses, simply beholding what is before us.

Percy did not advocate an abandonment of science, but he did see the need for another way of knowing, or at least another means of investigation—one that recognized the possibility of a different kind of truth. There are some insights that cannot be captured in terms of sensory data and therefore prove less immediately apparent. They cannot be weighed or measured or even captured in words. They are best likened to glimpses, perhaps intimations.

To pursue such truths is not to abandon rationality but to recognize the true subtlety and complexity of the reality we hope to recognize. To apprehend them we need to reset our tuners to a different frequency, one that resembles not a statistic but a narrative. When it comes to such truths, we must set aside our microscopes and CT scanners and behold through a quite different approach to exploration and discovery.

To be opened to wonder, we need what Christopher Yates, following Percy, calls a "reentry." The world turns out to be richer and more beautiful than any purely scientific account would suggest, and only by ceasing our rationalization can it wend its way into our consciousness. In effect, we need to develop a new set of expectations focused less on reasoning and more on beholding something that we cannot create for ourselves.

In MG, Binx loves his crippled half-brother Lonnie, perhaps the sickest character in the entire narrative. He does not see the boy as someone he can make use of. Instead he sees him as someone who has, through his suffering, beheld something that Binx himself senses to be most real and significant. Lonnie knows he will die and accepts his death, even to the point of wishing to die for those he loves. In so doing, he helps Binx to see what it means to live for others.

There is wonder in this. In a sense, Lonnie is useless. But in another sense, Lonnie's orbit is closer to the real meaning of human life than any other character in the book. Through Lonnie, the inconsequentiality of success and all its trappings become most apparent to Binx. He sees that the utility of a thing is not the measure of its significance, but that, as Aristotle said, the most important things in life are useless—good for no other purpose beyond themselves.

Stacey Ake points to the possibility that an awareness of the separate existence of all that is around us might awaken a sense of responsibility for it. Lonnie's hold on existence is weak, but this very weakness enables him to intuit things that entirely escape the hale and hearty, including the realization that real life is not possible so long as we think only of ourselves. It is through the crippled boy who will never reach maturity that Binx, the war veteran and playboy, sees what it really means to be a man.

Is Percy warning us that philosophical enlightenment is incompatible with the practice of medicine? I think not. Instead he is inviting us to see that, when it comes to becoming a more humane doctor and leading a more fully humane life in medicine, it is not enough to be merely a physician. As Rhonda McDonnell and Scott Cunningham remind us, we must also be anthropologists. With our eyes opened, we see not just biological specimens but human beings. But first, we must open ourselves to wonder.

Consider another tale, full of its own kind of wonder. A nurse in an assisted living facility is undergoing her semi-annual review, in the course of which her supervisor has accompanied her on her daily rounds. At the end of the day, the two meet to review her performance. To the nurse's surprise, she receives a formal reprimand. The reason the supervisor gives is this: "You are spending too much of your time looking at the patient, when you should be entering data into the electronic medical record."

This tale reminds us that medicine can serve at least two different masters, one focused on the disease, its management, and the collection of revenue, and the other focused on the patient and the patient's fears and joys. The former may be the more sophisticated and lucrative path, but from Percy's point of view it is also, humanly speaking, the path to perdition. Only by keeping our minds and hearts open can we hope to behold the truly wondrous.

Karey Perkins points to the essential role of community in solving the existential problem. When students applying to medical school write their personal statements, they typically think in terms of their own life story, writing in the first-person singular. Yet to find real meaning in medicine, they must learn to practice and live in the first-person plural, in community, and come to see their own stories as parts of still larger narrative wholes.

Alone, human beings long for companionship, friendship, and community. Hearts ache for the chance to serve some purpose beyond self, one that might reveal an underlying unity. Percy is not merely a physician or a semiotician. He is also a Christian. For him, perhaps it is finally in the table fellowship of bread and wine that authentic communion becomes possible, making possible a different kind of wholeness and opening up a wondrous community of divinely sanctioned love.

Indianapolis, IN, USA   Richard Gunderman

ACKNOWLEDGMENTS

I'm most grateful to Rod Dreher and his family, James Fox-Smith, Nancy Vinci, Julie and Mitch Brashier, Missy Couhig, Lisa Dobson Noland, Derek Gilbert, Oliver Hartner, the late Peter Augustine Lawler, Ralph Wood, Mary Keith Sentell, Lenore Ealy, Helen and Bill Campbell, Griffin Campbell, Adam Whatley, Jeanne and Ron Griggs and many others associated with that most congenial of conferences—the annual Walker Percy Weekend—and for the kind hospitality of the town of St. Francisville. Others who have been immensely generous with their support include Todd Breyfogle, Ben Alexander, Rhoda Faust, Chris Harris, Henry Mills (The Walker Percy Project), Jacques Rodrigue and Wayne Fernandez (George Rodrigue Foundation of the Arts), Mary Pratt Percy Lobdell, Ann Percy Moores, Win Riley, and Margaret Lovecraft. Thanks also to Shira Hoffman and Amelia Appel (McIntosh & Otis, Inc.). I'm most indebted to the encouragement and support from the Palgrave team— Laura Pace, Philip Getz, Amy Invernizzi and most especially Arun Prakash, project manager extraordinaire, for his patience and support. Last, but not least, my profound thanks to Elizabeth Corey who first (and unintentionally) turned me onto Walker Percy—and to Shannon Selin, for all else.

Contents

NOTES ON CONTRIBUTORS

Stacey E. Ake is Co-Director of the Certificate Program in Medical Humanities and Associate Teaching Professor of Philosophy in the Department of English and Philosophy at Drexel University.

Nathan P. Carson is Assistant Professor of Philosophy at Fresno Pacific University.

Patrick L. Connelly is Associate Professor of History and Department Chair of the History and Political Science Department at Mississippi College.

Carolyn Culbertson is Assistant Professor in the Department of Communication and Philosophy at Florida Gulf Coast University.

Scott R. Cunningham is Assistant Director for Operations at the Institute for Studies in Pragmaticism at Texas Tech University.

Richard Gunderman is Chancellor's Professor of Radiology, Pediatrics, Medical Education, Philosophy, Liberal Arts, Philanthropy, and Medical Humanities and Health Studies at Indiana University, where he also serves as the John A. Campbell Professor of Radiology.

Kenneth Laine Ketner is Founding Director of the Institute for Studies in Pragmaticism, Paul Whitfield Horn Professor within the Institute, and is Charles Sanders Peirce Interdisciplinary Professor in the Perry School of Nursing in Texas Tech University Health Sciences Center.

Leslie Marsh is Senior Researcher with the International Academy of Pathology at The University of British Columbia Medical School.

Rhonda R. McDonnell is Professor of English at Scottsdale Community College and is also a member of the Institute for Studies in Pragmaticism at Texas Tech University.

Karey Perkins Professor in the English Faculty at the University of South Carolina Beaufort and a member of the Institute for Studies in Pragmaticism at Texas Tech University.

Brian A. Smith is Managing Editor of *Law & Liberty* at the Liberty Fund, Inc.

Stephen Utz is Roger Sherman Professor of Law at the University of Connecticut School of Law.

Christopher Yates is Assistant Professor of Philosophy, Aesthetics, and Art Theory at the Institute for Doctoral Studies in the Visual Arts.

Abbreviations

CWP	*Conversations with Walker Percy*
L	*Lancelot*
LC	*Lost in the Cosmos*
LG	*The Last Gentleman*
LR	*Love in the Ruins*
MB	*The Message in the Bottle*
MCWP	*More Conversations with Walker Percy*
MG	*The Moviegoer*
SC	*The Second Coming*
SSL	*Signposts in a Strange Land*
TS	*The Thanatos Syndrome*

CHAPTER 1

Introduction: Philosopher of Precision and Soul

Leslie Marsh

That Percy falls within a long line of eminent physician-novelists is unremarkable; like Percy some authors *did* actually complete their medical studies (Chekhov, Bulgakov, Conan Doyle, Wendell Holmes, Sr., Robin Cook, Michael Crichton, William Carlos Williams, Khaled Hosseini, W. Somerset Maugham, Rabelais, Namwal El Saadawi, Schiller, Schnitzler, and Abraham Verghese) while others did not (Oliver Goldsmith, John Keats, and Gertrude Stein). Though Percy was a philosophical autodidact, he was first and foremost a fully-fledged philosopher whose longest-standing and deepest concerns congealed around the relationship between science and the understanding of man's place in the world and the cosmos, as a sentient being most distinctively mediated by language. Thus, the phrase "precision and soul" of the title (which I borrow from Robert Musil 1995), broadly connotes the idea of scientific method and the study of man *qua* man, the former a tradition of theorizing that for Percy has shed little or no light on the latter.

L. Marsh (✉)
International Academy of Pathology, Faculty of Medicine,
The University of British Columbia Hospital, Vancouver, BC, Canada
e-mail: leslie.marsh@ubc.ca

© The Author(s) 2018
L. Marsh (ed.), *Walker Percy, Philosopher*,
https://doi.org/10.1007/978-3-319-77968-3_1

1

A Biographical Sketch

One of three brothers, Walker Percy (1916–1990) was born into a most distinguished family, with ancestry going back to the Norman William de Percy who arrived in England soon after the Norman Conquest of 1066. Percy's father, Leroy Pratt Percy, was an attorney and general counsel for a major American steel manufacturer headquartered in Birmingham, AL. Conscious of their civic status, the family adhered to the notion of "noblesse oblige," a High Toryism that had its roots in the English aristocracy. Leroy, who suffered from what we'd term these days as manic depression or bipolar disorder (somewhat of a family trait), committed suicide aged 40; Walker who'd have been 13 was profoundly marked by this event his whole life. (There has been some speculation that Walker's mother might have been a suicidee as well, but nothing definitive has been established—she died in a car crash when Walker was 15). Either way, suicide seeped into the deepest recesses of Walker's mind, a bête noire that was to be the source of a great deal of ongoing personal consternation but equally it was the philosophical seed that germinated into his becoming a philosopher, suicide being a prominent theme in the work of philosophical-novelists Albert Camus and Jean-Paul Sartre.

Walker and his two younger brothers were subsequently adopted by Leroy's first cousin, William Alexander Percy. William (or uncle Will) was an extraordinarily cultivated, cultured, bohemian, and kind man, and yet, was someone who was equally worldly, having as a soldier witnessed first-hand the gruesomeness of the First World War earning the *Croix de Guerre*. William's learnedness had a profound influence on Walker, who in turn displayed a voracious rabbinical-like thirst for study across the sciences and the humanities. Percy attended medical school at Columbia, specializing in pathology. It has been said that he chose pathology on the grounds that he preferred not to have contact with patients (Majeres 2002). As my colleague Professor David Hardwick himself a distinguished pathologist often jokingly says, "My patients don't complain." Another interest of Walker's was psychiatry, Percy submitting himself to regular analysis while at Columbia in an attempt to quash the demons that were to continue to plague him all his life. Soon after Walker's graduation, his beloved uncle Will died.

While fulfilling his residency in pathology at Bellevue Hospital, Walker contracted tuberculosis. While in convalescence and with much time on his hands to read, the realization dawned upon him that he was more interested in philosophy than in medicine. Now married, Walker and his wife Bunt converted to Catholicism and settled down in the undistinguished locale of Covington well away from the hubbub of—but still within easy reach of—New Orleans, where he lived for the rest of his life. As his father before him, Walker was very civic-minded and was engaged in the life of his adopted town. (Interestingly enough, Walker testified as an expert witness in the US District Court, concluding that the Confederate flag by and large *did* connote a racist outlook. The view he took predated the current controversies by half a century!) After having a few philosophical papers published in some leading journals of the time (and still are), it became apparent to Walker that not only were his career prospects slim, but that his desire to become a philosophical novelist better suited his temperament. By 1961, Walker had become a reasonably well-known novelist if only because of MG (1961) getting a boost by, as a late outsider, winning the National Book Award. His follow-up LG (1966) was a finalist as was his next work LR (1971). His next three novels L (1977), SC (1980), and his last, TS (1987), didn't seem to garner the attention and support of the literati establishment that the first three did—perhaps by then they resented his mordant criticism of their worldview and had deemed his concerns and themes, at best unfashionable, and perhaps at worst, even reactionary. All attempts to have MG adapted as a cinematic feature have floundered—and perhaps that's not such a bad thing given Hollywood's ham-fisted way of going about things. There was even talk until quite recently of the philosophically literate filmmaker Wim Wenders and his collaborator novelist Peter Handke adapting *The Second Coming*. This too came to nothing.

THE PHILOSOPHER AS NOVELIST

I'm inclined to view Percy as a philosophical novelist much in the tradition of (in no particular order) John Henry Newman (*Loss and Gain*), Walter Pater (*Marius the Epicurean*), Robert Musil (*The Man Without Qualities*), Thomas Mann (*The Magic Mountain*), Yukio Mishima (*The Sailor Who Fell from Grace with the Sea*), and Hermann Broch (*The Sleepwalkers*), and as a philosopher-essayist, Percy has much in common with Miguel de Unamuno (*Tragic Sense of Life*).

For Percy, the serious writer, by definition, must be open to the "mystery of his art" and should not be shoehorned into any one world of ideas, weighed down by some thesis or other heavy-handed didactic exercise, an intellectual honesty he rigorously abided by. Moreover, for Walker, the serious writer should not be in the business of writing edifying tales. The implicit Catholicism in Percy's novels reflects the philosophical malleability of the tradition—in this sense he's so much more than merely a Catholic writer. With Percy's medical training echoing in the deep background, he took the view that the novelist is a diagnostician, "a literary clinician" so to speak, identifying "the particular [cultural] lesion of the age." Percy extends the analogy by going on to say that "the artist's work in such times is surely not that of the pathologist whose subject matter is a corpse and whose question is not 'What is wrong?' but 'What did the patient die of?'" (SSL, p. 206). Consonant with this sentiment, my colleague, the aforementioned David Hardwick, has repeatedly expressed the view that pathology is *the* Natural Science of Medicine. And perhaps it really was the pathologist's perspective that Percy distinctively carried though to make him the novelist that be became (Nash 2013b; Ahuja 2013). As Percy himself colorfully put it, pathology was "the beautiful theatre of disease" (Tolson 1992, p. 148). Bioethicist Carl Elliott remarks that Percy's

> novels often portray medicine as a profession in decline, sold out to greedy capitalists and narrow scientists. The most appealing doctors in the novels are often burned-out and dispirited; the worst of them are quacks or crooks. … Yet Percy's experience as a doctor and a patient shows through in more subtle ways, and perhaps ultimately more important ones. It shows through in the doctorly way that Percy writes, for example—the wry, clinical detachment with which he describes his characters and the circumstances in which they find themselves. Percy's style is reminiscent of the way doctors often describe their patients: sometimes with affection, occasionally with condescension, often with humor-but always with an eye toward diagnosing their particular pathology. Percy himself described it as "the stance of a diagnostician." (Elliott and Lantos 1999, pp. 4–5)

This is hardly a unique outlook. As engineer-philosopher-novelist Robert Musil put it:

> Recently I invented a very fine name for myself: "monsieur le vivisecteur." … "Monsieur le vivisecteur"–that's who I am! My life: the wanderings and adventures of a vivisectionist of souls at the beginning of the twentieth century! (Musil 1998, p. 3)

Percy's cultural diagnostic bears a striking resemblance to Musil's notion of *eigenschaftslosigkeit*, taken to connote the dual idea that a diagnosis is the beginning of the remedy. The diagnosis (for both Percy and Musil) points to the liberal penchant for abstraction; the remedy is a return (in the current argot) to the social situatedness of the individual, or in some sense, communitarianism. The idea of *eigenschaftslosigkeit* as exemplified in Musil's masterwork *The Man Without Qualities* has been articulated by cultural critic and philosopher Roger Scruton (2009, p. 165) as follows:

> Musil shows the individual conscience, surrounded by a society kept in place by empty routines. In this demoralized order the conscience becomes subjective, vacillating, profoundly unsure of anything save its own impressions. The man without qualities is in fact a man without substance, a subjectivity without a self.

Again, this idea resonates deeply throughout Percy's writing as we shall soon see.

For those who want a closer-grained documentation and explication of Walker Percy's life and philosophical work (assuming of course that one's interest has been piqued via his novels and essays) I'd recommend reading William Percy's achingly beautiful memoir—it gives immediate context to the world Walker Percy found himself thrown into and sheds light on the most influential person in his life, his uncle Will (Percy 1941). For a wider historical conspectus I'd suggest the very erudite and masterful Wyatt-Brown (1994). For those inclined to take the biographical route there are two players: Tolson (1992) is a very elegantly conceived and executed biography; Samway (1997) is more pedestrian and though it has been the subject of some derision, it has value. Though there is a veritable cottage industry of books and articles on Walker Percy, much of it middling, some bordering on the crass (some things don't have to be explicitly said), there are gems to be discovered and savored. The most recent, most elegant, and insightful philosophical offering is by Brian Smith (2017), who takes Percy to be a very subtle rhapsodist of complexity, a position analogous to the view I will proffer shortly: that is, Percy's primary concern was that of abstraction in theorizing.

I'm often asked by the Percy novice what would be the best way into Percy. Perhaps the best overview of his life and work is via a documentary that features several prominent Percy scholars and intimates.[1] Reading-wise I typically suggest to begin at the beginning—that is, MG—but given the political climate that we are currently experiencing,

LR would have a great deal of resonance. Given how profoundly polarized the US political landscape is, this is the book that might just be the ticket. LR took wing from the schism that opened up in the televised Buckley-Vidal exchanges of 1968, when the center ground seemed to give way and has since become so obviously deeply corroded by both sides. Percy, though, subtly recast this polarization into notions concerning the pursuit of happiness, short-term fixes provided by consumerism, new age self-help guides, *and* ideological zealotry. These themes were unleashed with even more force a decade later (L, pp. 217–220).

Mindful of the discussion's organizing principle—abstraction—a qualification is in order. Much like the Mississippi, while we can pretty much identify the intellectual tributaries that feed the Walker Percy river, it becomes ever so difficult to get a definitive and convenient handle on the overlapping concerns once it has reached the distributary phase. I would concede that there are several ways one could carve up Percy; he does unfortunately labor under one or more of these Procrustian labels— Christian, existentialist, semiotician, Catholic, Conservative, Southerner, and permutations thereof—as ill-defined by some of his more hagiographical supporters as by his detractors. While each of these labels are not totally incorrect, they are certainly one-dimensional and I'd caution the novice to be alert to this: Percy himself was well aware of this tendency to label him but sadly it continues to this day. As a wide-ranging and subtle philosophical mind, Percy suffers the indignity of being cherry-picked and appropriated in the service of others' more myopic agendas, especially since many of the sociopolitical issues that animated Percy are still very much with us, and indeed, as indicated a little earlier, are starker than ever before.

Capturing Percy's overriding concern under the aspect of abstraction has the virtue of admitting the aforementioned tally of labels and crosscurrents, but hopefully in my approach, is more contextually appropriate, thereby avoiding too gratuitous a skewing of his concerns.

The Abstract Self

The theme of abstraction operates in a twofold way in Percy: abstraction in the sense of being alienated from one's true or more authentic way of being/self and abstraction in a methodological sense, the inherent abstraction of scientific method and the more vulgar invocations of methodological individualism—i.e. social atomism. These issues interpenetrate one another making it difficult to tease out the strands in Percy's writings.

The alienation that so animated Percy is deeply connected to the Cartesian tradition. Noted Harvard child psychiatrist and Percyean Robert Coles (1999, p. 127) quotes Percy: "The abstract mind feeds on itself, takes things apart, leaves in its wake all of us, trying to live a life, get from the here of now, today, to the there of tomorrow." It entails an estrangement of the self both from the world and from itself. Walker Percy discerned what he took to be a distinctively twentieth-century (peculiarly Western) form of disquieted consciousness—a miasmic *malaise*—consisting in a loss of the self brought about by three inextricably linked phenomena: (a) our inherited bifurcated Cartesian self and, derivatively, (b) an uncritical assimilation and extension of scientific *a priorism*; and (c) atomistic social abstraction in the form of *homo economicus*. The upshot to these unremittingly abstract conceptions of being is that despite living in an age of considerable scientific achievement and attendant technological enhancement along with material abundance, we have been lulled into a false sense of well-being. This shallow or inauthentic "well-being" is often manifest more as a distraction from boredom, a social palliative or stupor to ameliorate our heightened anomie and desiccated inner life—a rampant consumerism that defines us by what we *want and by what we acquire*. But the "consumer" that Percy has in mind is not just of the commonplace "retail therapy" variety but also the consumer of ideas—junk science, conspiracy theorists, the New Age movement, cults, gurus of all sorts, fundamentalism, evangelicalism, zealotry of all kinds—all offering salvation that can be institutionalized as political, religious, or *even* academic charlatanism, the latter having a willing supply of vociferous illiberal student acolytes to do their bidding. It should be noted that though the root of our Western existential malaise is our Cartesian inheritance, I emphasize the adjectival form so as not to cast Descartes as the whipping boy—that was certainly not Percy's intention. (Woods Nash 2013a nicely riffs on the metaphor of the Cartesian theater in Percy's MG.)

Perhaps the most successfully and broadly assimilated and therefore the most damaging form of abstraction is the misplaced *idolatrous* faith in science (or scientism) across a range of sociopolitical and economic rationalisms, all vying for dominance under their exclusive and imperialistic monometric descriptions of the human good. (Even in some quarters, an affected humanities scientism is seen as a badge of honor; Hughes 2012). For Percy, this flattening tendency inevitably depreciates the perennial epistemic gap that surely is a mark of the human condition and indeed is corrosive of the liberal/civil condition, scientism being a sociocultural symptom of this disorder (Ketner 1999; Simone 2005). For Percy, a reputable science of man must surely have as a major part of its brief an explanation that accommodates the ubiquitous meaningfulness to our lives, a distinctly human trait. Whether or not it ever can is quite a different story.

It is at this juncture that we need to forestall any unduly quick inferences. First, Percy was certainly not anti-science. He had a deep appreciation of its elegance, explanatory power, and translational achievements—in point of fact, he sought to preserve its integrity from corrupting intrusions. Percy wanted to defend the truth value of science from the relativistic excesses of the social constructivist and the sociology of scientific knowledge fraternity. Second, Percy was *not* looking for some reconciliation between "science" and "religion": if one understands each to be in a totally different line of business, each with its own teleology and epistemic character, then the ostensible fault line dissolves. So far as Percy was concerned, if there is a schism, it is artificially induced by those who are not comfortable with the plurality of experience and perhaps unwittingly succumb to one or other monometric rationalistic worldview, be it from the religious side or the scientific side (Percy's outlook and temperament has much in common with the modal outlook of Michael Oakeshott; see Marsh 2009). Third, though Percy constantly affirms the moral unity of the human species, he is certainly not dispensing with the prime liberal notion that individuals are the ultimate units of moral value—but he doesn't do that at the expense of a historically and culturally *situated* individualism. Finally, Percy was not anti-market—he merely rejected the abstract atomism of neoclassical economics and, in some quarters, the tendency to view the market as the sole or primary arbiter of value (i.e. radical or unfettered libertarianism).

Keeping all this in mind, the existentialist themes of alienation and authenticity come into play. Broadly speaking, the notion of alienation implies that there is some meaningful essence that can be retrieved or can come to be realized, a more authentic self that manifests a genuine flowering of one's individuality (*adverbial* to individualism) in contradistinction to a self that is sunk in gray everydayness. This development of individuality typically takes place in and through practices, activities, and traditions: the communitarian emphasis on the essentially embedded and embodied conception of the individual person, offering a truer and more accurate model than described by atomistic liberal individualism or indeed of science.

The self comes into sharp relief in two of Percy's novels, LG and its sequel, SC. Here Percy deploys a fictionalized psychiatric disorder which he terms "Hausmann's Syndrome." "Hausmann's Syndrome," which actually connotes a dissociative fugue, is a specifier of dissociative amnesia, a pathology of *identity continuity* (American Psychiatric Association 2013), is salient to discussion of the Lockean memory criterion, a major player in personal identity talk. Used as a literary device it points to a deeper philosophical quarry that found full expression in his book LC. Replete with thought experiments, the bread and butter of personal identity theorizing in the analytical tradition of philosophy, Percy traffics in *aporia* that cuts across first-person phenomenology and third-person heterophenomenology.[2]

Percy wants to get beyond the idea that the explanation of my going to the drinks cabinet to get a bourbon can be exhausted by a neurophysiological account of the firings in my brain, without reference to the content of my beliefs and the broad tissue of human convention. This situated concrete dimension must surely be accommodated because reflexive thought, self-consciousness, and most importantly language, are distinctively human capacities. Percy takes a distinctly Peircean-Wittgensteinian "meaning as use" approach to the vexed notion of language and meaning. Were Percy around today, he may well take some comfort from the growing, but nonetheless still heterodox, rejection of the Cartesian tradition, namely, the situated cognition wing of cognitive science (much of it taking inspiration from Heidegger) and to a lesser extent the so-called Austrian (and behavioral) economics program. What binds this broad "movement" is the view that notions of autonomy, sense-making, embodiment, emergence, and the phenomenological must be factored into any explanatory model of man worth its salt.

SCIENTISM AS HANDMAIDEN TO PROGRESSIVISM

As already indicated, Percy across his novels and nonfiction writings waged an ongoing battle against "scientism," the idea that every intelligible question has either a scientific solution or no solution at all. Scientism for Percy was meant to be taken as a pejorative term, since on his account it embodies a dogmatic overconfidence, brimming with ideological fervor, its immodesty leaving no place for transcendence. Susan Haack, one of the very few (perhaps only) mainstream analytical epistemologist to have referenced Percy, shared some of his concerns. For Haack scientism is actually two casts of mind. In one guise, it consists in an exaggerated deference toward science, "an excessive readiness to accept as authoritative any claim made by the sciences, and to dismiss every kind of criticism of science or its practitioners as anti-scientific prejudice." In its other guise, it is *anti*-science, an exaggerated suspicion of science, "an excessive readiness to see the interests of the powerful at work ... and to accept every kind of criticism of science or its practitioners as undermining its pretensions to tell us how the world is" (Haack 2003, pp. 17–18), the latter connoting the radical postmodern relativistic outlook that was mentioned earlier.

So what has this to do with progressivism? Epistemic humility is not seen as a cultural virtue: it is the *zeitgeist* of the modern age that we exist in a (misperceived) linear trajectory of progress, progress here taken to be coextensive with *improvement*—morally, socially, technologically, economically, and scientifically. Progressivism thus conceived is clearly a "grand narrative" notion which on closer scrutiny is subject to all the weaknesses of such constructions. It is impossible to determine whether a change for the better in one part or aspect of the system is progressive for the overall system since there is no Archimedean point from which progress can be assessed. Every change alters some state of affairs, destroying or modifying it—that much one can accept. Once again we defer to Musil who captures this idea thus:

> "It seems to me," Ulrich said, "that every progressive step is also a retrogressive step. Progress exists always in one particular sense. And since our life as a whole has no sense, there is as a whole no progress either."

> Leo Fischel lowered his newspaper. "Do you think it better to be able to cross the Atlantic in six days or to have to spend six week[s] on it?"

> "I should probably say it's definitely progress to be able to do both." (Musil 1995)

Or as Chesterton (1908) put it:

Progress itself cannot progress. It is worth remark, in passing that when Tennyson, in a wild and rather weak manner, welcomed the idea of infinite alteration in society, he instinctively took a metaphor which suggests an imprisoned tedium. He wrote – "Let the great world spin for ever down the ringing grooves of change."

He thought of change itself as an unchangeable groove; and so it is. Change is about the narrowest and hardest groove that a man can get into.

The main point here, however, is that this idea of a fundamental alteration in the standard is one of the things that make thought about the past or future simply impossible. The theory of a complete change of standards in human history does not merely deprive us of the pleasure of honouring our fathers; it deprives us even of the more modern and aristocratic pleasure of despising them.

Granted we live, in some real sense, in the best of times (e.g. reductions in child mortality, vaccine-preventable diseases, access to safe water and sanitation, malaria prevention and control, prevention and control of HIV/AIDS, tuberculosis control, and declining poverty; WHO 1998). But we *also* live in the worst of times—Auschwitz-Birkenau, Holodomor, Cambodia, and more besides—the dark side to technocracy. In his excellent little book Slaboch (2018) broadly distinguishes between *sceptical* critics of progress (Schopenhauer, Burchhardt, Nietzsche, Tolstoy, Solzhenitsyn et al.) and *cyclical* theorists (Spengler, Vico, amongst others); each grouping having a corresponding view of human nature as the driver, a topic I discuss in detail in Marsh (in press). This is the thrust to Percy's highly disturbing novel TS, reflecting a culture that in its theoretical reduction of man to matter, *in practice*, "kills our capacity for triadic signification – the source of our sense of self – as a 'cure' for psychological suffering" (Mattix 2013, p. 146). The widespread implementation of, say, the drug methylphenidate seems to be implicitly justified on purely utilitarian grounds (Pratt et al. 2011, pp. 1–8).

Nowhere is this techno-ebullience more evidently false than in coming to grips with the subjective felt experience of, for example, pain or beauty, what in philosophical jargon are termed *qualia* (Wyatt-Brown 1994, p. 304)—let alone the issues of meaning and intentionality that we mentioned earlier. It may well be that the very idea of the mind explaining itself entails a logical contradiction (Hayek 1952), forever doomed to self-referentiality, a position disparagingly called "new mysterianism." As Percy repeatedly says, the "self can perceive, formulate, symbolize, everything under the sun except itself" (SSL, p. 127) and

> [w]hy it is possible to learn more in ten minutes about the Crab Nebula in Taurus, which is 6,000 light-years away, than you presently know about yourself, even though you've been stuck with yourself all your life (LC, p. 1).

This situated concrete (embodied) intentionality must surely be accommodated because reflexive thought, self-consciousness, and most importantly language are distinctively human capacities. Percy takes a distinctly Peircean-Wittgensteinian "meaning as use" approach to the vexed notion of language and meaning. Percy is of the view that where science loses its coherence is to blithely extend its explanatory reach across both *dyadic* and *triadic* organisms. Science is eminently well equipped to say something about spatiotemporally located entities, be it physiology or neurology, Venus and Mars, or even Halley's Comet—the dyadic—a two-way relation of the observed and the observer. But … when it comes to the linguistic, the sociological, or the anthropological, all partaking in symbol mongering *and* attendant intentionality, then a dyadic relation fails miserably. It makes no sense whatsoever in saying that a tiger is alienated or that a fish should consider the nature of water. Man on the other hand inhabits a world of symbolic forms that is triadic, a tripartite relation between things > the observer/interpreter > a community, of which the observer is a part. Even if there were known bridging laws between physics, chemistry, biology, psychology, and sociology something of the self would always be left over. As Elliott writes: "One reason is that even if we know all that there is to know about neurochemistry, we cannot explain everything about human behavior that is relevant to psychiatric disorders within the vocabulary of neurochemistry" (Elliott 1992, p. 245). Percy would no doubt be in accord with Wittgenstein's dictum that "[w]e feel that even once all *possible* scientific questions are answered, our problems of life have still not been touched upon" (Wittgenstein 1922, p. 652).

It is the recognition of the disjunction between the dyadic and the triadic that constitutes the beginnings of the search—man as wayfarer and *homo viator*—an ongoing theme in Percy's work.

As has already been made abundantly clear, Percy had a deep appreciation of science. Indeed, he sought to *preserve* its integrity. Given science's incredible success, not surprisingly, it gets coopted and perverted from within science—scientists themselves are no less immune to the full range of human failings. But of *more* concern to Percy is the charlatanism prevalent within society at large: "there is no piece of nonsense that will not be believed by some and no guru or radio preacher, however corrupt, who will not attract a following" (LC, p. 172). Science can be compromised by market pressures (Hardwick and Marsh 2012): data massage and article retractions are now commonplace. Equally common is the phenomenon of science being made functional to some sociopolitical agenda be it from the *il*liberal or "regressive" Left or the *il*liberal Right—as Haack (2003, p. 175) rightly says, "advocacy is not inquiry, and a fortiori not science" and this is applicable to the whole political spectrum—assuming of course that these terms Left/Right/Socialist/Conservative retain any meaning beyond the prevailing terms of mutual abuse (SSL, pp. 58, 248, 416). In this vein, Percy gives short shrift to, for example, "scientific creationism" (and other junk science): Percy is absolutely firm in his stance that "Darwin was right about the fact of evolution, and his contribution was unprecedented. Evolution is not a theory but a fact." Walker Percy, therefore, offers cold comfort to the zealous brand of religiosity characteristic of fundamentalism across the full spectrum of religious adherence. In Percy's view, religious vocabulary has also been so cheapened and is divorced from reason, notably scientific reason.[3]

A Danse Macabre of Wants and Satisfactions

Cartesian abstraction has a socioeconomic analog manifest in the guise of *homo economicus* so favored by orthodox economics: that is, agents are conceived as purely formalized rational maximizers without any situated and cognitive constraint. However critical Percy is of scientism, he is equally (perhaps more so) critical of the prevailing socioeconomic mores, a critique wielded with a blisteringly mordant wit. He pours scorn not only on the North Eastern sophisticates but also on the so-called "bible belt" of the South: "A flatulent Christendom and Yankee money grubbing," Percy himself feeling "like Lancelot in search of the Holy Grail who finds himself at the end of his quest at a Tupperware party" (SSL, pp. 180, 182).

Percy was dismayed by vast swathes of the populace lost in an unreflective sunkenness seemingly driven by veracious and vacuous consumerist appetites, cannon fodder in the service of economic growth: "A great culture is known through its artists and its saints and not by its GDP," he writes (SSL, p. 182). If ever there was a television show that captured Percy's scathing humor it was the 1970s BBC adaptation of David Nobbs' biting satire *The Fall and Rise of Reginald Perrin*.[4] We pick up the action when Reggie is interviewed about his new venture:

Colin Pillock:	Tell me, Mr. Perrin, are you running this community for the benefit of humanity, or simply to make money, or is it a giant confidence trick?
Reggie Perrin:	Yes.
CP:	I hope you're not going to tie yourself to this monosyllabic repetition of 'yes'.
RP:	No.
CP:	Oh good, because our viewers might think it a waste of time for you to come here and say nothing BUT 'yes'.
RP:	Yes.
CP:	So, which of them is it, Mr. Perrin? A social venture for the benefit of mankind? Purely a commercial venture? Or a con trick?
RP:	Yes. It's all three of them. That's the beauty of it.
CP:	What kind of people come to this community?
RP:	Well, at the moment we've got a stockbroker, an overworked doctor, an underworked antiques shop owner, a disillusioned imports manager, and an even more disillusioned exports manager. Three sacked football managers, a fortune teller who's going to have a nervous breakdown next April, a schoolteacher who's desperate because he can't get a job, a schoolteacher who's even more desperate because he has got a job, an extremely shy vet, an overstressed car salesman and a pre-stressed concrete salesman. People with sexual problems, people with social problems, people with work problems, people with identity problems. People with sexual, social, work and identity problems. People who live above their garages, and above their incomes, in little boxes on prestige estates where families are two-tone, two-car and two-faced. Money has replaced sex as a driving force, death has replaced sex as a taboo, and sex has replaced bridge as a social event for mixed foursomes, and large deep freezes are empty except for

twelve sausages. They come to Perrins (see Note 4) in the hope that they won't be ridiculed as petty snobs, but as human beings who are bewildered at the complexity of social development, castrated by the conformity of a century of mass production, and dwarfed by the immensity of technological progress which has advanced more in fifty years than in the rest of human existence put together, so that when they take their first tentative steps into an adult society shaped by humans but not for humans, their personalities shrivel up like private parts in an April sea.

Though this show was set in the suburbia of 1970s Greater London, it is pretty much an extension of 1950s American suburban homogenization populated by routinized ghostly bipedal life forms that so animated Percy.

Writing two decades in advance of the Internet becoming mainstream and before the rise of the ubiquitous "selfie" Percy wryly observed that "people in the modern age took photographs by the million: to prove despite their deepest suspicions to the contrary that they were not invisible" (MB, p. 26). Again we hark back to Percy's notion of the lost and disembodied self. Percy, for deep psychological reasons (Hawellek 2006) that we've only hinted at, recognized the grim drudgery of Reggie Perrin's (or MG's Binx Bolling's) middle-class life. For Percy, Wednesday was totemic of a nondescript day, the greater part of our experience, the "in-between" times which "ought to be the best of times" but are for the most part strangely diminished and devalued (SSL, p. 163)—a zombie-like existence deprived of life *and not knowing it*. As Percy so starkly put it in LG:

> Where he probably goes wrong, mused the engineer sleepily, is in the extremity of his alternatives: God and not-God, getting under women's dresses and blowing your brains out. Whereas and in fact my problem is how to live from one ordinary minute to the next on a Wednesday afternoon. Has not this been the case with all "religious" people? (LG, pp. 354–355; SSL, p. 311).

What Percy is getting at is some notion of Kierkegaardian existential authenticity and individuality, something that is not part and parcel of subhuman organisms' experience—our tiger and fish examples of earlier.

To live one's life in imitation, merely expressing the lowest common denominator cultural features of an age is, in Percy's view, a profoundly mediocre form of existence for a human being. Percy, it should be noted, is in no way deriding the common touch or experience (Wyatt-Brown 1994, p. 322); nor is he recommending the grandiloquence of what passes for the intelligentsia, those subscribing to some off-the-peg, ideologically brittle, worldview that too must stifle the individual's "search." Indeed as Wyatt-Brown (1994, p. 311) put it, Percy

> [c]alled attention to the vacuity of "everydayness," the monotonous routines that dulled the senses and the minds of ordinary people, but most especially the upper-class professional heroes of his novels.

Epilogue

Given Percy's existential bent and his debt to Kierkegaard, one could be forgiven in thinking that Percy would have a Kierkegaardian-like dourness: nothing could be further from the truth. Percy wields a blisteringly mordant wit targeting all comers—few are spared—especially in his nonfiction. It is no surprise then that it was Walker Percy who saw the comedic genius of John Kennedy Toole's posthumously published Pulitzer prize-winning novel *A Confederacy of Dunces*, Percy being instrumental in the process (Marsh 2013).

For Percy, man is *homo symbolificus*, living in a *Welt* (world) rather than merely in an *Unwelt* (environment). Man *qua* man can only plausibly be studied and understood as a situated being, not as an abstract entity. The modern liberal *cive* exists at the nexus of science, religion, politics, markets, art, and more besides, and liberalism's greatest achievement was to wrest independence from epistemic monopolies such as the theocratic state, or the expansive and centralized state, or corporate monopolies. So far as Percy was concerned, if there is a schism between religion and science it is artificially induced by those who are not comfortable with the plurality of experience and perhaps unwittingly succumb to one or other monometric rationalistic worldview, be it from the religious side or the scientific side. Though Percy's intuitions match those who are of the view with the idea that the phenomenology of experience cannot be (and may in all probability never be) accounted for by science, his ambitious project was to reconcile the abstract Cartesianism ("a disembodied barren intellectuality"; Wyatt-Brown 1994, p. 320) characteristic of most philosophy of mind with a more nuanced situated understanding of cognition and notions of social identity, without falling prey to positing bloated or irrelevant/divisive social ontologies, i.e. so-called identity politics.[5]

NOTES

1. This documentary can be purchased or rented via http://www.walkerpercy-movie.com. Some of these general themes are touched upon in Percy's Jefferson Lecture of 1989 (http://www.c-span.org/video/?c4356254/walker-percy-jefferson-lecture), the transcript published in SSL.

2. Whether or not Percy was familiar with philosophical classics in the genre such as Bernard Williams' *Problems of the Self* (1973); Thomas Nagel's "What is it like to be a bat?" (1974); Frank Jackson's "Epiphenomenal Qualia" (1982); Derek Parfit's *Reasons and Persons* (1984); Kathleen Wilkes' *Real People: Personal Identity without Thought Experiments* (1988); and several more besides, I cannot definitively say.

3. Some 30 years ago it was the so-called new Right that was the source of much of the anti-science rhetoric; this tendency has now been subsumed by the "regressive" (radical) Left.

4. Series three, episode five. Here the protagonist Reggie Perrin is interviewed on a program entitled "Pillock Talk," pillock being a colloquial Briticism for an idiot. (This will have resonance to those who viewed the infamous Cathy Newman-Jordan Peterson exchange on Channel 4). The background to the series in brief: Our hero lives the highly routine life of a suburban commuter to "that bastion of boredom, inertia and restlessness, the workplace" (Temple and Darkwood 2001, p. 102). The stresses of his mundane life begin to surface, with Reggie leaving his clothes on a beach in an apparent suicide. Reggie, alive and well, tours the countryside under various guises, but realizes that he misses his wife Elizabeth. Reggie attends his own memorial service in the guise of "long-lost friend" Martin Wellbourne. Elizabeth realizes that he is Reggie, but doesn't let on to anyone else, and they become engaged. Martin Wellbourne is then employed at Reggie's previous employer Sunshine Desserts, but like his old self Reggie, gets bored. Reggie (now back as himself) opens a shop called Grot, selling useless Dadaist products. To his amazement it is a raging success and soon has a chain of stores nationwide. Yet again he realizes that he is back in the routine he tried so hard to escape. Bored, Reggie tries to destroy Grot by employing unsuitable people in unsuitable roles. The upshot—even more success! Reggie then has a new idea: a community for the middle-class and middle-aged where people can learn to live in peace and harmony.

5. This chapter is a reworked version of Marsh 2016.

REFERENCES

Ahuja, Nitin K. 2013. It Feels Good to Be Measured: Clinical Role-Play, Walker Percy, and the Tingles. *Perspectives in Biology and Medicine* 56: 442–451.

American Psychiatric Association. 2013. *Diagnostic and Statistical Manual of Mental Disorders*. 5th ed. Arlington: American Psychiatric Publishing.

Chesterton, G. K. 1908. *Orthodoxy*. London: William Clowes.

Coles, Robert. 1999. *The Secular Mind*. Princeton: Princeton University Press.

Elliott, Carl. 1992. On Psychiatry and Souls: Walker Percy and the Ontological Lapsometer. *Perspectives in Biology and Medicine* 35: 236–248.

Elliott, Carl, and John Lantos. 1999. *The Last Physician: Walker Percy and the Moral Life of Medicine*. Durham: Duke University Press.

Haack, Susan. 2003. *Defending Science—Within Reason: Between Scientism and Cynicism*. Amherst: Prometheus Books.

Hardwick, David F. and Leslie Marsh. 2012. Clash of the Titans: When the Market and Science Collide. *Experts and Epistemic Monopolies. Advances in Austrian Economics* 17: 37–60.

Hawellek, Barbara. 2006. Suicide in the Literary Work of Walker Percy/Der Selbstmord im literarischen Werk. *Fortschritte der Neurologie-Psychiatrie* 74: 101–106.

Hayek, Friedrich. 1952/2017. *The Sensory Order and Other Writings on the Foundations of Theoretical Psychology*. Ed. with a Foreword Viktor J. Vanberg. Chicago: Chicago University Press.

Hughes, Austin L. 2012. The Folly of Scientism. *The New Atlantis* 37: 32–50.

Jackson, Frank. 1982. Epiphenomenal Qualia. *The Philosophical Quarterly* 32 (127): 127–136.

Ketner, Laine Kenneth. 1999. Rescuing Science from Scientism: The Achievement of Walker Percy. *The Intercollegiate Review* 35 (1): 22–27.

Majeres, Kevin D. 2002. The Doctor and the 'Delta Factor': Walker Percy and the Dilemma of Modern Medicine. *Perspectives in Biology and Medicine* 45: 579–592.

Marsh, Leslie. 2009. Reflecting on Michael Oakeshott: Introduction to the Symposium. *Zygon: Journal of Religion and Science* 44: 133–138.

———. 2013. Review of *Butterfly in the Typewriter: The Tragic Life of John Kennedy Toole and the Remarkable Story of A Confederacy of Dunces. The Journal of Mind and Behavior* 34: 285–298.

———. 2016. Walker Percy: Pathologist, Philosopher and Novelist. *Zygon: Journal of Religion & Science* Volume 51, Issue 4: 983–998.

———. In Press. Pathologizing Ideology, Epistemic Modesty and Instrumental Rationality. In: *The Mystery of Rationality: Minds, Beliefs and the Social Sciences*. Eds. Gérald Bronner and Francesco Di Iorio. Berlin: Springer.

Mattix, Micah. 2013. Walker Percy's Alternative to Scientism in *The Thanatos Syndrome*. In: *A Political Companion to Walker Percy*. Eds. Peter Augustine Lawler and Brian A. Smith, 145–157. Lexington: University Press of Kentucky.

Musil, Robert. [1930–1943] 1995. *The Man Without Qualities*. Trans. Sophie Wilkins. 2 Vols. New York: Alfred A. Knopf.

———. 1998. In: *Diaries, 1899–1941*, Ed. Philip Payne and Mark Mirsky. New York: Basic Books.

Nagel, Thomas. 1974. What Is It Like to Be a Bat? *The Philosophical Review* 83 (4): 435–450.

Nash, Woods. 2013a. *The Moviegoer's* Cartesian Theatre: Moviegoing as Walker Percy's Metaphor for the Cartesian Mind. In: *A Political Companion to Walker Percy*, Eds. Peter Augustine Lawler and Brian A. Smith, 29–45. Lexington: University Press of Kentucky.

———. 2013b. Searching for Medicine in Walker Percy's *The Moviegoer*. *Literature and Medicine* 31: 114–141.

Parfit, Derek. 1984. *Reasons and Persons*. Oxford: Oxford University Press.

Percy, William Alexander. [1941] 1973. *Lanterns on the Levee: Recollections of a Planter's Son*. Baton Rouge: Louisiana State University Press.

Percy, Walker. 1961. *The Moviegoer*. New York: Alfred A. Knopf.

———. 1966. *The Last Gentleman*. New York: Farrar, Straus and Giroux.

———. 1971. *Love in the Ruins: The Adventures of a Bad Catholic at a Time Near the End of the World*. New York: Farrar, Straus and Giroux.

———. 1975. *The Message in the Bottle: How Queer Man Is, How Queer Language Is, and What One Has to Do With the Other*. New York: Farrar, Straus and Giroux.

———. 1977. *Lancelot*. New York: Farrar, Straus and Giroux.

———. 1980. *The Second Coming*. New York: Farrar, Straus and Giroux.

———. 1983. *Lost in the Cosmos: The Last Self-Help Book*. New York: Farrar, Straus and Giroux.

———. 1987. *The Thanatos Syndrome*. New York: Farrar, Straus and Giroux.

———. 1991. In: *Signposts in a Strange Land: Essays*, ed. Patrick Samway. New York: Farrar, Straus and Giroux.

Pratt, Laura A., Debra J. Brody, and Qiuping Gu. 2011. *Antidepressant Use in Persons Aged 12 and Over: United States, 2005–2008*. NCHS Data Brief No. 76, October. Available at http://www.cdc.gov/nchs/products/databriefs/db76.htm.

Samway, Patrick H. 1997. *Walker Percy: A Life*. New York: Farrar, Straus and Giroux.

Scruton, Roger. 2009. *Understanding Music: Philosophy and Interpretation*. London: Continuum.

Simone, Joseph V. 2005. Walker Percy: Physician Homo Viator. *Oncology Times* 27: 5–6.

Slaboch, Matthew W. 2018. *A Road to Nowhere: The Idea of Progress and Its Critics.* Philadelphia: University of Pennsylvania Press.

Smith, Brian C. 2017. *Walker Percy and the Politics of the Wayfarer.* Lanham: Lexington Books.

Temple, Gustav, and Vic Darkwood. 2001. *The Chap Manifesto: Revolutionary Etiquette for the Modern Gentleman.* London: Forth Estate.

Tolson, Jay. 1992. *Pilgrim in the Ruins: A Life of Walker Percy.* New York: Simon and Schuster.

Wilkes, Kathleen. 1988. *Real People: Personal Identity Without Thought Experiments.* Oxford: Oxford University Press.

Williams, Bernard. 1973. *Problems of the Self.* Cambridge: Cambridge University Press.

Wittgenstein, Ludwig. 1922. *Tractatus Logico-Philosophicus.* London: Kegan Paul.

World Health Organization. 1998. *The World Health Report—Life in the 21st Century: A Vision for All.* Geneva: World Health Organization.

Wyatt-Brown, Bertram. 1994. *The House of Percy: Honor, Melancholy and Imagination in a Southern Family.* Oxford: Oxford University Press.

CHAPTER 2

Percy, Peirce, and Parsifal: Intuition's Farther Shore

Stephen Utz

In his novels Walker Percy vaunted the philosophical dimension of his art. He was of course wholeheartedly an artist. But the core of the literary mission as he saw it was to breathe air into and at least hint at a solution of fundamental questions. To that end, the plot of each novel deals with the quest of a character for knowledge of a special sort, a "sentience" that goes beyond the frame of everyday life and connects the humbler aspect of things with the sublime. That design required Percy to link his artistic projects with something like a theory of knowledge. In essays he addressed this theoretical interest explicitly and a little clumsily, having dealt elsewhere with aesthetics. There is also something puzzling in his choice of philosophical issues. Theoretical aspects of meaning and symbolism, and not of epistemology, are virtually always to the fore. Here, I attempt to show how these seemingly disparate problem clusters converged for him.

More specifically, this article will show that Percy fully understood the difficulty of Noam Chomsky's and Charles Sanders Peirce's claims that only a built-in bias makes it possible for us to learn both at the most ordinary level and as scientists. Percy seems to have foreseen the general shape

S. Utz (✉)
University of Connecticut School of Law, Hartford, CT, USA
e-mail: stephen.utz@uconn.edu

© The Author(s) 2018
L. Marsh (ed.), *Walker Percy, Philosopher*,
https://doi.org/10.1007/978-3-319-77968-3_2

of later developments in cognitive science and robotic learning that would transform the puzzle of apparently hard-wired learning. His persistent interest in Peirce's philosophy ultimately provided him with a bridge between symbolism and the theory of knowledge. In particular, he dwelt on the complementarity of the philosopher's triadic theory of meaning and novel views on "abduction." In a series of late essays, Percy wrote about how this might be so. Moreover, a close comparison of Peirce's theological comments with the views Percy revealed in his nontheoretical literary works shows them to have been on the same path, even though Percy never declared this to be the case.

A general view of the essays must be our starting point. Percy's sources of inspiration belong instead to celebrated philosophical traditions in epistemology and, especially, the philosophy of science. He was fascinated by the introspective phenomenalism developed in the writings of Leibniz, Descartes, and the British phenomenalists. He soon found most of them inadequate, perhaps because they had little interest in knowing the subject. Percy's theoretical writings on linguistics and semiotics emphasize the variable relationship between the subject and experience. The success of these writings, despite their overstated claims, is discoverable through comparison of his very specific interest in language and symbolism with the quests of his characters in the novels. This paper places that discussion in context and evaluates Percy's philosophical contribution. Perhaps not surprisingly, this topic had a theological dimension for Peirce. We can only speculate whether Percy had this in mind as well.

In the essays Percy abandoned the novels' subtlety. He joyfully blurted out what was on his mind, sometimes with such enthusiasm that he faltered in expressing his conclusions. The lack of inhibition is engaging and adventurous until we try to paraphrase the essays' content. He is patently a brilliant conversationalist, not a professional philosopher, and the argument is never straightforward. An essay will begin with an intriguing observation or a bold challenge to the status quo of some complex philosophical trend, and brandish a dazzling array of examples, while the reader is often not able to tell which of several theoretical issues he is addressing. Making matters more dramatic, he often treats celebrated philosophers as if they had been more certain of their ground, more assertive of background assumptions, than they were.[1]

The striking difference between the caution with which Percy introduced philosophical themes in the novels and his almost bantering celebration of them in his essays and correspondence can also be puzzling.

One expects to find arguments akin to those of the philosophers Percy is discussing. On reflection, however, it becomes clear that the *novels* are his philosophical laboratory. In them he conducts experiments in which the reader comes to identify with a central character's odd bafflement at life as a whole or with some circumstantial mystery. Percy, who liked to drop names, gives that of Parsifal to the taciturn character who engages in dialogue with the eponymous hero of his L. The novels' almost magical achievement is to make the reader experience a main character's *anomie*, always a dazed state of unknowing, just as the character does. Percy must gently spread the fragments of possible enlightenment through the narrative, to further the reader's identification with the predicament. His quiet control of all this is not polite restraint but a structural necessity; without it the reader could not share the hero's awakening. The essays allow him to embrace the learning curve rather than represent it dispassionately.

Percy's first diatribes against objectivists' attitudes toward thought and language did not at first introduce his views on the topic of meaning or symbolism or portend their importance in the later essays. MB, however, in the book of the same name is one of his more sure-footed essays; many of the others are exploratory without finding a clear theme. In the title essay, he imagines a castaway on an island going through the "messages" contained in many bottles that wash up on shore.[2]

The contents of some of the bottles are a list of sentences Rudolf Carnap had used to illustrate the variety of sentences in an essay that expounded what philosophers would call a verificationist theory of meaning, the theory that the meaning of a sentence (or of the proposition it expresses) is to be found in the conditions that would verify the sentence (Carnap 1928). Percy begins with Carnap because he finds Carnap's narrow focus on verification foreign to human experience. He argues that the castaway would divide the bottled messages into two categories: those that may be true *sub specie aeternitatis* and those "announcing a piece of news that bears directly on his life" (MB, p. 128). Percy then gives a plausible account of how someone in the castaway's circumstances would sort out which pieces of news he should take seriously and *treat* as truths, even though he cannot be sure.

It would not be fatuous to compare Percy's apparently spontaneous discussion of the castaway's pursuit of news with work by his contemporaries who philosophized about rational belief. Percy probably was not aware that this sort of departure from earlier programs like the Carnapian one Percy parodied was well under way at about the time he created the construct of a castaway. In fact, Carnap himself had moved on to such a project. In the late 1960s, the emerging field of artificial intelligence cross-pollinated with philosophical work that used Carnap's work on inductive logic (Carnap 1945; 1952) and more recent borrowings from game theory (Levi 1967) to attempt to explain how probability and context might make beliefs rational without dispositive evidence.

In brief, Percy had come upon something by an outsider's route that insiders were also pursuing. This problem area, regardless of the framework insiders and outsiders adopted, was concerned not so much with linguistic meaning or symbolism more broadly but with our risky path toward a workable set of practical as well as theoretical beliefs. We might describe this broadly as the theory of learning, but it would have to be made clear that not only modest and practical types of learning but also sophisticated projects like the development and testing of scientific theories were within the theoretical scope.

Although he paid close attention to a wide range of philosophers in these essays, Charles Sanders Peirce stands out above the rest, and Percy strove to develop his own version of Peirce's "triadic theory of meaning," expressly criticizing everyday thought and mainstream linguistics for taking a dyadic view of meaning. He plainly intended at the outset to do justice to the phenomenon of language.[3]

Superficially, the essays on the themes Percy borrowed from Peirce are rather opaque. He seems to pound the lectern as he asserts that meaning must be a three-way relationship, without unpacking that claim very well. From the novels, it was already clear that he saw our civilization's preoccupation with objectivity not only as mistaken, but as falsifying a central feature of our conscious lives. Elsewhere, especially in the early novels, this stand against objectivism gave him a tenuous link with existentialism (Abadi-Nagy 1987, p. 5).

As animals, humans are both subjects and objects. The world both includes us and stands apart from us. We all encounter this dualism, usually without noticing it as such, when experiences, especially of language, convey more than their "surface" content. Literary and philosophical existentialists stressed the bifocal consciousness of heroic quests for engagement of individual minds with the arbitrary facts of their settings. Dostoevsky's dysfunctional characters, Camus's despairing intellectuals, and others like them stepped aside from the mainstream, obsessed with their need to unify the trivial and the sublime wherever they happened to find themselves.

To resolve the antithesis between action and objectivity, a theory of meaning might play a central role.

As has been mentioned, Percy was on the same wavelength as the current set of thinkers who had emerged from the groundbreaking work of early symbolic logic and logical positivism (Carnap 1952; Levi 1967). Had he known that, however, he would probably still have wanted to distance himself from them. Their interests in learning were far more prosaic than he believed his were.

The term "meaning" in the triadic theory alludes to symbolism in a broad sense. Linguistic meaning of course implies that language users play a part in connecting the meaningful and the meant. But knowledge of the world and the ability to make things happen within the world also depend on one thing standing for another. Meaning in this sense provides a grounding for knowledge, action, and reflection on the world. Peirce makes this clear in several of his comments on his own version of the triadic theory of meaning.[4]

Peirce believed symbolism or meaning is central to several branches of scientific and artistic inquiry.[5] He of course thought it important for understanding language and, more generally, the content of thought. But he also thought the puzzle of how perception supports rational belief about unperceived things could only be solved by focusing on how a certain perception comes to stand for another, which he considered as much a form of symbolism as that of words for thoughts and objects. His insistence on linking the theoretical problems of symbolism with the theory of knowledge was eccentric for a philosopher with roots in the British empiricist tradition. Hume, Berkeley, Locke, and others in that tradition had tacitly assumed that the key to understanding how bits of our experience support rational belief in states of affairs we do not directly experience is purely a question of evidence. About the nature of that evidence they either had nothing to say or were, as in Hume's case, skeptical that there could be any rational justification. For these empiricists, the central question about experience was how we can rationally conclude from what we can see of (what we believe to be) a physical object that it will still be there when we turn our gaze away from it. But these philosophers were all but ignorant of the scope of science in their own time (Berkeley's interest in optics was exceptional). By Peirce's time, earlier empiricism could be seen to have limited itself to a small part of the puzzle of empirical knowledge, principally because philosophers now had become aware that everyday knowledge of things in the world around us must have some connection with the knowledge at which astronomy, physics, optics, and other emerging sciences aimed. Peirce is in fact one of the first philosophers who can without special pleading be called a philosopher of science. That field otherwise sprang up during or after his lifetime in reaction against the more limited view of the scope of philosophical epistemology during Enlightenment. It must be mentioned here that John Stuart Mill's *A System of Logic* gave an account of causal laws of nature that prefigured the more comprehensive approach to science taken by Peirce and others later in the nineteenth century; but Mill, as the title of his book makes clear, thought of the puzzling nature of causal statements as primarily logical or semantical; in developing one of the first modern approaches to induction, Mill did not couple his insights with his views of causation and related epistemological problems (Mill 1842, pp. 143–86).

Against this backdrop, it is at first hard to see why Peirce's theory of meaning (for which Peirce had coined the now widely used term "semiotic") would have held any interest for Percy. From Percy's own first essays on the triadic theory, coming as they did after earlier essays in which he had discussed symbolism as an artistic matter, it could seem he had simply misunderstood why Peirce made such a point of the general fact that the apprehending subject must be considered one of the things related to the symbol and what it symbolized.

On looking into Percy's views about meaning and knowledge in more detail, it is important to bear in mind that at the time when Percy wrote on these subjects, there were seemingly radical disagreements among schools of academic philosophers, who nevertheless were not very good at expressing their differences. Philosophy departments in the United States were sometimes described as "zoos," because they housed representatives of traditions that were hard to compare or differentiate, because they did not communicate at all with each other. Beginning in the 1950s, but with special rancor in the 1960s and 1970s, there were at least two mainstream approaches: the Anglo-American and the Continental European. The former had absorbed some aspects and prejudices of Viennese logical positivism but had moved on to "linguistic analysis," which analyzed traditional philosophical problems by examining everyday speech patterns about the underlying concepts involved in these problems. This tradition was more problem-oriented than the Continental tradition and had fewer "popes" or academic names to conjure with. The Continental tradition celebrated the work of Edmund Husserl, Martin Heidegger,[6] Jean-Paul Sartre, and other system builders, who addressed many of the same traditional problems of ontology, epistemology, aesthetics, and so on as the Anglo-Americans but usually did so with theories that had a single underlying core thought. These two mainstream groups included many subgroups. The Anglo-Americans, at least in the United States, were often dominated by exiled members of the Vienna Circle—Rudolf Carnap, Herbert Feigl, Gustav Bergmann, Friedrich Waismann—and later their younger followers W. V. O. Quine, Carl Gustav Hempel, and Ernest Nagel (Rorty 1967, Introduction). Many of these had begun as philosophers of science, as the Vienna Circle virtually made its main theme. Later British philosophers, following the lead of Bertrand Russell and his student Wittgenstein, had taken an interest in a wider range of philosophical problems. The big names in the Anglo-American tradition, however, were on the whole treated only as coworkers by others in the tradition, though sometimes as having accomplished important things. It seemed, at least from the US perspective, that the standouts among continental philosophers were gurus whose followers stayed rather strictly within their folds.

Against this backdrop, Percy referred to the views of thinkers from a selection of these schools. He was interested in Kierkegaard and Ernst Cassirer, but also of course in Peirce and Chomsky,[7] allotting serious consideration to Strawson and Ryle. For most philosophers of the time, it would have been a marginal activity to cross the divisions between schools in this way. Consequently, a philosophical contemporary who read Percy would probably have regarded his apparent search for consensus or at least common ground as quixotic.

By Percy's own account in his first three semiotic essays (MB, Ch. 8), he blamed the tradition of viewing relations of meaning as *dyadic* for much that was unsatisfactory or incoherent in both the philosophy of science (which for him included scientists' own views about what they were doing) and art. In all of his semiotic essays, he celebrates with a flurry of examples the multiplicity of functions language is able to serve, and he argues by example that this contradicts the implicit assumption of overly simplistic accounts of language that words (nouns, especially, in the examples he favors) just stand for objects. On the contrary, he argues, the correct view recognizes that words have "denotation." He uses the term idiosyncratically. In the most influential philosophical accounts of his century, philosophers *had* recognized that words and phrases have both connotation and denotation, or sense and reference, what Frege most famously had used the ordinary German words *Sinn* and *Bedeutung* to express. On these accounts, a word "denotes" or "refers to" something that it simply stands for (Frege 1892; Geach and Black 1980). The meaning of words or phrases, however, can also have an additional dimension, which allows statements like "The Morning Star is the Evening Star" to convey information, despite their assertion of an identity of the things to which the phrases they contain refer. Thus, it seems that what Percy meant by "denotation" is more like what others had called "sense" or "connotation." In fact, he had in mind a wider range of ways in which meaningful bits of language have a function that goes beyond simply standing for things. Another of Percy's ways of expressing this is to say that linguistic expressions are not merely "signs" but also "symbols." I take it from his choice of words that for him a symbol brings something more to its setting than its correspondence with something of which it is the symbol.

> A sign is something that directs our attention to something else. If you or I or a dog or a cicada hears a clap of thunder, we will expect rain and seek cover. ... But what is a symbol? A symbol does not direct our attention to something else, as a sign does, it does not direct at all. It "means" something else. It somehow comes to contain within itself the thing it means. (MB, p. 166)

He goes on to say that "modern semioticists" explain symbols as if they were signs, but that "[the] thing that is left out is the relation of denotation" (MB, p. 167). His rapturous accounts of this open-ended function of language is nevertheless a bit vague about what distinguishes the symbolic component. For instance, he lists seven "meanings of the telegraph sentence *baby chair*" (MB, p. 170). They include several alternative statements of fact, one question, and two commands. Of course, the example also suggests that this subtle variety of function clings to words as "symbols" even as the baby learns them, and not only manifests itself at a later stage of language use.

It appears that Percy meant something more complex than Frege meant by *Sinn* by the content of a "symbol". From the outset he emphasizes that when words function as symbols, a social setting is often required and perhaps always partly constituted by the symbolic function. Percy seems to have thought that relatively few theorists, like himself, had noticed how the complexity of linguistic meaning depends on context and on the capacity of language to be shaped by human beings in response to context. In fact, Percy in some of his essays cites and restates the broad theses of Ernst Cassirer, "the great German philosopher of the symbol" (MB, p. 154), and his disciple

Susanne Langer, whose *Philosophy in a New Key* argued that the human propensity for metaphor is grounded in a continuous process by which our minds "make" meaning by spontaneously seeing one thing as a symbol of others (Langer 1942). Cassirer (1946) and Langer (1942), but not Percy, made it clear that their views were in part a protest against the simplistic tenets of logical positivism. Interestingly, Percy also invoked Wittgenstein's later work for its similar rejection of the flat view of language that Wittgenstein had earlier assumed, if not defended, in the *Tractatus*. Chomsky also caught Percy's attention as a central culprit in what Percy saw as the wrongheadedness of contemporary linguistics. The Chomsky connection is of critical importance, as we will see, to Percy's high evaluation of Peirce's semiotic, which he believed capable of correcting a shortcoming in Chomsky's "hardwired" Cartesianism.

It is also worthy of mention that one of the grounds cited by Cassirer, Langer, and Percy for rejecting the view that words are simple signs for their referents is that individuals may use words to mean something not included in conventional usage. Someone may say "It's waning" to communicate that it's raining (Cartwright 1962). This is a relative minor problem for the dyadic theory of meaning, but it does point to a crucial triadic relation between the speaker, the words used, and what is meant. In any case, Percy seized upon Peirce's general view that linguistic meaning and other forms of symbolism depend on a triadic relationship.

When Percy embraced Peirce's interest in symbolism in later essays, he moved from Cassirer's and Langer's unspecific enthusiasm for the phenomenon of symbolism to a more succinct set of claims about how symbolism works. Notably, he identified his own view of the phenomenon with Peirce's "triadic theory of meaning." In more than one long essay, Percy sets forth his version of that theory. Percy seems to understand the role of their shared "theory" as an affirmative account of what meaning is. But Peirce's theory does not aspire to this.

His version of the triadic theory is more properly understood as a "model" of the relation of meaning. In Peirce's words, "I define a sign as anything which is so determined by something else, called its Object, and so determines an effect upon a person, which effect I call its interpretant, that the latter is thereby mediately determined by the former" (Peirce 1998, p. 478). This definition is not intended to explain or make any positive contribution to our understanding about how meaning works or what it is. Instead, Peirce merely wished to emphasize that what he called an "interpretant" is necessary for one thing to mean another, or to be a sign or symbol of another. The interpretant is the necessary third member of the relation between sign and signified. As the *Stanford Encyclopedia of Philosophy* expresses this point, "the meaning of a sign is manifest in the interpretation that it generates in sign users" (Atkin 2013, § 1). While this is an important fact about the meaning of signs and symbols, it is not something any earlier or later theorist would have denied or failed to notice. Peirce's reason for insisting that we consider the role of the interpretant in all discussions of meaning is to ensure that we do not ignore its importance.

How might we forget the role of the interpretant? As Percy's scorn for dyadic accounts of meaning rightly suggests, some standard approaches in linguistics and logic give the impression that signs and symbols do not require a human audience or that the part played by the human audience is so bland and unvarying that it can be ignored. Given Percy's enthusiasm for Cassirer's and Langer's protests against just this sort of thing, it is not surprising that he attached great importance to Peirce's pronouncement that the three-term relation of interpretant, sign, and object is central for a wide range of investigations: "It has never been in my power to study anything,—mathematics, ethics, metaphysics, gravitation, thermodynamics, optics, chemistry, comparative anatomy, astronomy, psychology, phonetics, economics, the history of science, whist, men and women, wine, metrology, except as a study of semiotic" (L, pp. 85–6).

What Peirce went on to do with his triadic theory confirms that he did not think of the theory's basic principle as particularly illuminating. His work on or with the theory consisted of developing lists of types of signs. In his earlier effort, he came up with a list of only three basic types. Later he expanded the list to ten and, in the last years of his life, to sixty-six (Atkin 2013, §§ 2., 3.4, and 4.3). The different types at each stage of his development of the theory referred to the levels of content the interpretant supplied to different kinds of sign. At the earliest stage, for example, he distinguished "icons," the types of sign that are simply likenesses of what they represent; "indices," the types that stand for something else in virtue of some connection in fact as when one is the cause of the other; and "symbols," which depend on human convention or stipulation, as in the symbolic function of words as signs of things or thoughts. (Neither Peirce nor Percy ever focused on the problematic nature of linguistic convention, to which Wittgenstein did devote a great deal of attention in the *Philosophical Investigations*, and David Lewis and other later philosophers have even more probingly examined (Wittgenstein 1967; Lewis 1969).

Percy seems to have thought Peirce's triadic theory somehow said more than Peirce ever aspired to say about how interpretants "make" symbols come to be. Percy was clearly eager for there to be some such payoff. Percy devotes the last half of *The Triadic Theory of Meaning* to reminiscence and reflection on the relationship between "psychiatrist" (in his time, presumably, this meant a Freudian psychotherapist) and patient. Summing up the illustrative relevance of such therapy plays on varied aspects of linguistic meaning, he says "the description of the psychiatrist as a participant-observer is in fact an accurate characterization of the semiotic options available 'in the therapist-patient encounter'" (MB, p. 175, citing Sullivan 1968) and then goes on to give several pages of examples, presumably from his own experience.

In brief, it would be tempting to think that Percy has simply misunderstood Peirce and mistakenly attributed to him Percy's own theoretical goals, which Percy was not equipped to achieve. The fact that Tom More in TS is said to have devised a theory of linguistic meaning that will transform linguistics and even epistemology suggests that Percy knew his own triadic theory was more a hope than a reality.

Another view, however, gives Percy more credit for treating Peirce's thoughts on semiotic and abduction as related and even as part of a single scheme. In MB, Percy made that connection without crediting Peirce for inspiring it. He did so by arguing (or assuming) a fuller view of linguistic meaning. How, he asks, would the castaway sort through the random messages he receives? He would prize those that seemed to convey "news," which of course he badly needs because of his isolation and lack of knowledge about what is going on in the world. Recall that Percy posits in the novels that a character in this agnostic predicament (Binx Bolling, Bill Barrett, Tom More) must make the best of it, grasping even for inconclusive support of the alternative bits of potential news.

Percy was in effect saying that linguistic meaning together with our need to acquire information makes this pattern of learning natural and perhaps inevitable. We may not need to know what to believe in the abstract, but we definitely need to choose premises for action, because we must act in order to live. Percy does not, however, overstate the utilitarian side of our need to learn. When he portrays its place in the castaway's life, he does so without offering any broad account of its place in human existence (just as he later suggests that a "Martian" might see things in the same way). Instead, he portrays the utilitarian and contingent side of life as underpinning the pursuit of knowledge for its own sake. This of course is inevitably prominent in narratives of quest. The writer follows where words lead, making associations among words based on the aspect of their meaning, not as "indices" in Peirce's sense, but as symbols. Percy thus makes a connection between meaning and learning. It is not a connection to which he calls attention explicitly, perhaps because he was not sure how to characterize its importance. Certainly, when he makes the connection in the essays (MB, Chapters 7–9), he seems merely to leave it to the reader to decide what to make of it; in effect, he ends these essays without stating a conclusion.

But finally, in his last essay on semiotic, he does focus on the connection and says something more directly about why it is important. Perhaps while exploring Peirce's semiotic work, Percy had come across another of Peirce's well-known inventions that fits extraordinarily well into a theoretical template Percy was developing independently and used in his novels. Peirce asserted that the development of science requires not only "induction," a way of evaluating empirical evidence that may support general hypotheses, but also a pattern of thought by which we select the hypotheses themselves—we need not only induction but also "abduction." In *A Theory of Language*, Percy discusses abduction's importance to his thought.[8] Moreover, his comment on the topic juxtaposed what Peirce had said about this scientific function with Chomsky's central claim that our minds must be biased in order to be capable of learning from experience at all. In brief, Percy made the connection between abduction and what Chomsky famously called the Cartesian element in how minds work.

Percy begins the essay by setting forth the problem of understanding how language learning can occur, given that a language acquirer faces a wildly open-ended (actually, an infinite) range of possible interpretations of others' linguistic behavior. He notes that Naom Chomsky (1956) and Jerrold Katz had posited the existence in our minds of a Language Acquisition Device (LAD) as capable of short-circuiting the frustration we would face if our minds were initially *tabulae rasae* as the empiricist and behaviorist approaches ("earlier Pavlovian and Watsonian versions"[9]) had supposed. He briefly sets forth the problem in this regard these earlier models of learning faced. Their solutions to the problem of learning have all the desirable features of such a theory "except one: [They are] wrong." Percy contrasts with them Chomsky's "transformational" model,[10] which of course Chomsky (1956) himself advanced as a fundamental corrective of behaviorism's crucial shortcoming. As Percy summarizes the LAD's role, "primary linguistic data → LAD → Grammar" (MB, p. 301). But he believes the LAD is a "black box" that merely stands for a solution of the problem of how language learning works without telling us what goes on inside the box (MB, p. 302). Percy's only comments on how this black box might be illuminated are in his *Theory of Language*, where he contrasts Chomsky's comments on the Cartesian nature of the language acquisition with Peirce's views on abduction in science.

Peirce had been the first to emphasize that the standards by which we test the evidence for a hypothesis or theory do not tell us which hypotheses or theories to test. From premises assumed to be true, deduction makes it possible to identify conclusively the consequences that must be true if the premises are true; but these consequences always contain less information than the premises—they are "non-ampliative." Philosophers since Aristotle have spoken of a form of inference that proceeds in the opposite direction, called "induction" in the literature since Isaac Newton (Newton 1687, vol. 3, General Scholium; translated in Motte 1729, vol. 2, p. 392). But our understanding of the standards of induction is still dolefully incomplete. Peirce was the first to emphasize that even if we were clear about the standards of both deduction and induction, these would not tell us how the hypotheses scientists entertain and test are selected. For any body of evidence an infinite number of hypotheses could be considered. But we could not possibly consider them all. In contrast with induction and deduction, Peirce elevated this selection process to equal status. In his words, "[a]bduction is the process of forming explanatory hypotheses. It is the only logical operation which introduces any new idea" (Peirce 1931–36, vol. 5, p. 172). Others had not focused on the fact that an infinite number of alternative and mutually inconsistent hypotheses could "cover" (account for, imply) any finite series of factual observations.[11] If we speak of finite amounts of evidence as supporting one or a small number of hypotheses, we must mean that an infinite number of others that are consistent with the evidence were not to be considered. Certainly, the evidence itself cannot select a single or small number of hypotheses as those best supported out of the infinite number of possible alternatives.

According to Peirce, there are "trillions of trillions of hypotheses" which might be made to account for [some new phenomenon in the laboratory], "of which only one is true" (Peirce 1958, vol. 7, p. 245). Yet as matters usually turn out, the physicist usually hits on the correct hypotheses "after two or three or at the very most a dozen guesses." This successful guessing or hypothesizing of scientists is not, according to Peirce, a matter of luck. Peirce's own explanation of the extraordinary success (in the face of such odds) of scientific theorizing is founded in his belief that general principles actually operate in nature apart from men's minds and that men's minds are nevertheless capable of knowing these principles. But how is this possible? Peirce hazards the guess that, since "the reasoning mind is a product of the universe," it is natural to suppose that the laws and uniformities that prevail throughout the universe should also be "incorporated in his own being." (Peirce 1931–36, vol. 6, p. 486)

Percy thinks Chomsky brings up the topic of abduction only in order to excuse his own failure to unpack how the LAD works (MB, p. 323). For this reason, Percy also refrains from approving Peirce's account, calling it "speculation," despite his otherwise unstinting endorsement here and elsewhere of Peirce's views on meaning and abduction. Percy presses the point home by saying that

> Chomsky's proposal to shift the burden of explanation from the linguist, the theorist of language as a phenomenon, to the child, the subject under study. Chomsky's theory of language is that the child is capable of forming a theory of language. (MB, p. 323)

In contrast with Chomsky, Peirce in Percy's view did not think we are hard-wired to select the right hypotheses. At least, that is what his climactic sentence apparently means: "[I]f one is seeking philosophical progenitors for Peirce's theory of abduction and [his view that our being part of the universe accounts for our ability to select the right hypotheses] one is inevitably led not to Descartes and a mind-body dualism but, according to Peirce, to Duns Scotus!" (MB, p. 324). Percy, however, says nothing further about Duns Scotus, and it is tempting to think he meant only this medieval philosopher had emphasized the "this-ness" of individual objects as holding information, so to speak, about their relations with abstract concepts.[12] The rest of Percy's essay sinks into obscurity. He returns to the triadic theory of meaning, offering examples of how a child might learn the meaning of "This is a balloon" from the child's father's utterance of the sentence. But it is possible that what he meant to say is that something in the context of language learning, comparable to the context of scientific hypothesis selection, is both capable of limiting the number of rival hypotheses we actually consider and does so justifiably.

Context in other words can reasonably limit the number of alternative hypotheses. What can he have meant by that?

Peirce visited the topic of abduction many times in uncoordinated writings, just as he did others of his favorite themes, including the triadic theory of meaning. We do not know which of Peirce's writings on abduction Percy had read. The most specific of Peirce's illustrations of how abduction works are drawn from the development of the kinetic theory of gases in the seventeenth and eighteenth centuries. In particular, he comments on how Boyle's Law—that a given mass of air or any other gas is proportional to the pressure to which it is subject—was subsumed by the later molecular theory of gases (Peirce 1982). This illustration of abduction does not tell us how Boyle's already striking hypothesis stood out from the infinite range of alternative hypotheses. It was, so to speak, a close description of the controllable aspects of the experiments Boyle conducted, and these aspects can even now be seen to suggest the hypothesis based on volume and pressure without qualification, rather than say the color of the container or the source of the pressure. Peirce goes on to trace how Boyle's Law was later subsumed under Daniel Bernoulli's kinetic theory of gases (1738) and the even later mechanical theory of heat (Peirce 2014, pp. 177–79). Peirce does not spell out how the choice of general concepts—mass, pressure, kinetic movement, temperature of a gas— seemed the only reasonable choices for the theorists in question to use in framing their theories. His point, however, is that there was some such pressure from the environment that made the observations possible, the setup of the experiments themselves.

Something similar is true of the original and later version of Snell's law, which states that the ratio of the angle of incidence of a ray of light in one medium to its angle of refraction at the interface of the first medium with a different medium is constant for the two media. When first proposed (during Snell's lifetime 1580–1628), before the mechanical theory of heat had been proposed, it seemed natural to consider only the identity of the media and angles of incidence and refraction as the terms worthy of variation in experimental testing. When the wave and particle theories of light had emerged, and the mechanical theory of heat had entered the stage by a different route of inquiry, it eventually occurred to optical theorists to wonder whether heat might affect Snell's constant for a pair of media. Experiments directly led to the reformulation of Snell's law to make the heat of the media, as well as their identities, variables on which the constant depended (Utz 1976, pp. 168–72). Both Boyle's and Snell's Laws illustrate that a very low-level scientific hypothesis may seem to be selected by the experimental setup necessary for testing the hypothesis. In Percy's terms, these contextual factors are what make the "news" or hypothesis worthy of closer scrutiny. They do not, however, make its success under testing inevitable.[13]

Percy understood that scientific inquiry is parallel in some ways, though not in all. The "experiments" he describes in his brief theoretical remarks about learning are incidental to everyday life—the child's interest in dogs and balloons, the castaway's need to know what the weather holds in store. He suggests that ordinary language in which some expressions are used more often than others, or perhaps are considered less biased than others, may nevertheless contain the sort of bias that gives hypotheses using those expressions a privileged priority for testing. He never develops this view of learning beyond giving a few examples.

The novels, however, do make it easy to grasp the attraction for Percy of something like abduction in the lives of his questing characters. Binx Bolling in MG celebrates the ordinary and boring elements of his life, the less than glamorous neighborhood in which he lives, the arbitrary contents of his pocket, and then announces cryptically to the reader that his chance encounter with movie actors on Royal Street in New Orleans is a vital piece of evidence in his quest for an understanding of life. Bill Barrett focuses a telescope he treasures as an adult toy on the façade of a building across Central Park in New York and acclaims "every grain and crack and excrescence" of the wall as needing to be "recovered," evidently for his quest (Percy 1966, p. 31). Bolling, Barrett, Tom More, and Lancelot Andrews Percival in TS have what appear to be hallucinations of a rain of "ravening particles" about them, perhaps reminiscent of the falling atoms in Lucretius's De Rerum Natura, and regard them as a clue of some sort (Percy 1966, pp. 26, 47, 69, 89, 127, 337; Percy 1961, p. 5; Percy 1987, p. 10).[14] Barrett calls his quest the "itch for omniscience." These characters continue to seize upon details of everyday life as significant, and each eventually finds that the hints converge to affirm some overarching vision of the world, or in the later novels, some more limited revelation about the characters' otherwise unsatisfactory existences (Utz 2016, pp. 150–61). It is not extravagant to identify the castaway of MB with these seekers.

What links Percy's strong admiration for Peirce's theories with the epistemological slant of the novels is the implicit theory of learning that Percy found both in the triadic theory of meaning and in the theory of abduction.

We should recall that Percy's agnostic response to Peirce's claim that our ability to find appropriate hypotheses is shared and "incorporated in [our] being." It seems likely that Percy did not know that Peirce himself linked this aspect of abduction with belief in God. In *A Neglected Argument for the Reality of God*, published in 1913, Peirce wrote that "retroduction," which he uses as a synonym for "abduction," consists of the "spontaneous conjectures of instinctive reason; and neither Deduction nor Induction contributes a single new concept to the structure" of empirical knowledge (Peirce 1931–1936, vol. 6, pp. 486–502). What abduction does for us it to pick out the plausible hypotheses that are worth testing, and to revise that selection as testing goes forward, as both scientists and ordinary learners do as trial and error eliminates some of the initially "plausible" hypotheses chosen by instinctive reason. Tentatively, but without hesitation, Peirce proposes that the shared pull of our musings, reverie, and thought that is "Pure Play" (Peirce 1931–1936, vol. 6, p. 488) and that lies at the core of abduction point to the "reality of God." His observation is that both the intuitive process itself and humanity's widely shared tendency to entertain and accept the existence of God show this overarching hypothesis to be plausible.

In conclusion, it seems fair to suggest that Percy and Peirce were on the same path in their view of the grounding to which language and learning point. They both saw this as having radical implications for the authority of science and of theology, although neither went so far as to hint that the two were or could become similarly clear and certain. Nevertheless, the common pattern of Percy's novels, the free association implicit in the quests of his characters for a higher understanding of life, can fairly be described as exemplifying Peirce's generalizations about abduction and belief in the reality of God.

NOTES

1. I mean primarily Chapters 7–15 of Percy 1975. The earlier essays are equally serious but only the last eight have a common set of common themes.

2. The castaway is certainly the counterpart of the Martian, an identity Percy feigned in the first few pages of *A Theory of Language* (MB, pp. 298–307, esp. pp. 298–301).

3. See, in particular, "The Message in the Bottle", "The Mystery of Language", and "The Triadic Theory of Meaning" (MB, Chapters 6–8).

4. Peirce 1931–36, 6.484; Peirce 2014, pp. 172–78.

5. In fact, he argues for the importance and similar significance of meaning to both science and art in Culture (MB, Chapter 10).

6. Percy mentions Kant, Husserl, and Heidegger as background figures for his own emphasis on the context of symbols in which symbols are used, and suggests that they were on the same path as Cassirer (MB, pp. 202–4).

7. Percy sometimes seems to describe Chomsky as failing to grasp the problem that a triadic theory of meaning solves but at others assigns importance to Chomsky's understanding of others' failure in this regard (Chomsky 1965; MB, p. 165).

8. "In what follows, the Martian will revive another idea. … Charles Peirce's theory of abduction, which is an analysis of scientific hypothesis formation, peculiarly apposite, as the Martian sees it, to linguistic theorizing" (MB, pp. 300–1).

9. The references are of course to the Russian psychologist Ivan Petrovich Pavlov's theory that learning in infants and animals is the result of "conditioning" or repetitive exposure to the juxtaposition of signs and the things they signify. John B. Watson of Columbia University, also an academic psychologist, gave this approach the name "behaviorism." The novel component of the theory they both stood for was that language learning is no more complex that the learning of connections between other nonlinguistic phenomena, as in animal and human learning of simple causal relations (causal "recipes") in the world around us.

10. Percy compares these, as Chomsky implicitly also did, with Bloomfield's, Harris's, and Fodor and Katz's non-behaviorist views of language acquisition.

11. To mention only two, Wittgenstein and Goodman were celebrated for their emphasis on this selection problem during the years when Percy was interested in this problem. *See* Wittgenstein, (1967); Goodman et al. (1965).

12. Scotus wrote on *haecceitas* (this-ness) in his *Ordinatio* 2, d. 3, pars 1, qq. 1–6 (Scotus 1302).

13. Nevertheless, relevant parts of the environment in which the hypothesis "crops up" seem to favor it. In statistical trials of low-level hypotheses, this reflection of the environment is found in the investigator's assumption that certain variables are logically independent of each other. If variables are not logically independent, their repeated cooccurrence cannot raise the probability that their cooccurrence is statistically significant.

14. Percy remarks with apparent approval on Foote's inclusion of Lucretius in a list of great scientists. (Tolson 1997, p. 280).

References

Abadi-Nagy, Zoltan. 1987. Walker Percy: The Art of Fiction, No. 97. *Paris Review* No. 103.

Atkin, Albert. 2013. Peirce's Theory of Signs. In: *The Stanford Encyclopedia of Philosophy*. Ed. Edward N. Zalta. URL = https://plato.stanford.edu/archives/sum2013/entries/peirce-semiotics/.

Carnap, Rudolf. 1928. *Der Logische Aufbau der Welt*. Leipzig: Felix Meiner Verlag. Trans. Rolf A. George. 1967. *The Logical Structure of the World*. Berkeley: University of California Press.

———. 1945. On Inductive Logic. *Philosophy of Science* 12: 72–97.

———. 1952. *The Continuum of Inductive Methods*. 2nd ed. Chicago: University of Chicago Press.

Cartwright, Richard. 1962. Propositions. In: *Analytical Philosophy: First Series*. Ed. R. J. Butler. Oxford: Blackwell.

Cassirer, Ernst. 1946. *Language and Myth*. Trans. Susanne Langer from *Sprache und Mythos* (1925). New York: Harper & Bros.

Chomsky, Naom. 1956. Three Models for the Description of Language. *Information Theory, IEEE Transactions* 2 (3): 113–124.

———. 1965. *Aspects of the Theory of Syntax*. Boston: MIT Press.

Frege, Gottlob. 1892. "Über Sinn und Bedeutung." Trans. as "On Sense and Reference" by Peter Thomas Geach and Max Black. In: Geach and Black 1980.

Geach, Peter Thomas and Max Black. 1980. *Translations from the Philosophical Writings of Gottlob Frege*. 3d. ed. London: Rowman & Littlefield Publishers, Inc.

Goodman, Nelson. 1965. *Fact, Fiction and Forecast*. Cambridge, MA: Harvard University Press.

Langer, Susanne. 1942. *Philosophy in a New Key: A Study in the Symbolism of Reason, Rite, and Art*. Cambridge, MA: Harvard University Press.

Levi, Isaac. 1967. *Gambling with Truth*. Cambridge, MA: MIT Press.

Lewis, David. 1969. *Convention: A Philosophical Study*. Boston: Harvard University Press.

Mill, John Stuart. 1842. *A System of Logic: Ratiocinative and Inductive*. London: John W. Parker.

Motte, Andrew. 1729. *Newton's The Principles of Mathematics of Natural Philosophy*. London: Benjamin Motte.

Newton, Isaac. 1687. *Philosophiae Naturalis Principia Mathematica*. See Motte 1729.

Peirce, Charles Sanders. 1931–1936. *The Collected Papers of Charles Sanders Peirce*. Eds. Charles Hartshorne and Paul Weiss. 6 vols. Cambridge, MA: The Belknap Press of Harvard University.

———. 1958. *The Collected Papers*. Ed. Arthur Burks. Vols. 7 & 8. Cambridge, MA: Harvard University Press.

———. 1977. *Semiotics and Significs*. Ed. Charles Hardwick. Bloomington: Indiana University Press.

———. 1982. *The Writings of Charles S. Peirce: A Chronological Edition*. Vols. 1–6. Peirce Edition Project. Bloomington: Indiana University Press.

———. 1998. The Essential Peirce. Eds. Peirce Edition Project. Vol. 2. Bloomington: Indiana University Press.

———. 2014. *Illustrations of the Logic of Science*. Ed. Cornelis de Waal. Chicago: Open Court Publishing Co.

Percy, Walker. 1961. *The Moviegoer*. New York: Vintage Books, Inc..

———. 1966. *The Last Gentleman*. New York: Farrar Straus & Giroux.

———. 1971. *Love in the Ruins: The Adventures of a Bad Catholic at a Time Near the End of the World*. New York: Farrar Straus & Giroux.

———. 1975. *The Message in the Bottle*. New York: Farrar Straus & Giroux.

———. 1977. *Lancelot*. New York: Farrar Straus & Giroux.

———. 1980. *The Second Coming*. New York: Farrar Straus & Giroux.

———. 1987. *The Thanatos Syndrome*. New York: Farrar Straus & Giroux.

Rorty, Richard. 1967. *The Linguistic Turn: Essays in Philosophical Method*. Chicago: Chicago University Press.

Scotus, John Duns. 1302. *Ordinatio* or *Opus Oxoniense*.

Sullivan, William Stack. 1968. *The Interpersonal Theory of Psychiatry*. New York: Norton Publishing Co.

Tolson, Jay, ed. 1997. *The Correspondence of Shelby Foote & Walker Percy*. New York: W. W. Norton & Co.

Utz, Stephen. 1976. *The Concept of Evidence in the Philosophy of Induction*. Unpublished Ph.D. dissertation, Cambridge University.

———. 2016. The Itch for Omniscience: Walker Percy on the Examined Life. XII *Explorations: The Twentieth Century*: 149–171.

Wittgenstein, Ludwig. 1967. *Philosophical Investigations*. Trans. G. E. M. Anscombe. Oxford: Basil Blackwell.

Wolter, Allan B. 1987. *Duns Scotus: Philosophical Writings*. Indianapolis: Hackett Publishing.

CHAPTER 3

Walker Percy, Phenomenology, and the Mystery of Language

Carolyn Culbertson

In his *Nicomachean Ethics*, the ancient Greek philosopher Aristotle describes the human being as *zōon logon echon*, the animal that has language (*logos*). For Aristotle, the capacity for language was so important to human life that no person could truly flourish in their being without actively putting it to work through reasoning and deliberation (Aristotle 1999, p. 9).[1] Indeed, despite the well-known antagonism between philosophers and rhetoricians of ancient Greece, it is worth remembering what the two sides of the battle had in common: both philosophers and rhetoricians alike believed strongly in the power of speech to rightly guide both individual and city.

This way of understanding the human being seems to have been about as intuitively right for the philosophers of ancient Greece as it is today intuitively wrong for us moderns. Whenever I have introduced this idea to students in philosophy classes, I have unfailingly heard the same objections. They will inevitably have heard of scientific studies about how animals communicate with one another, so they conclude that an old thinker like Aristotle must have come to a faulty conclusion based on the fact that he

C. Culbertson (✉)
Department of Communication and Philosophy,
Florida Gulf Coast University, Fort Myers, FL, USA
e-mail: cculbertson@fgcu.edu

© The Author(s) 2018
L. Marsh (ed.), *Walker Percy, Philosopher*,
https://doi.org/10.1007/978-3-319-77968-3_3

41

did not have access to these scientific studies. Birds clearly send songs to one another; other birds understand and respond to those songs. Humans have even trained some animals to communicate with them. Chimpanzees use hand signals. Even pet dogs are often trained by their human companions to understand a range of different words. The idea, then, that language is the most distinctively human trait seems thoroughly unconvincing.

From this perspective, the very idea of *philosophy of language* makes little sense. After all, if one wants to understand how language works, then it seems that one ought to just observe what happens—mentally or behaviorally—when a person learns a word, hears and understands a sentence, successfully makes a request of another, and so forth. In each case, the measure of successful communication will be something independent of the linguistic world: Did the child in fact point to the right animal when asked to identify the "whale"? Did the request for salt successfully yield the salt? In other words, it seems that we can understand how language works just fine by approaching it as an observable process that can be broken up into a series of observable events—some that we observe within the subject, others that we observe in the world outside of the subject. Understood along these lines, it seems like the tools of science are perfectly adequate for the task and that *philosophy* is unnecessary for it.

But are such questions appropriate for thinking about everything that human beings do with language? As I write these words, for example, I know that there will be no easily observable measure by which to gauge their success. If the evaluative measure were obvious, then what I've written will not have broken any really significant ground. Of course, what fuels a writer is something different. A writer would like to say something that has not been said—to prompt the readers to think about things in a new way. As you read this paragraph, for example, what I hope is happening is not just what transpires with a dog when it goes to fetch upon hearing a human's command. No, the task of understanding for the reader is clearly different, as it is for the one listening to another in the course of conversation. We humans delight in those conversations that take us to unexpected places, just as we delight in the book that says something different each time we read it. It would seem to be this feature of our relationship to language, then, that requires a *philosophical* examination, since the theoretical models currently available are not capable of accounting for it.

Yet it should not be surprising that it was a writer, not a specialist in the discipline of philosophy, who expressed the need for a philosophical reexamination of language most powerfully. In addition to his novels, the Louisiana writer, Walker Percy, wrote dozens of theoretical essays over the course of his lifetime examining the subject matter of language. It was his craft as a writer that inspired Percy in this undertaking. As an essayist and a novelist, he had a burning curiosity about the phenomenon of human language or, as he puts it in his essay "The Delta Factor," (MB, p. 14) about "what happens when people talk, when one person names something or says a sentence about something and another person understands him." Percy spent decades of his life examining the major developments in linguistics and the philosophy of language taking place in the twentieth century, searching for something that could account for linguistic activity that is creative yet conducive to understanding and for the distinctive form of life that such beings who engage in such creative linguistic activity have. This becomes, on Percy's own account, a "mild obsession" that occupies the writer for decades. As a novelist, of course, Percy very well might have refrained from such investigations—submitting to the muse of writing without questioning the grounds and the ends of his own craft. Or, he could have limited his readings of theory to literary theory, focusing on language in its literary mode. Instead, for decades he diligently examines many of the most important contributions being made to linguistics and the philosophy of language during his lifetime. Among the theorists that he engages in his essays are Rudolf Carnap, Ernst Cassirer, Noam Chomsky, Susanne Langer, Charles Peirce, Alfred Tarski, and Benjamin Lee Whorf. As is well known, he found the writings of Peirce particularly illuminating and drew a good deal from Peirce's semiotic theory in his own writing. Less understood, however, is the deep kinship that Percy found with the philosophy of language offered by the German phenomenologist, Martin Heidegger. Indeed, scholarship on Percy and Heidegger has focused almost entirely on Percy's reception of the Kierkegaardian, existentialist themes in Heidegger's *Being and Time*, within which language is of only secondary importance.[2] This is no doubt in part because Percy himself tended to read Heidegger through the lens of Kierkegaard,[3] having been introduced to Heidegger's work through Werner Brock's *Existence and Being*.[4] Indeed, it was not until later on in his career that Heidegger himself recognized the centrality of the topic of language for his own work. This, however, makes Percy's appreciation for this dimension of Heidegger's project all the more impressive. In the small selection of Heidegger's texts available to him, Percy recognizes a valuable set of reflections that speak to the peculiar sort of thing that language is and, in light of this, the peculiar kind of existence that the human being, as a linguistic being, has. As we shall see, it is this connection—the "mystery of language"—that, on Percy's view, linguistic research tends to overlook.

Percy on the Life of the Linguistic Being

Language is one of the most fundamental and ubiquitous elements of human experience. It is literally everywhere for us to see. Yet, as Percy explains, this situation does not make it easier for us to understand the integral role of language in our lives. "The difficulty," he writes, "is that it *is* under our noses; it is too close and too familiar. Language, symbolization, is the stuff of which our knowledge and awareness of the world are made, the medium through which we see the world. Trying to see it is like trying to see the mirror by which we see everything else" (MB, p. 151). If this is right, then it would appear that we need another "mirror" to get a look at this mirror of language. In fact, Percy devises several schemes for this purpose. In the essay "The Delta Factor," for example, Percy invites us to view human behavior through the eyes of a Martian who has come to earth to study human beings. The first thing that would stand out to the visitor about our behavior, Percy (MB, p. 13) explains, is how constantly we humans are involved with linguistic activity in some way.

> Imagine the Martian's astonishment after landing when he observes that earthlings talk all the time or otherwise traffic in symbols: gossip, tell jokes, argue, make reports, deliver lectures, listen to lectures, take notes, write books, read books, paint pictures, look at pictures, stage plays, attend plays, tell stories, listen to stories, cover blackboards with math symbols – and even at night dream dreams that are a very tissue of symbols.

Now, Percy's description of human behavior makes two things clear. First, of course, the description is meant to show how frequently all of us are engaged in linguistic activity of some kind. We are engaged not only when we are constructing statements and producing them as physical utterances but also when we are absorbed in a book, when we are dreaming, when we are engaged in abstract symbolization, and so on. In each case we are interpreting—and in some cases producing—signs with socially shared meanings. Indeed, one is even "speaking" in this sense when one chooses to keep silent, say, as an expression of defiance or frustration. The sheer amount of time that we spend engaged in such activity already suggests that language plays a distinctive role in our lives, and this is something—as Percy points out—even a Martian would immediately see. What may be harder to notice, though, is that we are actually engaged in linguistic activity toward a variety of ends. We "traffic in symbols" in order to deepen our understanding, to articulate formal truths, for amusement, for humor, for artistic expression, for the sake of dialogue with others, and so on.

What is even more difficult to notice is that many of these ends are completely dependent on language and would not exist without it. Take the activity of scientific inquiry. When we think of scientific inquiry, we are likely to focus on the interaction between a researcher and objects of research, say, in the natural world. However, the objects and concepts with which science deals are inevitably social and result in part from social discourse. Thus, as Charles Bigger explains it, "[t]he truth conditions for the human sciences lie within those conditions of language, essentially spiritual, which constitute knower and known, self and other, man and world. This is the great theme of the *logos* itself" (Bigger 1989, p. 56). Likewise, there could be no pursuit of formal truth without a formal language like mathematics or logic in which to construct proofs. Similarly, there would be no artistic expression or humorous performances without a range of symbols—that is, signs with socially shared meanings—from which to draw. All of these pursuits draw from the social activity of language and would be incomprehensible without it. In light of this, we can see that language is not just a tool that can help us accomplish certain ends; it is also, importantly, a source of ends itself.

This is why, for Percy, it is important to consider what a transformative event language acquisition is. The tendency, of course, is to think about what happens in this process as the gradual acquisition of a set of tools and to imagine that the person learning a language is motivated to acquire these tools because they are instrumental to their existing goals. Certainly this is the most popular way of describing the rationale of language acquisition to adult language-learners. For example, one common rationale given for teaching college-level reading and writing is that this curriculum offers a set of skills that are beneficial for communicating in the job place, in public discourse, and in our interpersonal relationships. The message to students, then, is that working on college-level reading and writing is valuable only as a means—a means to perform more effectively in these spheres of action. A similar message is often given to students about the value of learning a foreign language. If language is itself a source of ends though, these arguments leave something important out. They fail to do justice to the transformative and creative effect of reading and writing.

This transformative effect is even clearer when we consider what happens when a child starts to acquire language. No doubt part of what the child does in this process mirrors what the dog does when it learns words like "fetch" and "heel." They learn to respond to certain verbal cues, and for the human child, to give verbal cues that will typically produce one kind of response. But the child is also undergoing something much more profound. They are entering into a veritable *world* of language—a development that has no parallel in the nonhuman animal world. What does this mean? Percy (SSL, p. 289) explains it thus:

> It, this strange new creature, not only has an environment, as do all creatures. It has a *world*. Its world is the totality of that which is named. This is different from its environment. An environment has gaps. There are no gaps in a world. Nectar is part of the environment of a bee. Cabbages and kings and Buicks are not. There are no gaps in the world of this new creature, because the gaps are called that, *gaps*, or *the unknown*, or out there, or *don't know*.

It is this, then, the emergence of a linguistic world that is distinctively human. When one has a linguistic world, one pushes for everything to have a place and meaning in language. In children, this is manifest as the desire to know the name for all things. In adults, it is the desire to expand one's understanding of this world through language—through the conversations one has, the books one reads, the jokes one hears, the letters one writes, and so on. The one who "has language" (*logon echon*) in this sense has it in a qualitatively different way than does a trained chimpanzee or, to be sure, a programmed computer.

This distinction is lost on us today for the most part. Because of a tendency to equate reality strictly with that which is observable by the empirical sciences, contemporary thinking rarely recognizes anything like the linguistic world at all. If language is recognized, it is only the objective works produced through linguistic activity—bridges built, homework assignments submitted, medical discoveries made, computer programs designed. What goes unnoticed and unanalyzed, by contrast, is the linguistic world that leads us to these products, without which none of these things would matter or even exist. A study, for example, on the correlation between meditative practice and certain brain wave readings only matters given a number of discourses already in circulation, for example, about the problems of stress and the importance of self-care.

Again, it is easy to overlook how fundamental discourse is in our lives, though, since, as Percy explains, it is the medium through which our understanding is constantly taking place. To bring this medium to light, it is helpful to think about how a person's life changes with the acquisition of language. A special case in point is the account that the famous writer, Helen Keller, gives of her own experience learning how to speak as a young child who, due to illness, had lost both her vision and her hearing in her second year of life. Percy is particularly fascinated with Keller's account of her experience and at times attributes some of his most important insights into language to Keller's story. What fascinates Percy is the nature of the breakthrough Keller famously experienced as an eight-year-old child—a development that fundamentally changed the form of her existence and the role of language in it. Percy points out that, prior to this, Keller had already possessed the ability to communicate basic messages with others. She could signal for a piece of cake when she wanted a piece of cake. She could use a set of symbols as tools to accomplish certain ends. It was not until that fateful day in 1887, however, that Keller developed a relationship to language that would eventually allow her to read, to lecture, to have conversations, and eventually to become an eloquent, sophisticated, and prodigious writer and activist—engaging with the important moral and political questions of the day. According to Keller's own account, the decisive moment occurred during a routine teaching procedure. Anne Sullivan and Keller were outside, and Sullivan, Keller's teacher, ran the young girl's hand under a stream of water from a spout, spelling the word "water" into her other hand. Keller recalls a "misty consciousness" coming upon her, revealing to her "the mystery of language." "I left the house eager to learn. Everything had a name, and each name gave birth to a new thought. As we returned to the house every object which I touched seemed to quiver with new life. That was because I saw everything with the strange, new sight that had come to me" (MB, p. 35).

For Percy, we can learn about what is distinctive in the human relationship to language by better understanding what happened with young Keller that day. He explains:

> Here in the well-house in Tuscambia in a small space and a short time, something extremely important and mysterious had happened. Eight-year-old Helen made her breakthrough from the good responding animal which

behaviorists study so successfully to the strange name-giving and sentence-uttering creature who begins by naming shoes and ships and sealing wax, and later tells jokes, curses, reads the paper, writes *La sua volontade e nostra pace*, or becomes a Hegel and composes an entire system of philosophy (Ibid.).

In other words, this new relationship to language transformed Keller's relationship to the world. Words were no longer just tools for communication; they became sources of meaning and understanding. The world changed too; it became a world whose meaning and truth now hinged upon the human practice of language.

It is easy to see from this example how *empowering* such a development is. To the young child who has not yet undergone this kind of transformation, the world is what it is, an ahistorical field of presence. Of course, it is hard to try to imagine for us now as linguistic beings what life was like without language. Imagine for a moment living in a world without any books, newspapers, or websites; without movies and television shows; without private conversations or even any inner monologue. Or, if you have ever traveled to a place where the language is totally foreign to you, recall how strange this experience can be, and now imagine that, on top of this, you also lacked the ability to reflect on this strangeness through talking, writing, or even thinking. Given how irregular this transformation would be for us, it is not surprising that, in her description of her breakthrough, Keller writes of a "new sight" that came to her. What she could now "see" was the world coming into "new life" through speech.[5]

Because of her unique situation, Keller underwent this transformation later and more abruptly than most. Still, in an important sense, it is something we all undergo. By acquiring language, we come to inhabit a new kind of world—a world that is constantly revitalized (brought into "new life") through speech. As soon as a child starts to learn the names for things, an empowering transformation begins to take place. The child has a frenzied interest early on in learning as many names as possible. We find the same interest evident in Keller's own account when she explains the insight that motivated her newfound eagerness to learn: "Everything had a name, and each name gave birth to a new thought." Recall Percy's description of the world of the human language user which, unlike the nonhuman animal, is a world without gaps. Keller had a basic vocabulary to use before this transformation occurred. She did not have was a sense of how with language the world formed a meaningful totality, nor how as a participant in that language she herself would play an active role in articulating that totality. Indeed, Keller now came to understand that the world she had taken for granted, including her inner world, would expand and change as she became a co-participant of language with others. It was this discovery that so thrilled Keller, making everything "quiver with new life."

Keller's story fascinates Percy in the way that it not only brings to view an essential function of language that we tend not to notice but also points to linguistic possibilities that, as a society, we tend not to cultivate. At any point, we *could* relate to language as Keller did—as a way to bring the world constantly into new life. Usually, however, we do not. We forget the word's original creative force, the fact that, in its early emergence, it brought forth something new for us to think. Instead, it becomes simply a way of referring to what is already familiar. Percy addresses this tendency in his essay "The Loss of the Creature." There he explores the tendency that we have to stop examining something closely as soon as we find the term that is functionally appropriate for it, that is, as soon as we are able to file it away in whatever inventory is appropriate for that practical, social context. He describes, for instance, a student who walks into biology class to find a set of materials on his desk: a dissecting board, a scalpel, a probe, a syringe, and one "specimen of *Squalus acanthias.*" In this context, the student is encouraged to see the creature before him as the experts see it and only as relevant to the practical task at hand. The name used by experts functions as a means of directing attention to that task. Through this process, though, Percy argues, we lose the creature itself, just as the lexicon of botany can make it so that the tree that we laypeople encounter "loses its proper density and mystery as a concrete existent, and, as merely another specimen of a species, becomes itself nugatory" (MB, p. 63). The point applies not only to objects in nature but to human artifacts as well. Regarding his own writing, Percy himself once remarked that the term "Southern novelist"—a term often used to describe the man behind his work—depressed him, "conjuring up as it does a creature both exotic and familiar and therefore boring, like a yak or a llama in a zoo" (SSL, p. 153).

To be sure, Percy's point is not that we should abandon the use of scientific, technical, or categorical terms. We should, however, be aware of the way that such terms can discourage us from interpreting a thing in new ways, finding new meaning in it and thus perhaps even treating it differently. Indeed, whenever we start to explore something—be it a new body of literature, a new tree, or a new place, Percy suggests, we should be prepared to struggle against the tendency to use such terms in a way that restricts all thought to a given practical context. We must not let the designation of Percy's work as "Southern literature" lead us to assume, without further investigation, that its primary purpose is to charm readers with nostalgia and wit, just as we ought not let the identification of a creature as "a specimen of *Squalus acanthias*" reduce the creature to an object whose purpose is to be dissected and studied for scientific research.

HEIDEGGER AND THE RECOVERY OF LANGUAGE AS LANGUAGE

Like Percy, the philosopher, Martin Heidegger, eventually came to understand his own project as an inquiry into the nature of language. While the subject matter is certainly raised in his early work, on Heidegger's own admission, it remained in the background of his philosophical writings until his 1934 lecture series on the topic of "Logic." It is in this lecture that Heidegger began for the first time finally to make central to his work an exploration of the nature of language, that phenomenon that the ancient Greek philosophers called *logos* (from which the word "logic" derives).[6] What is especially relevant for our purposes is the way Heidegger accounts for how long it took him to finally focus on the topic. Later he explains that "because reflection on language, and on Being, has determined my path of thinking from early on, therefore their discussion has stayed as far as possible in the background" (Heidegger 1971, p. 7).

That said, it is not hard to see how, a reader of *Being and Time* like Percy could find in its phenomenological exposition of worldhood a model for thinking about the fundamental transformation that occurs with language acquisition. Indeed, Percy cites Heidegger's discussion of *Dasein*'s worldhood in *Being and Time* as instructive for his own thinking. "There is Heidegger," Percy writes, "who uses the word '*Dasein*' to describe him, the human creature, a being there. The *Dasein*, moreover, inhabits not only an *Umwelt*, an environment, but a *Welt*, a world" (SSL, pp. 289–90). This conceptual distinction, as we have seen, proves to be extremely helpful to Percy in his quest for understanding what is distinctive about the human relationship to language.

Although Percy drew extensively from the concepts presented in *Being and Time*, it was Heidegger's later work focusing specifically on the question of language where the affinity shines most clearly. This is strikingly the case for the lectures and essays that Heidegger produced throughout the 1950s on the topic of language that are collected in the volume *On the Way to Language* (*Unterwegs zur Sprache*). It is in this set of works where

Heidegger, like Percy, tries to bring to light what is left out from the dominant conception of language operative in both linguistic research and contemporary philosophical discourse, and it is here where he explains, in light of this, the need to "make our way to language" despite the fact that language is "originarily familiar" to us.

For example, in one contribution to the volume, "A Dialogue on Language," two interlocutors ("a Japanese and an Inquirer") explore how the Western concept of language leaves something about the nature of language and its relevance for human existence "unthought." Thus, they reason, if one really wants to understand the essence of language, one must forge a path—a *way*—to it. However, as the interlocutors attempt to think through what is missing from contemporary thinking about language, they find that what they are after cannot be easily apprehended. Even the term "language" (*Sprache*) itself can be a stumbling block for their exploration, since in hearing it, it is easy to assume that what is to be thought is something already ready-to-hand and thus easily grasped. Moreover, Heidegger insists that the nature of language "will never be found as long as we demand information in the form of theorems and cue words (*Leitsätzen und Merkworten*)" (Heidegger 1971, p. 54). To enter into the essence of language, Heidegger suggests, we will need to reorient ourselves in how we listen to words in general. We cannot take words simply as supersensuous concepts that correspond to a sensuous reality understood as immediate or given, that is, as merely instrumental signs. Rather, Heidegger suggests, we must learn to take them as "hints and gestures" (Heidegger 1971, p. 27). What does this mean? We might define a hint as something expressive that does not exhaust what it expresses but keeps its disclosure in suspense. It is, as Heidegger explains in "The Nature of Language," what "lets us only suspect at first the memorable thing toward which it beckons us, as a thought-worthy matter for which the fitting mode of thinking is still lacking" Heidegger 1971, p. 96). To take words as hints or gestures, then, would entail seeing them as meaningful yet incomplete disclosures in that they reveal what is still "thought-worthy," "still lacking" from the realm of present disclosure.

Of course, such a way of orienting ourselves to language sounds strange to us today in an age where thinking increasingly takes its lead from the logic of technological rationalization. Consider how common it is today to take computer language as a paradigm for language as such. When we take computer language as a model for all language, we then see language as a set of rules that, if followed, allows one to produce in another an intended representation or response, just as a programming language allows one to successfully communicate instructions to a machine. Given how common it is for linguistic research to approach language in this way, it is striking to hear in Heidegger's dialogue that language, in its essence, speaks like a hint or a gesture. When asked by the Inquirer about whether there is a word in Japanese for "language," however, it is precisely this description of language as a hint and a gesture that eventually "emboldens" the unnamed Japanese character to offer a response. The response: language is "*Koto ba*," an old Japanese word that the speaker gradually translates through a series of sequential interpretations. As the interpretation unfolds, the inquirer exclaims that the term appears indeed to be a "wondrous word, and therefore inexhaustible to our thinking" (Heidegger 1971, p. 47). What the dialogue praises, then, is a kind of speaking that opens up something inexhaustible for thought.

This point requires some clarification though. After all, it might seem that such a concept of language does nothing more than to turn language into the very opposite of what we normally take it to be. Instead of making something clear to our thinking, it confounds our thinking and forces it to confront its own limits. Instead of the domain of language being the domain of what is intelligible, language is now presented as defying our habitual demand for intelligibility.[7] I suggest, however, that we ought to understand the claim that language is a hint, instead, in terms of the hermeneutic relationship between language and what it opens up. It is Heidegger's student, Hans-Georg Gadamer, who develops this point mostly clearly. In his work, Gadamer explores the distinctive type of understanding called for by our encounters with language. Such understanding, Gadamer argues, does not entail the grasping of something finite. When I read a book or listen to a lecture, Gadamer argues, I do not try to get inside the head of the speaker or the author. That is, the task of understanding in this case is not to grasp some finite content. No, unless I am listening as a therapist or an interrogator, what I am doing is thinking along with the *logos*. I am thinking about the subject matter at issue—be it the educational model that my colleagues are talking through with me or the adventure that I am reading about in a book. Indeed, as I listen to what is said about it, I find that the subject matter has not been exhausted by what I have heard said about it. It becomes a subject matter about which more can be said and written. It shows up, to use Heidegger's term, as "thought-worthy," and, in doing so, encourages me to stretch out the present limits of my understanding. In this way, the words that I hear can be said to provide a "hint" in the sense described above. They bring forth a subject matter and, in so doing, reveal things about it; however, they do so in a way that invites further interpretation, which leaves room for further disclosures.

This is nowhere more evident than in the case of translation. Because there is no one-to-one correspondence between languages, as a translator, I cannot hope to simply render the text word-for-word into the new language without giving any thought to the subject matter itself. No, in translating the text, I am necessarily engaging in the work of interpretation. The same goes, Gadamer says, for my interaction with any text. In reading written documents—be it religious scripture, legal documents, or philosophical texts—I am not just allowing my mind to be imprinted with a set of letters or even a set of words. I am participating in a process of understanding, of interpretation. Encountering the finite character of the text is, then, a necessary step in the process of understanding, since it is through these encounters that we can develop new insights into the subject matter in each case. It is, in other words, by grappling with, say, particular religious or philosophical texts that speak to the nature of virtue that I am pushed to develop fresh insights about this topic. This is why Gadamer says that, while historical texts lack the immediacy of other historical artifacts, their lack of immediacy is actually not a defect; "rather, this apparent lack, the abstract alienness of all 'texts,' uniquely expresses the fact that everything in language belongs to the process of understanding" (Gadamer 2013, p. 407).

In light of Gadamer's argument, let us return to Heidegger's point that the essential power of a word is to offer a hint or a gesture. Following Gadamer, what this now means is that language is constantly soliciting interpretation from us, an interpretive process that is never complete insofar as there is no intrinsic limit to what can be said about any given subject matter. The point is not, then, that the most powerful form of language is that which defies intelligibility and thwarts our attempts to understand it. Language speaks as a hint or a mystery because it is never finite. When we are claimed by another's words, we find ourselves interpreting for ourselves the subject brought forward and in turn able to contribute something to the discussion ourselves.[8]

To be sure, Heidegger himself is not as clear on this point as Gadamer. In the interest of accenting the strange, question-worthy character of words and in disabusing us of that tendency to restrict language to a purely instrumental function, his formulations in his later work sometimes misconstrue the basis for the mystery of language—presenting, for example, language as a power whose force and meanings exist entirely independently of human language users and as impenetrable to all interpretation or translation.[9] However, when interpreting Heidegger's philosophy of language, one must look not only to these conspicuous formulations but also, I would insist, to what he does and does not do with language in his lectures.

Consider the conversation that transpires in "The Dialogue on Language," for example. The conversation in the dialogue begins when a request is made to translate *Sprache* into Japanese. In the dialogue, the two interlocutors do not simply conclude that the task is futile, refusing any attempt at translation. No, instead, the Japanese interlocutor takes the encounter with the Western concept of language as an opportunity to bring into play and to interrogate his own linguistic and cultural horizons. What results is a creative translation of "language" as *Koto ba*, and a deeper understanding of the subject matter through this interpretation. Moreover, what Heidegger clearly wants to show in the dialogue is that the interlocutors can only make progress in understanding the topic at hand if they both refrain from an immediate translation of the strange into the familiar, allowing the words to open up something new for their thinking.

The dialogue represents, in fact, what Heidegger himself hoped to do with the scholars from Japan who had been coming to Germany to study with or collaborate with him, scholars like Yuasa Seinosuke, Tezuka Tomio, and Hisamatsu Shin'ichi. Heidegger was quite interested in Japanese culture and the Japanese intellectual tradition but, even with a constant stream of guests from Japan, proceeded with extreme caution in his attempt to understand this tradition which he found so markedly different from that of Western metaphysics. He clearly did not wish to rush into an interpretation of the Japanese philosophical tradition, so he sought dialogues with his guests and showed particular interest in the interpretation of Japanese language.[10]

One finds a similar orientation in the other essays and lectures that comprise Heidegger's *On the Way to Language*. The collection includes three lectures structured around an interpretation of a poem: "The Nature of Language," "Words," and "Language in the Poem." In his interpretations of poetry, Heidegger demonstrates the point that listening to language requires undertaking the task of interpretation. For he does not approach any of the poems he takes up by asking what among the things already familiar it signifies. As he reads the lines of poems by Friedrich

Hölderlin, Georg Trakl, and Stefan George, he is careful to look out for what is "strange" in the thoughts that they bring forth, that is, for what challenges the very preconceptions that he necessarily brings with him as a reader. This is why he draws so much attention in his readings of the poems to what withholds itself from immediate interpretation. In his reading of a poem from George, for example, he is careful to search out what in the poem resists an immediate rendering of its meaning. Of the poem's last stanza, for example, Heidegger insists that "we must be careful not to force the vibration of the poetic saying into the rigid groove of a univocal statement, and so destroy it" (1971, p. 64).

While it is structured neither as a dialogue nor as an interpretation of a poem, one can find the same approach developed in the final lecture course included in the collection "The Way to Language." This time, however, Heidegger's task is to show how the concept of "language" (*Sprache*) itself calls for a careful, interpretive approach—the same kind that poetry requires. As Heidegger explains, this is because, since the birth of modern linguistics, we have consistently failed to think language *as language*. We have analyzed it as a human activity, a cultural worldview, a system of communication, and a physical process, but, in so doing, we have missed what is distinctive about it. Of course, to define something is always to define it in terms of other things. Heidegger's point, though, is not that we ought to limit ourselves to producing only tautological utterances about language (e.g., "language is language, period"). The point is, rather, to recognize the world-formative capacity of discourse, that is, the way that we dwell in a world that is the product of an ongoing process of interpretation. As Heidegger says in his reading of George's poem, the word is "that which makes the thing be a thing," that which "first brings what presences to its presence" (1971, p. 155).

Again, this is difficult to think today, given our habit to take what really *is* as a reality independent of language and to take language as something especially lacking and opposed to reality. Words are *mere* words. Deliberation is *mere* talk. Interpretation is *mere* interpretation. The human's capacity for language is, then, nothing special at all. Phenomenological investigations into language, though, powerfully challenge such everyday attitudes, and it is this that draws Percy to such investigations. Indeed, despite their stylistic differences, as we have seen, Percy and Heidegger were engaged in very similar inquiries within the philosophy of language. Both recognized that language was more than a set of names to be learned and used as means for certain actions, that it is also a source of ends. This is what the writer grasps best, according to Heidegger. "The poet experiences his poetic calling as a call to the word as the source, as the bourn of Being" (1971, p. 68). But it is not only the literary writer that has this calling. As we have seen, Heidegger attempts to embody this same comportment in his attentiveness to language—be it the language of a poem or of an interlocutor in dialogue, for he understands that such attentiveness to language is essential for expanding and deepening our understanding of the world. For, as Percy's analysis of the Helen Keller story shows, becoming a linguistic being (*zōon logon echon*) means becoming a species of an entirely new kind. It means acquiring meaning and direction from the human exchange of ideas. And it is this comportment that we human beings manifest when we delight in having conversation, reading books, listening to lectures, and so on.

Now, it should be clear that this transformation is not something that we accomplish in a day or even several semesters but is something that we work at our entire lives. Even Helen Keller felt a significant change in her world again when, upon entering college at Radcliffe, she found herself truly immersed for the first time in "a world of books." Moreover, after this development has begun to take place, it can be tempting to want to regress to a life uncomplicated by the unpredictable life of *logos*. I am referring to the leveling down of language that concerned both Heidegger and Percy. Percy, as we have seen, recognized the danger of allowing a term—be it "Southern novelist" or *Squalus acanthias*—to rid us of the need for interpretation and thus to thwart the development of an understanding that is intrinsically historical and intersubjective. In his essay "Naming and Being," Percy (SSL, p. 135) explains:

> The symbol "sparrow" is, at first, the means by which a creature is known and affirmed and by which you and I become its co-celebrants. Later, however, the same symbol may serve to conceal the creature until it finally becomes invisible. A sparrow becomes invisible in ordinary life because it disappears behind its symbol. If one sees a movement in a tree and recognizes it and says it is "only a sparrow," one is disposing of the creature through its symbolic formulation.

Percy cites in this essay Heidegger's discussion in *Being and Time* of the tendency of *Dasein*, that being for whom being is a question, to flee from itself. Heidegger argues here that it is largely through a certain use of language that *Dasein* tries to flee from itself, that is, from its lot as the being for whom being is a question. The potential of language to open up new ends and new understanding is leveled down, and language is reduced to "idle talk" (*das Gerede*). With idle talk, a conversation becomes simply an opportunity to reassert what is already familiar and commonly said, regardless of whether one has any understanding of the subject matter. Idle talk, Heidegger (1962, p. 213) explains, "not only releases one from the task of genuine understanding, but develops an undifferentiated kind of intelligibility, for which nothing is closed off any longer."

Heidegger's classic example of a subject matter that might elicit idle talk is death. In talking about death, it is common for people to speak about its inevitability, treating it as a most familiar and well-documented event (e.g., "we all know that eventually we will die"). What this obscures though is the fact that nobody can relate to their own death as an event that will occur. When one speaks of death this way, one is indeed attempting to turn death into what is familiar—an event that occurs like other events and that can be accordingly anticipated and prepared for. Thus, in subjecting the topic of death to idle talk, one is attempting to flee precisely from being that creature for whom being is a question. Although the case of death is paradigmatic in many ways, it is not the only subject matter in connection with which idle talk arises. There is a danger of idle talk present whenever one encounters an account that has the potential to challenge the horizons of their thinking. For example, in taking up a difficult philosophical text— one that challenges me to rethink some of the basic assumptions operative in my thinking—it may be tempting to dismiss the importance of the text by appealing to simple, summary criticisms of it that are in wide circulation. Similarly, in hearing about some disturbing event taking place in the world—say, state-sanctioned murder in the Philippines—it can be tempting to invoke common ways of minimizing the level of concern that is due, say, by remarking on how commonplace such violence is in the third world. This too is what Percy has in mind when he speaks about disposing of the subject through its symbolic formation.

Through their craft, writers like Percy work against this leveling, striving to make the world once again something curious and thought-provoking for us. Philosophers too, though, have their way of disrupting the force of idle talk. Like Percy, Heidegger aims for a reinvigoration of language, attempting to use words in a way that salvage their disclosive force. Like the essayist, the aim of Heidegger's philosophical language then is rarely the unequivocal transmission of a message, whose meaning is bound to an assumed practical context (e.g., a classroom dissection). He aims instead for language that makes us think.

For both Percy and Heidegger, the stakes of preserving this attunement to language are great indeed. Without it, after all, understanding becomes disconnected from the process of human inquiry, deliberation, and interpretation. The meaning and the ends of our existence become independent of these basic human activities. As a result, the world we live in gives us fewer and fewer questions. Indeed, even we ourselves—as individuals and as human beings—become less of a question to ourselves. This predicament is even more familiar to us today than it was to Heidegger and Percy. One need only think about the lack of support for rigorous public debate or for humanities and arts programs to know that the problem has worsened over the last few decades. Indeed, we find ourselves more now than ever lacking any sense for what is distinctive about the human's capacity for language. As Percy (MB, p. 9) puts it, "[m]an knows he is something more than an organism in an environment. ... Yet he no longer has the means of understanding the traditional Judeo-Christian teaching that the 'something more' is a soul somehow locked in the organism like a ghost in a machine. What is he then? He has not the faintest idea." Philosophers of language, then, have a tremendous responsibility on their hands, for if Percy is right that it is only this strange gift of language that allows us a meaningful way of dwelling—of inhabiting the world as a constant source of new disclosures—then it is the task not only of essayists but of philosophers too to make this connection clear.

NOTES

1. Aristotle (1098b) here argues that it is not the capacity for survival or perception that is distinctively human but the capacity for action in accordance with *logos* (language, speech, reasoning).
2. Lushchei 1972; Lawson 1979, pp. 219–244; Lawry 1980, pp. 547–557; Crowley, 1989, pp. 225–242; Crowley and Crowley 1989, pp. 225–242; Lauder, 1996.
3. This is evident, for example, in "Symbol as Hermeneutic in Existentialism," where Percy considers a number of Heideggerean concepts as characteristic of the broader school of "European existentialism" (MB, pp. 277–287). See also Dewey 1972, p. 278.
4. Brock (1949) contained the first translations of Heidegger's work in English. It included four essays in translation ("Remembrance of the Poet," "Hölderlin and the Essence of Poetry," "On the Essence of Truth," and "What Is Metaphysics") and Brock's own explanation of Heidegger's philosophy, particularly, *Being and Time*). Percy owned *Existence and*

Being and took extensive notes in his copy of it. Brock, a student of Karl Jaspers, reads Heidegger's work through the lens of Kierkegaard. In his earlier book, Brock (1935) presents Heidegger as an inheritor of Kierkegaard's existentialism, particularly Kierkegaard's insistence that philosophy must begin with the study of the distinctive features of human existence.

5. Keller was insistent on using metaphors of vision and rejected the idea that they were inaccessible to the blind. In *The World I Live In*, Keller responds to the policy of the *Matilda Ziegler Magazine for the Blind* to omit stories and poems that make allusions to visually stunning scenes that would, according to the magazine, only "serve to emphasize the blind man's sense of his affliction." Keller responds: "That is to say, I may not talk about beautiful mansions and gardens because I am poor. I may not read about Paris and the West Indies because I cannot visit them in territorial reality. I may not dream of heaven because it is possible that I may never go there. Yet a venturesome spirit impels me to use words of sight and sound whose meaning I can guess only from analogy and fancy. This hazardous game is half the delight, the frolic, of daily life. I glow as I read of splendors which the eye alone can survey" (Keller 2005, p. 32).

6. The text of the lecture has been reconstructed on the basis of student transcripts. See Heidegger 2009.

7. Feldman (2006, p. 88) argues that in *Being and Time* Heidegger attempts to use language to reveal the limits of language and thus that the book is ultimately not a discussion of being but a performance of language's inability to represent being. She observes that, in Heidegger's book, "the very words of the investigation into being are wrested out of readiness-to-hand, in part by devices such as italics, scare quotes, hyphenation, invention, and etymology, which thematize or make conspicuous the word-character of the words."

8. One thinks here of Helen Keller's reflection on what prepares one to become a writer. "You see, there is but one road to authorship," Keller writes. "It remains for ever a way in which each man must go a-pioneering. ... What I mean is, we can follow where literary folk have gone; but, in order to be authors ourselves, to be followed, we must strike into a path where no one has preceded us" (Keller, 1913, p. 120).

9. For example, Heidegger writes (1971, p. 81): "There is some evidence that the essential nature of language flatly refuses to express itself in words – in the language, that is, in which we make statements about language". Likewise, "The Way to Language" begins with a reverential invocation of a line from Novalis (Georg Philipp Friedrich von Hardenberg) that Heidegger hopes will encourage his listeners to keep the strangeness of language in mind throughout his lecture: "The peculiar

property of language, namely that language is concerned exclusively with itself – precisely that is known to no one" (Heidegger 1971, p. 111).

10. In his interactions with his guests from Japan, the topic of language was naturally important, since several of the guests were involved with the translation of Heidegger's works into Japanese. Heidegger's attention to this particular language, then, reflects his interest in these translation projects. It is worth recalling too that Heidegger's work was first translated into Japanese in 1930, 19 years before the first English translation.

REFERENCES

Aristotle. 1999. *Nicomachean Ethics*. Trans. Terence Irwin. Indianapolis: Hackett.

Bigger, Charles P. 1989. Logos and Epiphany: Walker Percy's Theology of Language. In: *Critical Essays on Walker Percy*, ed. J. Donald Crowley and Sue Mitchell Crowley. Boston: G. K. Hall & Company.

Brock, Wener. [1935] 2014. *An Introduction to Contemporary German Philosophy*. Cambridge: Cambridge University Press.

———. 1949. *Existence and Being*. Washington, DC: Regnery Gateway.

Crowley, Sue Mitchell. 1989. Walker Percy's Wager: *The Second Coming*. In *Critical Essays on Walker Percy*, ed. J. Donald Crowley and Sue Mitchell Crowley. Boston: G. K. Hall & Company.

Dewey, Bradley R. 1972. Walker Percy Talks about Kierkegaard: An Annotated Interview. *The Journal of Religion* 54 (3): 273–298.

Feldman, Karen S. 2006. *Binding Words: Conscience and Rhetoric in Hobbes, Hegel, and Heidegger*. Evanston: Northwestern University Press.

Gadamer, Hans-Georg. 2013. *Truth and Method*. Trans. Joel Weinsheimer and Donald G. Marshall. London: Bloomsbury.

Heidegger, Martin. 1962. *Being and Time*. Trans. John Macquarrie and Edward Robinson. New York: Harper and Row.

———. 1971. A Dialogue on Language. In *On the Way to Language*. Trans. Peter D. Hertz. New York: Harper and Row.

———. 2009. *Logic as the Question Concerning the Essence of Language*. Trans. Wanda Torres Gregory and Yvonne Unna. Albany: State University of New York Press.

Keller, Helen. 1913. *Out of the Dark*. London: Hodder & Stoughton.

———. 2005. The World I Live In. In *Helen Keller: Selected Writings*, ed. Kim E. Nielsen. New York: New York University Press.

Lauder, Robert E. 1996. *Walker Percy: Prophetic, Existentialist, Catholic Storyteller*. New York: Lang.

Lawry, Edward G. 1980. Literature as Philosophy: *The Moviegoer*. *The Monist* 63 (4, 1): 547–557.

Lawson, Lewis A. 1979. The Fall of the House of Lamar. In: *The Art of Walker Percy: Stratagems for Being*, ed. Panthea Reid Broughton. Baton Rouge: Louisiana State University Press.

Lushchei, Martin. 1972. *The Sovereign Wayfarer: Walker Percy's Diagnosis of the Malaise*. Baton Rouge: Louisiana State University Press.

Percy, Walker. 1975. *Message in the Bottle: How Queer Man Is, How Queer Language Is, and What One Has to Do with the Other*. New York: Farrar, Straus, & Giroux.

———. 1991. *Signposts in a Strange Land*. New York: Picador.

CHAPTER 4

That Mystery Category "Fourthness" and Its Relationship to the Work of C. S. Peirce

Stacey E. Ake

Part One: An Overview of Peirce's Semiotics

In an 1897 manuscript, Peirce defines "logic, in its general sense," as semiotics or the "formal, doctrine of signs" (*Collected Papers* 2.227, hereafter CP). For Peirce, there are three elements within this logical or semiotic relation: a sign, an object, and an interpretant. The sign or *Representamen*, which is also called a First, stands in a genuine triadic relation to something called a Second and something else called a Third. In this triadic relation, the Second is the First's *Object*, and the relationship between the First and the Second is capable of determining a Third. This Third, also known as the First's *Interpretant*, must also assume the same triadic relation to its Object with which the First stands in relation to the same Object (CP 2.274). Furthermore, the triadic relation is considered *genuine* only when "its three members are bound together by [the relation in such] a way that does not consist in any complexus of dyadic relations" (Ibid.).

Moreover, according to Peirce, a sign, or more technically a *representamen*, is "something which stands to somebody for something in some

S. E. Ake (✉)
Department of English and Philosophy, Drexel University,
Philadelphia, PA, USA
e-mail: sea29@drexel.edu

© The Author(s) 2018
L. Marsh (ed.), *Walker Percy, Philosopher*,
https://doi.org/10.1007/978-3-319-77968-3_4

respect or capacity. It addresses somebody, that is, creates in the mind of that person an equivalent sign, or perhaps a more developed sign. That sign which it creates [is called] the *interpretant* of the first sign. The sign stands for something, its object" (CP 2.228). By way of example, let me type the word "ball." Now, if Peirce is correct, as a sign or representamen, the word "ball" should have conjured up in the reader's mind conceptions of balls, whether beach balls, tennis balls, billiard balls, or crystal balls. These images, in the mind of the reader, are interpretants of the word-sign "ball," which in my mind is the representamen. Furthermore, just to point out the vagaries of semiotics, "logic in general", and human communication, the object of the sign in question was not a spherical object; rather, it was that wonderful midnight dance where Cinderella met her Prince Charming—a fancy-dress ball.

The above example also underlines something else which Peirce stresses in his semiotics—namely that a sign "can only represent the Object and tell about it. It cannot furnish acquaintance with or recognition of that Object" (CP 2.231). Because a sign can only convey *further* information about its object, there appears to be a certain "givenness" to Peirce's semiotics. This combination of what might be considered "givenness" as well as the predominantly descriptive nature of Peirce's philosophy gives rise in his work to a phenomenological analogue to the semiotic First, Second, and Third. These phaneroscopic (i.e., phenomenological)[1] categories are known as Firstness, Secondness, and Thirdness, respectively.

Part Two (A): Firstness—(Perception of) Quality

Firstness, like its semiotic analogue, can be considered the category of quality, where quality is something that is not necessarily realized. According to Peirce, quality "is not in itself an occurrence, as seeing a red object is; it is a mere may-be. Its only being consists in the fact that there *might be* such a peculiar, positive suchness in a phaneron [Peirce's technical word for a phenomenon]" (CP 1.304). In other words, the Firstness of the red object is its redness—a redness which would not exist without the occurrence of the object itself. In this sense, redness is a "may-be," a possibility, whose realization is impossible without the object's existence.[2]

In other words, I cannot have "redness" unless I have a red ball or a red shirt or a red car. But what about "Beauty" or "Truth" or "Justice"? These seem to have existences separate from things beautiful, true, or just. Why not "Red"?

Such questions aside for now, another aspect of Firstness that must be considered is that it is first met by the perceiver without concomitant analysis. Firstness just *is*—not merely the quality perceived but the moment itself. In this way, Firstness may also be viewed as the state of immediate consciousness, devoid of thought and reflection.

Part Two (B): Secondness—(Experience of) Struggle

Secondness, the middle category of Peirce's phenomenological triad, is fundamentally antithetical to Firstness. It is the state of encountering the other, the Object, in all its glorious alterity. As such, Secondness reflects "the element of struggle," (CP 1.322) where struggle is defined by Peirce as the "mutual action between two things regardless of any sort of third or medium, and in particular regardless of any law of action" (Ibid.). Moreover, Secondness also reflects that "which we especially experience—the kind of thing to which the word 'experience' is more particularly applied" (CP 1.336). Furthermore, Secondness is not merely the category of experience, it is also the category of cold, hard fact—quite literally. In Secondness, we "are conscious of (…) getting hit, of meeting with a *fact*" (CP 1.376).

According to Peirce, such a violent encounter with the factual will create "a sense of commotion, an action and reaction, between our soul and the stimulus" (CP 1.322). This commotion is the result of the factual nature of the stimulus' unrelenting alterity. The nature of the stimulus, the object, is such as to undermine all our prior perceptions. The object's nature is the absolute constraint upon our fancy, and we must change our thinking about the object as a result of our encounter with it. Peirce considers "such forcible modification of our ways of thinking the influence of the world of fact or *experience*," (CP 1.321) because it is this very act of coming to think "otherwise than we have been thinking that [definitionally] constitutes experience" (CP 1.336).

Part Two (C): Thirdness—(Cognitive) Mediation

Thirdness is mediation, and, as such, it is the category of thought and learning. For Peirce, Thirdness is the middle term between the extremes of Firstness and Secondness, and it is, in fact, best represented by thought. In a very early paper, dated 1868, Peirce writes that in thought, there are "three elements: first, the representative function which makes it a *representation*; second, the pure denotative application, or real connection, which brings one thought into *relation* with another; and third, the material quality, or how it feels, which gives thought its quality" (CP 5.290). The particular kind of quality found in Thirdness itself is not substantive in the sense of a quality or a First *quâ* Third, but adjectival in relation to thought itself, and this is what gives Thirdness its special place in the genuine triad of both Peircean semiotics and phenomenology. By imbuing thought with quality, thought may then go on to serve as a representamen in subsequent semiotic triads and as a true quality in subsequent phenomenological triads.

But before we can continue with the discussion of the phenomenological (and, consequently, existential) ramifications of this breach in Peirce's semiotics, I think it is necessary to draw out a few of the implications for communication and human self-knowledge (and, hence, human existence) which lie embedded in Peirce's semiotic phenomenology. To do this, it is necessary to discuss Peirce's view on how one comes to "fix belief" and thus arrive at knowledge. While this appears to be a singularly epistemological endeavor, it should be noted that it is through this epistemological method that Peirce first posits that we come to self-knowledge: by finding out that we are wrong. For Peirce, the self is known and made aware of itself via negation. I know myself through the errors I ~~amke~~ make. This is the "Apollonian demise."

It is the most Greek of all demises just as Apollo is often considered the most Greek of all the gods. He is the god of the sun, yet he is not. Helios is. He is the god of healing, yet he is not. Asclepius is. He is a god of truth and wisdom, and yet capable of incredible wanton cruelty. In other words, he is, fundamentally, neither true nor wise. He links gods and men, just as the Peircean "individual" relates the cosmos back to itself, and yet he does not. He simply speaks this relation through an oracle. His death? Not precisely known. Some say he became Dionysus.[3]

In other words, either Apollo was subsumed into all that with which he identified (health, wisdom, etc.) or he evolved into his exact opposite (Dionysus). Either way, Apollo *quâ* individual is gone and not a trace remains. Every attribute pertaining to Apollo has been co-opted by some other, including, in the end, his very identity: that is, he *becomes* Dionysus. Apollo becomes ~(Apollo). He is negated unto death, unto non-existence. And this negation unto death for a human engaged in semiotic praxis is a direct result of combining Peirce's *via negativa* to self-identity with his formulation for a scientific community. Such a combination is neither forced nor arbitrary. The creation of a self is a semiotic process whereby "self" is simply another word for the Third or interpretant that results from the interaction between the child (and his representamen) and the stove (the object). The resulting Third is a negation of the child's original First, and Peirce calls this Third a self.

Such a never-ending cycle of phenomenology would be incredibly painful if it were a matter of positively establishing a self.[4] However, we know from Peirce that the result of this process is not the creation but the diminution of the self into nothingness. But there is a noteworthy peculiarity in Peirce's concept of Thirdness, and therefore a Third; namely, that a Third "in semiotic terms is the interpretant which, when perceived in the *mind of an other* (again, a third), explains the relation between the First and the Second."

I would like to point out that the above reveals an aspect of Thirdness that distinguishes it drastically from either Firstness or Secondness: specifically, the fact that Thirdness moves in two different directions. Firstness, for example, exists in the object and moves toward the perceiver, who perceives it *quâ* representamen. Secondness exists in the mind of the perceiver toward the object, where the object counters it, resulting in the affirmation or negation of the perceiver's current representamen. Note that the representamen can be either affirmed or negated, resulting in an interpretant. Yet Peirce's fundamental assumption is that it will be negated. Thus, Secondness is not simply a matter of alterity for Peirce, but the *brutality*, the *struggle* of and with alterity.

Thirdness, on the other hand, does two things. This is brought to light if we again consider the little boy and the stove. There are actually two types of Thirds that are mediated in this anecdote: an epistemological one and an existential one; namely, "The stove is hot" (an epistemological Third) and "I am wrong" (an existential—or, perhaps, phenomenological?—Third). But what if the stove had been cold? Then, the two resulting Thirds would have been "The stove is cold" and "I am right". That Peirce does not develop this possibility simply reflects his strong prejudice toward the violence of Secondness.[5]

In other words, Peirce's semiotics and phenomenology depend on intersubjectivity, and the best he will do is articulate an inter*object*ivity. This lack of true intersubjectivity grounds the existential failings of Peirce's semiotics. This is why it is nothing more than a phenomenology—a semiotic description of existence. It is lacking in true sociality, in real intersubjectivity. Yet, as I mentioned above, there are glimpses of true intersubjectivity and positive individuality within the Peircean canon. That intersubjectivity which is present, unarticulated, in the Peircean canon is dubbed "Fourthness" by Walker Percy. And it is precisely such Fourthness that is necessary if Peirce (or anyone) is going to attempt to draw out what it means to be human as an individual, a particular, and not merely as a member, a participant, in a larger aggregate.

PART THREE: THE NEED FOR FOURTHNESS

In order to begin to explain Fourthness consider the scenario of a semiotic community made up of two people regarding a box. Here are two individuals who have established that the object is for all intents and purposes a box. In fact, we could call our two interlocutors "Those who call the object in question a box." Perhaps we call them "The Boxers" for short. In fact, they might even call each other that. "We are the boxers," they say. They have, then, between themselves, established knowledge of themselves by means of creating an identity.[6]

Yet in doing so, they have not only gone beyond simple knowledge of the other due to opposition (Secondness), they have also gone beyond Thirdness because their discovery of mutual understanding is the mediation that mediates their mediation. In retrospect, one can see that it is the existence of this Fourthness, a thing which presupposes Firstness, Secondness, and Thirdness, that allows the lesser forms of belief fixation to flourish. Were it not for Fourthness, neither tenacity (trust only in oneself either by ego or by default), nor authority (trust in the other to the detriment of the self and reality itself), nor the *a priori* method (trust in the articulation of Fourthness without actually going through the process requisite to achieve and affirm it, that is—trust in prior trust) could have survived as methods. In all of these cases, the social aspect of Fourthness has, in one form or another, vanquished the process of scientific inquiry. Fourthness, legitimately or otherwise, has triumphed.

Fourthness is (at best) a true abduction, since one can only guess and then experiment as to whether the other is trustworthy. In elaborating Fourthness, one engages in the scientific method. However, one cannot do so when one is establishing one's identity in the midst of Fourthness. Just as Peircean self-consciousness is created in the moment of negation, self-awareness via Fourthness exists in the moment, unmediated. One may discover later that this is how it came about by reflecting on the moment of Fourthness, but there is no reflection during the moment itself—just as there is no reflection on Secondness until after the moment has passed and been mediated.

Moreover, just as self-consciousness as negation occurs during the experience of Secondness, self-consciousness as identity occurs during the moment of Fourthness. "What?!! You play shortstop, too!" "I'm from Poughkeepsie as well." "You're kidding! You also have a kid-brother named Rudiger?" Such are the moments of Fourthness. And, although both Secondness and Fourthness are relational, unlike instances of Secondness that only serve to distance us from the universe, moments of Fourthness draw us back into it. It is unfortunate that Peirce, with the law of mind and its concomitant continuity, as well as his presentation of an agapastic creative universe, should have failed to develop thoughts of this nature. But perhaps such a Fourthness is not readily prescinded from an existence based on logic. Such an abduction to Fourthness requires, perhaps, more of a basis in the existential. I think this is seen in the work of Walker Percy, where he presents his theory of the "Delta Factor." In this, the human being moves from being a semiotic creature to a languaged creature.

PART FOUR: THE DELTA FACTOR

In his 1975 book MB, Walker Percy begins his first essay, entitled "The Delta Factor", with this exhortation:

> In the beginning was Alpha and the end is Omega, but somewhere between occurred Delta, which was nothing less than the arrival of man himself and his breakthrough into the daylight of language and consciousness and knowing, of happiness and sadness, of being with and being alone, of being right and being wrong, of being himself and being not himself, and of being at home and being a stranger (MB, p. 3).

Obviously, whatever this *Delta Factor* is, it is extremely important for Percy. Moreover, it seems to be required to bear a lot of weight so far as human relations and human being is concerned. Percy himself knows this, but for him the Delta Factor is the only key he can find to help him answer a fairly simple question, "What is man?"

And what is man that we are mindful of him? That man is a biological organism cannot be doubted. Percy would say that man is, obviously, an organism. But, for Percy, who is opposing the Skinnerian behaviorists, it should also be noted that man is much more than an organism in an environment; man is also a creature in a world, a world made up of symbols.

Percy's first premise is that we live in an age where all previously held theories concerning man have broken down:

> What does man do when he finds himself living after an age has ended and he can no longer understand himself because the theories of man of the former age no longer work and the theories of the new age are not yet known, for not even the name of the new age is known,[7] and so everything is upside down, people feeling bad when they should feel good, good when they should feel bad?
>
> What a man does is start afresh as if he were newly come into a new world, which in fact it is: start with what he knows for sure, look at the birds and beasts, and like a visitor from Mars newly landed on earth notice what is different about man (MB, p. 7).

So, Percy, taking his own advice, observes his fellow humans as if he were a Martian and discovers that the singular thing that causes them to stand apart is language: their obsession with it and ignorance of it. For Percy, it is a matter of *oro ergo sum*:

> Why is it that men speak and animals don't?
>
> What does it entail to be a speaking creature, that is a creature who names things and utters sentences about things which other similar creatures understand and misunderstand?
>
> Why is it that every normal man on earth speaks, that is, can utter an unlimited number of sentences in a complex language, and that not one single beast has ever uttered a word?
>
> Why are there not some "higher" animals which have acquired a primitive language?
>
> Why are there not some "lower" men who speak a crude, primitive language?
>
> Why is there no such thing as a primitive language?
>
> Why is there such a gap between non-speaking animals and speaking man, when there is no other such gap in nature?[8]
>
> ...
>
> Is it possible that a theory of man is nothing more nor less than a theory of the speaking creature? (MB, p. 8).

His second premise is stated as the conclusion above: "Is it possible that a theory of man is nothing more than a theory of the speaking creature?" If this is the case, then for Percy, it is quite possible that understanding man as a languaged creature will give insight into man's problems in the late twentieth century, as well as in the early twenty-first century.

Percy's own insight into the relationship between humans and their language came as he contemplated a particular event in the life of Helen Keller, namely her experience with Anne Sullivan in a well house in Tuscumbia, Alabama, in 1887. Percy notes that prior to her experience in the well house, Helen had learned basic stimulus-response signing. "When she wanted a piece of cake, she spelled the word in Miss Sullivan's hand and Miss Sullivan fetched her the cake (like the chimp Washoe, who gives hand signals: tickle, banana, etc.)." But before continuing on to the events of the well house, I would like to perform a quick Peircean analysis of Helen's "cake behavior."

Obviously, the object in question is the cake. So, we have cake as the object, the Second, in this semiotic translation. The hand-sign "c-a-k-e" is for Helen Keller a representamen and for Anne Sullivan an interpretant; however, the question is open whether this hand-sign is a representamen-interpretant for the object cake or for something else.

Note the fact that when Helen signs c-a-k-e to Anne, Miss Sullivan does not, in fact, reinforce the veracity of this sign, she instead *gets Helen a piece of cake.* Helen has not given the name or concept for an object; she has *issued an order for an activity.* There is no Firstness to Thirdness move in any real sense.[9] An order has been obeyed. A stimulus has produced a response.

Let's consider Helen's predicament from another Peircean angle. Helen is hungry (a First). She tries to assuage her hunger (a movement to Thirdness) by wanting cake (an object). So far, so good. So, she signs c-a-k-e (a representamen). Anne Sullivan gets her the cake (a very true interpretant in the sense of interpretation; Miss Sullivan has quite accurately interpreted Helen's demand). Here, the object in question is not the cake, but the *getting of* cake. In both these cases, a Thirdness or mediation is achieved without the presence of *thought.* As a matter of fact, the getting of cake for Helen is not a triadic event, but a sequence of dyads:

Helen is hungry B> Helen signs c-a-k-e
Helen signs c-a-k-e B> Anne Sullivan gives her a piece of cake.

Nothing in this series of relations bespeaks Peircean genuineness or triadicity. As a matter of fact, if this were a logical syllogism, Helen's signing would be superfluous.

In other words, nothing in this interaction comes back to affect or effect Helen as a person. She is not integrated into her universe; she merely commands it, and then becomes frustrated when it denies her wishes (as will be shown below).

It is all very well and good to say that Helen is experiencing Peircean negation (Secondness) without the necessary faculty of mediation (Thirdness). But how can this be if she is capable of signing her way to a piece of cake? How can she be capable of semiotic Thirdness (knowing the word "c-a-k-e") and not phenomenological Thirdness (knowing the word "H-e-l-e-n")? I suspect that it is because Helen, at this point in her life, is capable of what Seboek calls communication—the semiotic activity of any higher animal—but not capable of the semiotic activity of humans, namely language.[10]

This is because humans in language are dealing not with signs but with symbols, which implies a relation other than that of triadicity.[11] It implies a need for sociality, for Fourthness, where the fourth factor in question is that very Peircean community of fellow inquirers, one's fellow humans. This need for the presence of one's fellow men in the activity of language is what Percy calls the Delta Factor, something that he discovered in the well-house experience of Helen Keller reported below:

> We walked down the path to the well-house, attracted by the fragrance of the honeysuckle with which it was covered. Someone was drawing water and my teacher placed my hand under the spout. As the cool stream gushed over one hand, she spelled into the other the word water, first slowly then rapidly. I stood still, my whole attention fixed upon the motion of her fingers. Suddenly I felt a misty consciousness as of something forgotten—a thrill of returning thought; and somehow the mystery of language was revealed to me. I knew then that "w-a-t-e-r" *meant* the wonderful cool something that was flowing over my hand (MB, pp. 34–35).[12]

Helen discovers that "w-a-t-e-r" means water. In other words, "w-a-t-e-r" is the *name* for water. Water now has an existence apart from Helen's own. It exists in itself, and not simply as something that quenches her thirst. There is something *called* water:

> That living word awakened my soul, gave it light hope, joy, set it free! There were barriers still, it is true, but barriers that could in time be swept away.
> I left the well-house eager to learn. Everything had a name, and each name gave birth to a new thought. As we returned to the house every object

which I touched seemed to quiver with life. That was because I saw everything with the strange, new sight that had come to me (Ibid.).[13]

Consider the delight with which the infant or toddler greets the information that "This is daddy" or "That is mommy." Helen was experiencing
this; the realization that the world and all that was in it was discontinuous
from her(self). If things can be named, they can be mentally ordered, and
not just in the presence of said things but also in their absence. Now, she did
not merely have to react to the world, she could act in and upon it:

> On entering the door I remembered the doll I had broken. [She had earlier
> destroyed the doll in a fit of temper.] I felt my way to the hearth and picked
> up the pieces. I tried vainly to put them back together. Then my eyes filled
> with tears; for I realized what I had done, and for the first time I felt repen-
> tance and sorrow (Ibid.).

Could it be that acknowledging the separate existence of all that is around
us also awakens a sense of response-ability to and for them? Could it be
that this sense of response-ability is not cognitive or intellectual but simply
grounded in the realization that others exist? Could it be that acknowledging the strong alterity of the other—that it does not exist for the sole
benefit of our existence—is what awakens what we call "the moral faculty"? And, when we talk about morality, we are in fact talking about
moral sentiments and not moral imperatives, propositions, or schema?
Helen goes on to say:

> I learned a great many new words that day. I do not remember what they all
> were; but I do know that mother, father, sister, teacher were among them—
> words that were to make the world blossom for me, "like Aaron's rod with
> flowers." It would have been difficult to find a happier child than I was as I
> lay in my crib at the close of that eventful day and lived over the joys it had
> brought me, and for the first time longed for a new day to come (Ibid.).

From this story, Percy deduces the two key elements and the two key
implications of the Delta Factor. The two key elements are reflected in
the fact (1) that the presence of Miss Sullivan was absolutely necessary to
convey to Helen the nature of the symbol "water," and (2) that by Miss
Sullivan's help Helen came to understand that "w-a-t-e-r" meant *water*.
These two facets of the Delta Factor Percy respectively dubs (1) "the
relation of intersubjectivity" between Miss Sullivan and Helen Keller, and

(2) "the relation of quasi-identity" between the object *water* and the word "w-a-t-e-r," and both will be discussed in more detail below.

Before discussing them, however, I would like to stress the two implications of Helen Keller's story: first, that by means of the well-house incident, Helen has moved from the realm of animal communication to that of human language and, second—something which is very strange—Helen, by means of this event, has somehow entered the realm of ethical activity. By means of the well-house experience, not only have objects received names for Helen, but actions have received values, *moral* values. It seems that when objects receive value, they get names, and when actions receive value, they get meaning.[14]

It is by means of this relationship between Helen's acquisition of language and her apparently simultaneous acquisition of ethical understanding (or existential angst?) that Percy ventures to hypothesize that man's uncertainty and ignorance about the nature of language directly mirrors man's concomitant uncertainty and ignorance about his own nature.

But the relation that I am here trying to point to is the metaphorical capability of Helen and her moral capability; I suspect that they are part and parcel of one another. Consider, for example, the sentence "This [a round blue object floating in the sky] is a balloon." Now consider the sentence "Beauty is but a flower." Both sentences consist in the linking of disparate entities by the copula "is." The second is "obviously" metaphorical, but why not the former? Is beauty any more or less like a flower than a round blue floating object is like the sound "balloon"? Fundamentally, all tradition aside, the answer is no. It is this metaphorical ability to link/liken names to objects that opens the mind to linking (and, hence, likening) other disparate objects to one another: beauty and a flower, flesh and grass, *Coke* and it, God and love, sin and death, and so on.

Note also, that in all cases of naming, of metaphor, real communication is completely dependent upon the ability of the observer of the metaphor to prescind away the correct relationship between the entities involved. For example, what if the little boy thought his father meant by "balloon" the string that attached the balloon to his little wrist? Moreover, is flesh like grass because flesh, too, is green? Is Coke "it" because it reminds one of the silent movie queen and "jazz baby" Clara Bow?

But the development of such a metaphoric or narrative capacity depends not on thought, but on a teacher. This teacher imparts an authority that, while it may or may not be overthrown by subsequent experience, nevertheless establishes the process of naming, of metaphor, of *human* being.[15] Here again we see Fourthness, sociality, the Delta Factor in operation.

To understand the Delta Factor, please remember the two interlocutors that are contemplating the box in front of them. The box is the Object of their inquiry and interlocutor #1's representamen "box" is received as an interpretant in the mind of interlocutor #2. What Peirce fails to take into account is the relationship between the sound "b-o-x" and the object at hand. He also fails to consider what relation, if any, exists between the interlocutors (such as if one were a liar). Percy, through his articulation of the Delta Factor, addresses both these questions, as we shall see below.

PART FIVE (A): THE AXIS OF THE RELATION OF INTERSUBJECTIVITY

Consider the triadic relation of an object, a representamen (and its inter-locutor), and an interpretant (and its interlocutor). If one draws a line linking all three members of the triadic relation, it is obvious that a triangle unites all three. However, the subject of our triad, the sign itself (namely, "box"), is not included in the triad triangle. Why not? Ostensibly because it exists in the minds of the interlocutors. All well and good.

But to travel from one mind to another, this sign must take some form; it must be expressed in either spoken, gestured, or written language (i.e., the sign must have its *own* sign). It must be represented by something. This something Percy calls this a symbol, where a symbol has the same relation-ship to the sign as that sign has to the object (MB, pp. 251–264). Because of this view of the symbol, what goes on intrapsychically in the minds of the interlocutors is secondary to Percy's purposes. Thus, all the entities involved in Percy's "language game" are "real-world" objects: a symbol, an object, and two interlocutors. All of these language-game players have existences apart from one another.[16]

If we begin drawing lines among the various members of Percy's lan-guage game, what we see is an expansion of Peirce's triangle into a dia-mond by the addition of the symbol. But we also see something else: there are two axes. One axis joins the two interlocutors and is the axis of inter-subjectivity; the other axis, that of quasi-identity, unites the symbol and the object.[17]

If we recall Helen's experience at the well house, we soon realize that it is the authority (and perseverance and trust and kindness and persistence) of Helen's teacher, Anne Sullivan, that both conveys and affirms Helen's experience with the water. Helen had no doubt played with the running water before, perhaps splashing around in it or drinking it. It is not the *experience* of *water* that is new to her. It is the *naming of it* that is new. And naming can only be done with one who is already a knower of names.

"Naming can only be done with one who is a knower of names" seems like a perfectly obvious, inane observation. Perhaps. But what lies unnamed in that very sentence is that the relationship between the knower of names and the learner thereof, between the teacher and the pupil, is one of authority and trust. And it is a very delicate balance. Consider the abject bewilderment and confused sorrow that strikes a child the first time he or she discovers that mommy or daddy is wrong or lied or does not know something. For the first time, the formerly unquestioned balance between authority and trust has been shaken.[18] The authority of the child's principal source of names has been undermined.

However, this undermining of the parent's or the teacher's authority is absolutely necessary; otherwise, the child or student runs the risk of succumbing to Peirce's error of authority. And it is the very possibility of the error of authority that reveals the tacit existence of some form of intersubjectivity in the more phenomenological dimensions of Peirce's semiotic.[19] Please note that the undermining of the teacher's authority does not eliminate the axis of intersubjectivity; it merely alters it.[20] Once one has participated in the human language game, one cannot escape it. Even when one is all alone, isolated on a desert island, one can still hear the voices of one's past. Remember: Robinson Crusoe begins his memoirs reminiscing about his parents and their goodness and their *authority* in virtue of their virtue. Sartre was almost right. It is not only hell that is others; the complementary half of our reality is others, even if it is only made up of our memories of them.

What thus becomes apparent is that the axis of intersubjectivity will always be with us. This seems to imply that part of optimal human functioning might be to learn how to discern among "authorities" and come to recognize those "authorities" whose "naming" is most beneficial to one's self. It would also seem, given Peirce's account of the four incapacities, that one must also keep an eye on the object at hand. I think Percy would add that one must also keep an eye on the symbol at hand.

PART FIVE (B): THE AXIS OF THE RELATION
OF QUASI-IDENTITY

A friend of mine, a non-philosopher, once asked me what I thought the most essential or most basic philosophical question was. I responded with my most pathetic infantile whine: "Whhhhhhhhhhhhhy?!" I then added that you had to say it like a four year old. This story becomes even more revealing when one takes into consideration something that happened during one of my finals in high school.

It was my final in philosophy. There were three questions. One had something to do with Aquinas and Heidegger, the second one totally escapes me, but the third question was extraordinary. Prof. Tapia simply wrote on the blackboard: *Por qué?* (Why?). What a perverse question. I watched as student after student went up to ask him about this question. Smiling, he sent them all back to their seats. I saw some of my fellows intensely writing long essays. But to answer the unanswerable discursively is already the wrong answer. This question did not require an answer; it required a *response*. Obviously, there were only two choices: *Porque.* (Because.) or *Por qué no?* (Why not?). I chose the latter.[21]

It seems to me that the object-symbol relation can best be illustrated by something drawn from these two stories. It is the four year old who asks: "Why is the sky blue?" "Why do I have to go to bed now?" "Why are oranges round?" "Why am I here?" "Why is this *corn?*" "Why? Why? Why?" What would happen if parents resorted to a cheery, confrontational "Why not?" (thus turning the tables on the occupant of the car seat) instead of the usual, firm, barely covered exasperation of "Because"? I think this would surely open up the world for Peircean inquiry in an almost exponential fashion.

I also think (given the open-endedness of the question "Why not?") that it reveals not simply the arbitrariness of any objective relationship between object and symbol (Is "brittle" really *brittle?* Can one actually write with the word "pencil" any better than one can write with the Spanish word *lapiz?*), but also the socially constructed nature of all symbols. "Why is this corn, dear? Well, because we are speakers of American English and the symbol that is agreed upon (or that we have agreed upon) for this comestible is the word 'corn'. British speakers of English, however, use the word 'corn' as a name for all grain, not just for maize. We have also agreed to use that same symbol to denote a particular affliction of the feet, but that isn't relevant here. Would you like some more watermelon, dear?"

Without the intersubjectivity that exists between two humans, the creation of a symbol-object axis (the naming of something) is impossible. This brings us back to the idea that Peirce *assumes* the existence of Fourthness, of true intersubjectivity, throughout his entire semiotic phenomenology. As a matter of fact, none of his incapacities would be possible if intersubjectivity did not precede semiosis or *symbolosis* itself. The use of signs (communication) does not require human language and, hence, humans; but the making of errors where signs are concerned is only possible where there are humans and symbols and, hence, where real language is involved.

A sign cannot be mistaken; only a symbol can be mistaken. Consider the vulgar practice of seventeenth-century English sailors in Japan drinking the water offered them in their fingerbowls. As a sign, they were perfectly in their right: one drinks water. As a symbol, they were completely wrong: this is special water for ceremonial ablutions. If one does not think this difference holds, consider the social (or semiotic) consequences of drinking "Holy Water" from the font at a Catholic Church.

The final point of interest concerning the axis of quasi-identity (remember: one cannot eat the word *oyster*; for this reason, the relation between object and symbol can only be one of *quasi*-identity) is that what may be arbitrary is nonetheless quite real. "Soft" looks *soft* to an English speaker.[22] "Suave" on the other hand looks somewhat unscrupulous to an English speaker; however, it looks *soft* to a Spanish speaker. This is the stuff which dreams and realities are made on. Consider, for example, the fact that in English the word "love" rhymes with "dove," "above," "shove," and "glove" (hence the safe-sex slogan: "no glove, no love"). Now consider that the Spanish word *amor* (love) rhymes with *rubor, calor, sudor, pudor, clamor,* and *fragor* (redness, heat, sweat, shame, din, and chaos, respectively) as well as many others. Is it possible that the linguistic-language possibilities that result from a name affect the perceptions of the named object within the language culture? I suspect so. Language is a creature that creates. In this, too, it is much like man. It identifies and creates identity simultaneously. The capacity of both man and language to name and identify will have a peculiar effect when the object of naming turns out to be the namer himself, namely, man.

In the Peircean semiotic world, the first disclosure of the existence of something that might be called a self occurs when the inquirer encounters error, his own personal error and ignorance (Hoopes 1991, pp. 44–45). When the inquirer discovers, despite his own belief to the contrary, that the stove is, in fact, hot, he is, according to Peirce, revealing the source of his self-consciousness: his misapprehension. But his reaction is not simply [~(stove cold)!]. Rather it is, "The stove is not cold. It is hot; therefore, I am wrong!" From this, Peirce tells us that we must assume the existence of a self wherein ignorance and error lie. Thus, for Peirce, the self is all that is not in step with the lovingly evolving cosmos. Thus, the error-filled self consists of a negation of the already existing. Yet, by virtue of the agapastically evolving cosmos, every aspect of the self that is in step with the universe will be subsumed (in almost Hegelian fashion) into the cosmos and then negated (in almost Buddhistic fashion). These two fates of the self are its only possibilities; consequently, the self in the Peircean universe succumbs to an Apollonian demise.

However, one should note something striking about Peirce's negation unto death; it starts out with the inquirer's admission that "I am wrong." This admission of identity presupposes an "I" that could possibly err. That the self may be revealed in negation is, perhaps, true; but that the self might be somehow created via negation is patently ludicrous. Also note that, in Peirce's example, the child persists in thinking that the stove might not be hot, despite what his parents say.

In other words, the child himself is involved in negation or, at the very least, contradiction—which is essentially negation prior to testing. Had the stove actually been cold, what would the child have discovered? He would have discovered that he did not belong to the group of people (i.e., his parents) who believe that stoves are hot. In modern parlance, we might say that he has effectively discovered his alienation from his parents. So, affirmation of his perspective has led to a fate considerably worse than mere negation; he is alienated.

But to be alienated, one must be alienated *from something*. Alienation implies that one has lost some sort of nativity, in the sense of indigenousness. In testing the heat of the stove, is the boy testing the stove or the veracity of his parents' statements? I suspect the latter. He is perhaps testing their authority or he simply no longer trusts their authority. Either way, the existence of the elements of Fourthness presupposes their testing.

Fourthness is (at best) a true abduction, since one can only guess and then experiment as to whether the other is trustworthy. But Fourthness must be established before it can be tested. I presume that the Peircean elements of Firstness, Secondness, and Thirdness are experienced by humans in much the same way that they are experienced by other members of the animal kingdom. They present themselves in humans as communication. A four-month-old baby may have two distinct cries when in distress— "Change me!" and "Feed me!"—just as a monkey might have two cries— "Up tree!" and "Under cover!"—for when a predator appears. And while both are engaged in communication, neither is yet engaged in language.

However, as the baby (but not the monkey) matures, she enters the world of intersubjectivity in which other humans respond and coach her feeble attempts at communication. This establishes and reinforces in her particular reactions that soon become habits of response. These rehearsed forms of communication will, one day, explode into language as soon as the infant or toddler has had her "Helen Keller moment." The relation of intersubjectivity has activated the pursuit of quasi-identity (naming). This pursuit is a form or habit of thought. The continuation of this habit of thought into adult life is tantamount to the translation of the infantile "Why?" question into the more adult or more philosophic question, "Yes, but what does it mean?", for meaning is the medium of quasi-identity.

Thus, it seems that in elaborating Fourthness—the medium of inter-subjectivity that surrounds us, precedes us, and to which we identify and contribute identities—one engages in a scientific method of sorts. This is the case inasmuch as Thirdness is said to impart a quality to our future thoughts. However, it is predominately a matter of Peirce's own prejudice (and, no doubt, his own experience) that all subsequent experiences of alterity are presumed to be negative.

Consider again the fact that Peircean self-consciousness is created in the moment of negation; does this imply that self-awareness via Fourthness exists in the moment, equally unmediated? For to discover one's own self-awareness, one must reflect, after the fact, upon the moment of negation—for example, "The stove is hot; therefore, I am wrong" alludes—in virtue of the "therefore"—to some sort of reflection or Thirdness which mediates the relation between the contradictory input ("hot stove!") and the existing entity which posited the contradictory input ("I"). And yet there is no reflection *during* the moment itself, for there can be no reflection upon Secondness until after the moment has passed and been mediated in Thirdness.

Self-consciousness as identity, on the other hand, occurs *during* the moment of Fourthness. Remember: "What?!! You play shortstop, too!" "I'm from Poughkeepsie as well." "You're kidding! You also have a kid-brother named Rudiger?" Such are the moments of Fourthness. But these are particular moments of Fourthness between two subjects and the relation between them. This differs from naming an unrelated object in that it is not an object that is being named by one subject for another subject; rather, one subject is naming himself in virtue of another subject, thus creating a relation between them.

Part Five (C): The Resultant "Positive" Creation of Identity via Social Interaction

In other words, if two people consider an object and the one says to the other: "That, my dear boy, is a piliated woodpecker!" the relation of intersubjectivity ("my dear boy") has been used in order to establish a relation of quasi-identity (That ... is a piliated woodpecker), the establishment of which will be more or less successful depending on whether the authority of the namer is strong (he's the president of the local Sierra Club or Audobon Society, for instance) or weak (he's your drunk uncle; moreover, he's obviously staring at a squirrel).

Now consider Watson and Crick racing Wilkes and Franklin to the discovery of DNA. There is an object: DNA. The name (a symbol) is known, the acid itself (an object) can be elaborated, but its structure (another symbol, although it fundamentally represents the object's objectivity) still eludes scientists. The relation of intersubjectivity is already quite intricate between Watson and Crick; together they work out a model of the structure of DNA, and create a moment of naming (or nomenclature), of revealing the structure of DNA. They have established a relation of quasi-identity: this (model) is (or represents) the structure of DNA. But note, they have also participated in a moment of intersubjectivity *qua* quasi-identity. They now call themselves the co-discoverers of DNA. But which is it? Have they merely named themselves? Their relationship now, in fact, turns on their having become the co-discoverers of DNA. What happens when we name ourselves?

And yet it is the very nature of the human being and his involvement in language that allows him to name himself as well as the objects which surround him. Sometimes, although both Secondness and Fourthness are relational (they each deal with alterity), and unlike instances of Secondness which serve to distance us from the universe, moments of Fourthness draw us back into it. However, one may ask: is it the same thing for me to experience Fourthness with another as it is to engage in Fourthness with myself? Is there a difference in the authority involved that changes this relation?

Given the impact of Fourthness on Peirce's categories, it is unfortunate that Peirce, with his law of mind and its concomitant continuity/discontinuity, as well as his presentation of an agapastic creative universe, should have failed to develop thoughts of this nature. A phenomenologically rich interpretation of semiosis and its categories, which took into account the socio-existential aspects of man as a languaged animal, could speak volumes.[23] But perhaps such a Fourthness is not readily prescinded from an existence based on logic, even a logic as semiotic.[24]

NOTES

1. While the terms phenomenological and phaneroscopic are frequently used interchangeably in the Peirce literature, as they will be here, I suspect they are not synonyms. Rather, like the distinction between pragmatism and pragmaticism, Peirce is stating a tangible difference between phenomenology (the study of appearances) and phaneroscopy (the observation of the obvious). The first is a discipline, while the second is a method.

2. N.B.—The occasion for the existence of a "mere may-be" as realized in a phaneron is not the same as the existence of a quality as a "mere may-be" itself. See CP 1.304.

3. In part, such a divine transformation makes sense. Much of what is attributed to Dionysus' later cult actually reflects values originally attributed to Apollo: health, poetry, peace, blessedness. Moreover, Dionysus, like Apollo, had an extremely cruel side. Again, perhaps, only an exaggeration of Apollo's. Unlike Apollo, however, Dionysus' death is well-documented. Either by the Titans or on the orders of Hera, Dionysus is fated to be torn to pieces, resurrected, and torn to pieces again—only to follow in the cycle with another resurrection, another sundering. In this, Dionysus becomes the suffering god. However, to explain the relationship between the awful fate of Dionysus and the matter of selfhood and identity is not the subject of this chapter but the next one.

4. Consider what happens when it is the individual who is the object of the community of scientists? Is a stone altered or affected if it is mistaken for cubic zirconium, even though it is, in all actuality, a diamond? No, it is merely an object beset by erring subjects. (Besides, for Peirce, evolutionary love, by means of the community of scientists, will eventually amend this discrepancy.) But a person, a true subject, who—although a mere instance of the cosmos' attempt to understand itself—may, indeed, suffer under such error. He may, in fact, be torn apart by mis-identification, only to be joyfully restored to wholeness by correct identification, a wholeness which is subsequently shattered by an error which is healed by correct recognition

which is then ... and so on. This is the Dionysian demise. When one's quest for identity, for selfhood, for individuality is dependent on alterity, the result is an almost infinite flux between not wanting to be whatever it is that is oneself and wanting to be whatever it is that you have been told is yourself. In other words, it is despair.

5. Another oddity is that Peirce requires an other to *affirm* the interpretant. Liars aside, one must need ask the question why other humans should be the only set of objects not hell-bent on negating the individual.

6. In other words, they have named themselves by naming the semiotic community to which they pertain. They have articulated and admitted the social nature of their semiotic interaction as members of the scientific community.

7. Something reflected in the presumptuous absurdity of the appellations modernity and post-modernity.

8. Missing sentences: How can a child learn to speak a language in three years without anyone taking trouble about it, that is, utter and understand an unlimited number of sentences, while a great deal of time and trouble is required to teach a chimpanzee a few hand signals?

Why is it that scientists, who know a great deal about the world, know less about language than about the back side of the moon, even though language is the one observable behavior which most clearly sets man apart from the beasts and the one activity in which all men, scientists included, engage more than in any other?

Why is it that scientists know a good deal about what it is to be an organism in an environment but very little about what it is to be a creature who names things and utters and understands sentences about things?

Why is it that scientists have a theory about everything under the sun but do not have a theory about man?

9. At best, the use of "c-a-k-e" can be viewed as an index—a second of a second. And even in this, the actual establishment of the sublated legisign aspect of the index was established by Annie Sullivan and not by Helen Keller. In a similar way, one might share the index "fetch!" with one's dog. Thus, there are two interesting things here: (1) The aspect of Thirdness in "c-a-k-e" was imported by means of a person, a subject: Annie Sullivan, and shared along the axis of intersubjectivity with Helen Keller; and (2) because the level of exchange falls shy of the symbolic (even by Peircean standards), it would not be considered as truly or fully human in the Percyean sense.

10. That such a difference between Peirce's semiotic and phenomenological Thirdness is even possible is perhaps reflected in his use of the category of thought as a weasel-term. I posit that there is a qualitative difference between "thought thinking itself" and my thinking the thought that

"thought thinks itself," and that these two types of thought are not immediately interchangeable.

11. What Percy will be drawing upon in his use of the word *symbol* as opposed
to the more common term *sign* is an observation made by Peirce himself
but not developed. Note the following (emphasis mine):

A man walking with a child points his arm up into the air and says,
"There is a balloon." *The pointing arm is an essential part of the symbol
without which the latter would convey no information* (See CP 1.33).

Why is the raised pointing arm essential to the symbol which is, ostensibly, nothing more than a particular kind of mediated thought? I suspect,
along with Percy, that it is not the raised arm conveying information, but
the *father's* arm conveying *authority* that is the essential part of the
symbol.

12. It should also be kept in mind that water or wa-wa was the first word Keller
learned as an infant. Thus, she lost her hearing and sight to illness *after* she
had begun the process of naming. Whether the same results would come
to someone who was born deaf and blind is another question entirely.

13. Emphasis mine.

14. It is, perhaps, easy to disregard this second contention on the hermeneuti-
cal grounds that it is Helen Keller, the adult, who is writing this memoir
and imbuing it with her own ethico-religious experience. I agree. I am sure
the seven-year-old Helen knew next to nothing about "Aaron's rod"; however, the seven-year-old Helen *did* go over to the hearth and cry. This is a
fact that can be corroborated by those around her. So that, regardless of
her own interpretation, we are still left with her empirical action.

15. I suspect that one of the reasons "feral children" fail to learn human language is not merely their missing the "language acquisition age," but missing the human company from which one might learn language. The "wild
boy of Aveyron" never learned to properly speak, but he could respond to
the cracking of a nutshell or the placing of plates on a table. He responded
by coming to the sound in the same, albeit inverted, way Helen Keller
signed c-a-k-e when she was hungry. But neither the "wild boy" nor the
pre-well-house Helen would have ever said, "I am hungry." The reason for
this, I contend, is that they both lacked the capability to have an "I" or
even a proper name. If one cannot comprehend that w-a-t-e-r is *water*,
how much less can one comprehend that H-e-l-e-n is—is what??? If one
cannot concede that the "I" is a socially learned phenomenon (and not
necessarily one acquired by negation, although it may be amplified by it),
consider the fact that a two year old does not learn "I am Sebastian," what
he learns is "My name is Sebastian." In other words, my "name" is
"Sebastian," my "fuzzy bedtime friend" is "Bamse the teddybear," the
"big noisy thing" is "tractor." Another observation concerning Sebastian:

when he was a little over two years' old, his mother was "mommy," his father was *far* (Danish for father), and "anybody who will help me get out of bed or will play with me and my toys or will take me for a walk" was *mor* (the Danish for mother). Why? I think it is because, if you are in Denmark and scream "Mooooooooooooooooor!" loud enough, somebody will come. Scream "Mommmmy" and you are left out in the cold—linguistically and existentially. One final observation concerning language, social interaction, and individual consciousness: a human toddler cannot go through the "no!" stage unless he or she has fellow humans to negate. This sounds quite trite, but it is not. Peirce posits that one comes to self-consciousness by *being* negated by the world. I suspect that it is quite the opposite. I believe self-awareness begins when the toddler discovers that he or she can control (negate) others and their actions by the word "no!" I remember a friend of mine's daughter whose "terrible twos" lasted merely two weeks. One day, sitting demurely in her high chair, she was told to eat her peas. "No!" came her rallying cry, and *everybody in the kitchen froze*. She just smiled. She had felt the power. A few days later she was told that she could say either "yes *or* no" to questions depending on what she wanted. Shortly thereafter, the "terrible twos" subsided. By use of the word "no" she had successfully individuated herself from those around her; by the option to use yes *or* no, she received the capacity to integrate or not to integrate as she saw fit. This is the true beginning of autonomy. The "wild boy" never gets to individuate; perhaps Helen Keller never gets to choose until the moment in the well house.

16. That symbols are twice removed from their objects and once removed from their signs can be supported by the utter unintelligibility of Egyptian hieroglyphics throughout most of modern history. Such a language of pictographs should have been easy to decode, if it was a set of signs. Instead, it was a set of symbols such that the interpretation in the minds of the interlocutors transmogrified the signs themselves. Let me give another example. If you are driving and a ball rolls out into the street, you slow down and/or stop, just in case a child might be following it. The ball is a sign to stop. If you approach an upside-down triangle street sign, you may stop, slow down, or continue depending on the traffic conditions. And, in the United States, that would be the right thing to do. Not so in parts of Europe where that sign means "Stop!" In the case of the "Stop signs," one sees that they are really "Stop symbols."

17. It should also be noted that Percy essentially collapses the representamen and the interpretant into the sign itself (which he calls the "symbol"), thus giving the symbol a life of its own in opposition to the object as particular. The symbol, then, becomes the shared item, the creator of identity between the two organisms/subjectivities involved in this process. Because identity

is clustered around the symbol and not around the object, the representamen, or the interpretant, the process of inquiry can move beyond questioning the nature of the process of inquiry or the semeiotic itself into questioning the relation between the object and the symbol, the object and other objects, the symbol and other symbols, and so on. In other words, where the sociality, the Fourthness, of the two interlocutors is assumed, a true scientific inquiry can proceed.

18. Consider the reaction of the electorate to the sexscapades of their leaders. Here is an almost quantifiable relationship between trust (public confidence) and authority (the probabilities of successful re-election). Public figures "name" our values. If they cannot be trusted in the little things, what right do they have to be entrusted with authority over the big things?

19. If one considers the nature of Percy's symbol, one notices something very strange. In Percy's account of *symbolosis* (semiosis), the assumption is made that there will be no difference between the symbol in the minds of the two interlocutors. In other words, the interpretant and the representamen are collapsed into one another. This leaves one wondering whether Percy's Fourthness which results from the Delta Factor is not simply a form of fixation of belief by authority. That it, in fact, is not can be shown by two things: (1) the fact that both of the interlocutors are concentrated upon the object at hand and that communication of this sort (i.e., naming) cannot occur in the absence of an object, and (2) that the explicit social nature of Percy's semiotic approach almost guarantees not the veracity or good will of the community at large, but its multivocity. Moreover, the attitude of trust assumed by the recipient (adult) interlocutor stands to judge the veracity and goodwill of any particular namer.

20. This is classically illustrated in teenage behavior. Either a teenager will retreat into their own little world (and indulge in the error of tenacity; a four year old will also do this) or the teenager will join a self-reifying peer group (and thus become involved in the *a priori* error; something that can readily become a lifetime occupation). However, in neither of these cases has the actual axis of intersubjectivity been diminished one whit.

21. I suspect that all philosophical antinomies, when you come right down to it, participate in this very dichotomy and difference of approach.

22. However, if you say the word "soft" a hundred times, it will not only stop to seem *soft*, it will cease to mean *anything*. Eventually, it will become "ofts" because the "o" is the strongest sound in the word. In this way, the concept or perception of "softness" can be experimentally separated from the word in which it inheres.

23. In positing logic as semeiotic, man as a sign, and logic as the third of the normative sciences, Peirce betrays a prejudice which undermines the real-order veracity of his project: a belief that life is logical or fully collapsible

onto logic. Existentially, this is not the case. Thus, while Peirce goes to great lengths to define and describe his categories discursively, he does not define them (in the sense of *bas-relief*) by setting them out existentially. Even Secondness is not valued for its existentiality *per se*. Rather, it is valued as an heuristic device that hones the precision of Firstness in its pursuit of Thirdness. Thus, reality is not to be valued in and of itself but for its tutorial abilities. However, such a criticism is not devastating to Peirce's project, since, as mentioned before, all the elements necessary to creating a definition of Fourthness are present within his writing—but not in such a way as to be readily discerned.

24. N.B.—But a logic as semiotic views man as a sign not as a man *per se*. Thus, one can see how the formative aspects of sociality may have escaped Peirce's notice.

REFERENCES

Hoopes, James. 1991. *Peirce on Signs*. Ed. James Hoopes. Chapel Hill: The University of North Carolina Press.

Peirce, Charles Sanders. 1932. *Collected Papers of Charles Sanders Peirce*. Eds. Charles Hartshorne and Paul Weiss. Cambridge, MA: Harvard University Press.

Percy, Walker. 1975. *Message in the Bottle: How Queer Man Is, How Queer Language Is, and What One Has to Do with the Other*. New York: Farrar, Straus, & Giroux.

CHAPTER 5

Diamonds in the Rough: The Peirce-Percy Semiotic in *The Second Coming*

Karey Perkins

As the author of six novels and a National Book Award winner (1960), Walker Percy is mostly known for his fiction in the tradition of the French existentialists—Camus, Sartre, Gabriel Marcel (CWP, pp. 183, 275; MCWP, p. 167). Claiming to be uniquely American in this endeavor, Percy credits existentialists Kierkegaard and Marcel as primary philosophical influences (CWP, p. 5; MCWP, pp. 166–67). However, he is more than a novelist with occasional random existential musings or themes. Although he begins in existentialism—life itself had made him so, as he battled a then life-threatening illness, tuberculosis, soon after medical school—his extensive readings as he recuperated in a Saranac Lake New York sanitarium introduced him to semiotic theory, the study of signs and symbol, first through Susanne Langer, then through Ernst Cassirer (CWP, p. 57; MCWP, p. 143). Langer and Cassirer sparked Percy's interest in language and the uniquely human activity, as Percy saw it, of symbol. But it is from American pragmatist Charles Sanders Peirce that Percy's own semiotic theory eventually emerges and thoroughly permeates his writing—both fiction and non-fiction—with layered meanings. Percy attempts a

K. Perkins (✉)
University of South Carolina - Beaufort, Beaufort, SC, USA

© The Author(s) 2018
L. Marsh (ed.), *Walker Percy, Philosopher*,
https://doi.org/10.1007/978-3-319-77968-3_5

systematic philosophy based in Peirce's semeiotic [Peirce's spelling], a philosophy he called the "Peirce-Percy Semiotic" (Samway 1995, p. xviii).

While it's fairly clear that Percy's non-fiction explores Peirce, the Peirce-Percy Semiotic has not been recognized in his fiction. Overlooked is that Percy is applying semiotic principles not just in his essays, but also in his novels—something rarely mentioned, even by Percy himself. As Percy becomes more and more convinced that it is Peirce who has the answer to the problem he wants to solve, and as he focuses more and more on Peirce's semiotic in his non-fiction research as his philosophical journey progresses, his novels reflect a similar shift. Percy's first three novels are primarily existentialist, but his last three are infused with the Peirce-Percy Semiotic.

THE PROBLEM: ANTHROPOLOGY'S FAILURE

Existential philosophy may have named the problem of the human condition, the angst and longing humans uniquely experience even when life is otherwise proceeding quite well. But Peirce's semiotic provided the answer to the problem, which is the inadequacy of current theories of science—whether biology, psychology, anthropology, even traditional semiotics—to fully describe humans and the human condition. Percy says: "[A]n individual man or woman cannot be encompassed by scientific theories ... after the last word is spoken by science, man remains a wayfarer" (MCWP, p. 129). Science cannot differentiate functional (survival, biological) purposes from ontological (existential, meaning) purposes using its current paradigm. Percy sought an adequate theory, a whole system—something he called a radical anthropology—to replace failed current scientific perspectives of human beings:

> A radical anthropology must take account of ontological levels more radical than the scope of the functional method .... Anthropology must be willing to accept not only functional criteria: what social and biological purpose is served by this or that cultural element or aesthetic criteria: whether or not a cultural element conforms to the prevailing cultural pattern and contributes to "cultural integration," but a normative criterion as well. It must not be afraid to deal with the fact that a man may flourish by one scale and languish by another—that he may be a good organism and an integrated culture member and at the same time live a trivial and anonymous life (MB, pp. 240–41).

Conversely, other humans will forgo basic needs at a biological level to flourish at an existential level. The starving artist sacrifices physical needs to create his work; the devoted monk will fast and take vows of poverty and chastity to become closer to God. How does science explain this behavior on a functional level? Not very well. Percy recognizes that science can explain certain characteristics of humans biologically—hunger, heart attacks, procreation—but completely fail to explain other characteristics, existential ones. Percy writes, "Modern anthropology deals with man as a physical organism and with the products of man as a culture member, but NOT with man himself in his distinctive activity as a culture member .... Modern anthropology has been everything except an anthropology" (MB, p. 239).

Percy thought traditional science failed because its methodological assumptions confined it to a "dyadic" understanding of human beings, including their symbolic capacity, whereas Peirce identified the "triadic" perspective that would correct this view. "Accordingly, like Charles Peirce, I insist on the irreducible difference between dyadic and triadic phenomena," Percy says (SSL, p. 283). While dyads represent two physical objects interacting in a discontinuous cause-effect, stimulus-response manner, triads represent a continuity of relations, a web of relations creating a fabric of life, enabling humans to have symbolic capacity, including language, art, culture, religion, self-awareness, even uniquely human consciousness. The dyadic and triadic distinction is the crux of Percy's argument, and it was Peirce who introduced the idea to Percy through his concepts of Secondness and Thirdness. For Percy, the concept of Thirdness was the missing answer to his existential questions about why science fails to account for the human psyche and its symbolic capacity. He explains:

Why is it that there's only one theory of pneumococcal pneumonia, and yet there are sixteen schools of psychotherapy, sixteen theories or views of the personality, and a patient can do just about the same in each of the different schools? One works as well as the other .... The point is that we don't know very much about the psyche, not much more than Plato .... My feeling is that the only way to get a hold of any "science of the psyche" is to approach it through triadic theory. Most traditional psychology, all science, tries to explain things dyadically, interaction, secondary causes, function ... which works fine for explaining the solar system or black holes or quasars and pulsars, the whole cosmos is a dyadic system. But it doesn't work fine for explaining other triadic creatures. It doesn't work at all for explaining consciousness, language, poetry, other triadic activity, e.g., uttering a sentence

.... Suppose someone took Charles Sanders Peirce seriously and tried to create a triadic science? (CWP, pp. 289–290).

And that's exactly what Percy did.

THE SOLUTION: THE PEIRCE-PERCY SEMIOTIC

One culprit responsible for the dyadic paradigm's domination of modern science was Descartes' dualism. Percy writes: "If modern man was split in two by Descartes' mind-body theory three hundred years ago, it is unlikely that he can be pasted back together by yet another theory. [We need] ... a new way of looking at things .... Charles Peirce's triadic theory applies mainly to man's strange and apparently unique capacity to use symbols and in particular, to his gift of language" (SSL, p. 117). This "new way of looking at things" is a paradigm shift toward the triadic mode. Percy cites many times his desire to make an objective model or develop a theory, a full system, of human beings to replace inadequate dyadic theory dominating anthropology and psychology today (CWP, pp. 221–222).

In part, the scientist in Percy is reacting against existentialist Kierkegaard's subjectivity. Although Percy agreed with Kierkegaard's criticism of science's inadequacy to describe humans, he felt Kierkegaard erred in his "opposition to Hegel's system—objectivity" (CWP, p. 119). Percy clarifies, "I was trying to systematize it ... having been brought up scientifically, I had a great respect for scientific rigor and precision of language" (SSL, p. 109). Charles Sanders Peirce's semiotic provided that objectivity. While Percy does not give a name to his system in this interview, he does elsewhere, writing in 1971 a letter to Shelby Foote about such a book:

> 100 years from now it could well be known as the *Peirce-Percy theory of meaning* [my italics] .... this guy laid it out a hundred years ago, exactly what language is all about and what the behaviorists and professors have got all wrong ever since—laid it out, albeit in a very obscure idiosyncratic style. I propose to take his insight, put it in modern behavioral terms plus a few items of my own, and unhorse an entire generation of behaviorists and grammarians. (Samway 1995, pp. xvi–xvii)

In 1977, Percy reemphasized to Foote his interest in pursuing the "Peirce-Percy Semiotic" (Tolson 1997, pp. 223–24; Samway 1995, p. xviii). Percy subscribed to Peirce's semiotic and wanted to pursue it, adopting a version of it as his own. To that end, in the last decade of his life, Percy corresponded with Peirce expert and semiotic mentor Kenneth Laine Ketner, seeking a greater understanding of Peirce and his concepts. Ketner refers to Percy's version of Peirce's theory in several papers, calling it variously the "Peirce-Percy Conjecture" (Samway 1995, p. 266) and the "Peirce-Percy Principle" (Samway 1995, pp. 273, 282). Percy's impression of Peirce's importance is conveyed in a letter to Ketner: "My own feeling is that what I could call Peirce's 'triadic' theory is of seminal importance as a formal schema for making sense of that distinctive human behavior which involves the use of symbols (sentences, literature, art, etc.) and that it has not even begun to be explored—despite all the lip service to Charles Sanders Peirce (CSP) by present-day semioticists—nor by literary theorists—nor by psychiatrists" (Samway 1995, p. 14). Percy also expresses a desire to write a book called *Thirdness*:

> The thesis is that CSP's Thirdness, triadicity, properly understood and properly applied, can go a long way in pointing some right directions in the current mess in which the social sciences find themselves .... The traditional paradigm (Cartesian and Newtonian), which has been so extraordinarily successful in the physical, chemical, and biological sciences, has proved quite a spectacularly unsuccessful in the so-called social sciences, i.e., the sciences of man qua man. (Samway 1995, pp. 17–18)

It was a conclusion that would only strengthen as time passed. By the end of his life, Percy said, "I think Charles Peirce, the American Philosopher, may be the best clue about it, which has not been pursued or developed ... I would like to ... become a recluse for the next four years and work on Charles Peirce's triadic theory of language" (MCWP, pp. 204). As time progressed, his philosophical focus on Peirce intensified. Percy's existential anthropology becomes a semiotic anthropology, and Charles Sanders Peirce becomes the foundation of Percy's philosophical system, the Peirce-Percy Semiotic.

Percy denies that one would have to read philosophy to understand his novels. In 1971, he says in separate interviews: "God forbid if we have to read philosophy in order to read a novel," and later, "I don't believe in enigmas and acrostics. I've read novels that you have to have read some sort of handbook in order to understand. I think if this sort of novel—the philosophical novel or whatever it is, the sort of thing that the French pioneered—is any good, then the philosophy is part and parcel of the novel, and there's no illustrating of theses" (CWP, pp. 53, 60–61). However, his latter three novels belie his words. A comprehension of his philosophy is necessary for an appreciation of the full impact of the Peirce-Percy Semiotic in L, SC, and TS.

THE PEIRCE-PERCY SEMIOTIC: FOUNDATIONS IN PEIRCE

Percy's semiotic was a classification system, with geometric shapes and their corresponding numbers as categorizing labels based in Peirce's concepts of Firstness, Secondness, and Thirdness. Percy didn't have much use for Peirce's monads or his concept of Firstness; it was Secondness (dyads) and Thirdness (triads) he was after.

Secondness is what happens when physical, material qualities knock into each other; Secondness includes physical cause-effect reactions that take place in different times and spaces. One billiard ball, in one space, begins at one point in time. It travels through space and time, and hits another ball in another space and time, causing a reaction. When two billiard balls or two cars collide, a cause-effect reaction that is consistent, orderly, and predictable occurs. Secondness is what we think of when we think of the physical world, that which acts according to the laws of Newtonian physics. Peirce explains, "The idea of second is predominant in the ideas of causation and of statical force. For cause and effect are two; and statical forces always occur between pairs. Constraint is a Secondness" (Houser and Kloesel 2009, p. 79). Secondness is undeniable. The world of Secondness is the world that traditional science examines and describes. Peirce writes: "The second category of elements of a phenomena comprises the actual facts .... Facts also concern subjects which are material substances .... we feel facts resist our will. That is why facts are proverbially called brutal. Now mere qualities [Firstness] do not resist. It is matter that resists" (Houser and Kloesel 2009, p. 77).

Percy says traditional science explains the physical world through dyadic models: "Dyadic events are, presumably, those energy exchanges conventionally studied by the natural sciences: subatomic particles colliding, chemical reactions, actions of force-fields on bodies, physical and chemical transactions across biological membranes, neuron discharges, etc." (MB, p. 162). In the "energic" world of classical matter, this works. However, "[s]omething usually went wrong with the behaviorist S-R model whenever it was applied to a characteristically symbolic transaction,

telling a story and listening to a story, looking at a painting and understanding it, a father pointing at a ball and naming it for his child, a poet
hitting on a superb metaphor and the reader 'getting' it with that old
authentic thrill Barfield speaks of .... To be blunt about it, it doesn't
work" (MB, p. 32). But Percy had found something that DID work: triadic theory.

When these material cause-effect reactions (Secondness) become regular and predictable, we can create "laws" or general principles about results
of these interactions. These consistent and repeated reactions of two particles or entities result in *Thirdness*—or the laws of the "habit-taking tendencies" of things. Newton's laws and what we generally think of
science—physics, yes, but also the social sciences such as behaviorism—
rely on the principles of Secondness to make sense, but the laws themselves, the laws that material entities follow and exhibit, are examples of
Thirdness.

Thirdness describes things that are real in the universe, but that are
non-material. For example, the law of gravity is a reality in the universe,
but it is not tangible. One cannot see the law of gravity with one's five
senses, only the results of that law. The law of gravity cannot "bump into"
anything and create a reaction, but it does describe and affect items in the
world in an undeniable and unalterable manner (e.g., if I release the ball I
am holding, it will fall to the ground.) Freedom is really found in the universe, and its presence makes a clear difference in the universe, but it is still
non-tangible. Hamlet is also real in the universe (with definite, unalterable
characteristics), but he, too, is non-tangible. Peirce explains:

> Take, for example, the relation of *giving*. A *gives* B to C. This does not con-
> sist in A's throwing B away and its accidentally hitting C, like the date-stone,
> which hit the Jinnee in the eye. If that were all, it would not be genuine
> triadic relation, but merely one dyadic relation followed by another. There
> need be no motion of the thing given. Giving is a transfer of the right of
> property. Now right is a matter of the law, and law is a matter of thought and
> meaning (Houser and Kloesel 2009, p. 92).

Thirdness is represented by a "triad," a three-place relation, and it is
essentially relationship—between anything, whether abstract principle or
material entity or both—and it creates "continuity" in the world.

Another Peircean doctrine is that Thirdness is primary and more
basic to the world—not Secondness, as is classically believed. A classical

physicist sees separate and distinct atoms or particles and their underlying elements as the first and primary components of the physical structure of the universe; a Peircean physicist sees relationship and connectedness (among any and all entities) as the primary component of the universe—which includes physical structure and far more.[1] Peirce applies this concept to human beings as well. All else, including atoms and individual human beings, is secondary to relationship. And, all is related. Ketner writes to Percy: "The basic stuff of the cosmos is relation; ... the cosmos is a bunch of relations and worlds and like .... Matter, in other words, is a just a certain kind of relational pattern or system (as is everything)" (Samway 1995, p. 32). While dyads represent two objects interacting in a discontinuous cause-effect manner, triads represent a continuity, a web of relations creating a "fabric of life." Without Thirdness, we would live in a world of disconnected dyadic events, not unlike Hume's Bundle of Perceptions, or what Percy considered the greatest danger, Nominalism, of which, he says, "[N]othing [is] really knowable or scientifically lawful or meaningful but a bunch of sensory impressions that we give names to" (MCWP, p. 64). Peirce says that "every genuine triadic relation involves meaning, as meaning is obviously a triadic relation" (Houser and Kloesel 2009, p. 91). Percy refers to Peircean Thirdness in his last novel: "The great American philosopher, Charles Sanders Peirce, said that the most amazing thing about the universe is that apparently disconnected events are in fact, not, that one can connect them. Amazing!" (TS, p. 68). It is this connection that gives life meaning. Percy realizes, like Peirce, that Thirdness is directly related to meaning, and human capacity for symbol entails the human existential need for meaning and ontological knowing—meaning of the word, meaning of the event, meaning of life.

THE PEIRCE-PERCY SEMIOTIC: PERCY'S ADAPTATION

Percy applies Peirce's metaphysical concepts to his own version of semiotic, in particular illuminating the unique act of "naming." He says, "What I object to is the social scientist—what I would call a 'triadic' creature, which is what all men are—demoting his subject to a 'dyadic' creature" (MCWP, p. 59). Structuralists and other language theorists transfer science's dyadic model (Peircean Secondness) to communication.

A *dyadic* language event includes two things, the signified (object) and the signifier (word). Percy uses the following example to show the dyadic theory of communication, as when the father points to a balloon and tells his child that that is a balloon (MB, p. 43); in this picture, the father utters the world "balloon" and the child then looks for the balloon (Fig. 5.1).

For Percy, however, dyadic models are not an accurate description of the human language event of symbolism, of naming, which includes a third element. What humans are doing, a triadic event, is qualitatively different from what animals are doing, dyadic sign.[2,3]

The San Francisco zoo's sign-language-using gorilla, Koko, was taught perhaps 100 words in human sign language,[4] but Percy argues that she was using dyadic *sign*, not triadic symbol. When Koko signed "banana," it was a dyadic event, an action or motion merely in order to get the banana (Fig. 5.2).

According to Percy, Koko's signing had only *two* components—the object "banana" and the word "banana." Her communication was a biological event, for survival, explainable by science; she signed it to satisfy her hunger, to *get* a banana. For her, it was a cause-effect event. The sign "banana" did not *become* the banana or *mean* the banana in Koko's mind; it was an action that produced a result. The sign (the cause) produced the banana (the effect), and they occurred at separate moments in time, one following the other. The event is not metaphysically different from two billiard balls hitting each other. The purpose of the event was to satisfy a physical need, not an existential or ontological one.

For Percy, traditional science and semiotics err in their attempt to understand symbol and language and human interactions dyadically. A dyadic event, or "sign," entails a space-time *separation* between word and object. In the triadic symbolic event, there is no space-time separation. The word and the object are actually *one*, occurring simultaneously, united within the individual by a coupler. To a human being, the word *is* the

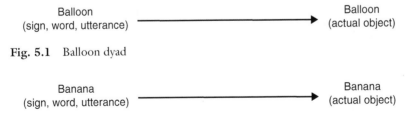

Balloon
(sign, word, utterance) ⟶ Balloon
(actual object)

Fig. 5.1   Balloon dyad

Banana
(sign, word, utterance) ⟶ Banana
(actual object)

Fig. 5.2   Banana dyad

object. Triadic symbol differs from dyadic sign in that the latter is a linear cause-effect, stimulus-response interaction, whereas the former is not. With dyadic phenomena, two separate entities directly relate to and interact with each other on a physical level and remain separate; with triadic symbol, there is no direct causal relation of signified (object) and signifier (word). Triadic symbol has two items, an object and a word, but they are "coupled," entailing a third element, a coupler. Symbol is a pairing, a simultaneous identification in which the symbol actually BECOMES the object symbolized—through the third element, the coupler. The object is contained *in alio esse*,[5] within the word. Percy elaborates:

> But what is a symbol? A symbol does not direct our attention to something else, as a sign does. It does not direct at all. It "means" something else. It somehow comes to contain within itself the thing it means. The word *ball* is a sign to my dog and a symbol to you. If I say *ball* to my dog, he will respond like a good Pavlovian organism and look under the sofa and fetch it … But if I say *ball* to you, you will simply look at me and, if you are patient, finally say, "What about it?" The dog responds to the word by looking for the thing; you conceive the ball through the word *ball*. (MB, p. 153)

So a symbol does not *direct* our attention to an object, but is rather a "vehicle of conception" that carries the essence of the object *in alio esse*, within it. Symbols don't *announce* or *point* to an object, they essentially *are* the object.

To clarify, Percy draws a triangle of a commonly mistaken impression of symbol. The triangle shows arrows from sign to organism (as the organism hears the sign) and then from organism to object (as the organism's attention is then directed toward the object). Percy here is drawing a linear process of "sign"—one which is erroneous when describing human symbol-mongering (MB, pp. 199, 252) (Fig. 5.3).

Fig. 5.3 Linear (dyadic) "symbol"

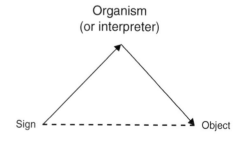

This diagram is not one triad, but rather, two dyads. The dotted line is an imputed relation; the solid lines represent a relation of cause. However, the second arrow is pointing in the wrong direction, according to Percy. The proper message (triadic symbol) does not merely "pass through" the organism as this drawing implies, which is still dyadic, still a linear and energic event, still cause and effect, just going through the organism as a human filter. In this mistaken view, sign and object are still separate, in both time and space, not united within the individual.

The correct depiction of symbol is with both arrows going directly to the organism, so that they are united within the individual *at once, simultaneously*. The symbolic event does not "pass through" the individual; in fact, without the individual, the symbolic event does not even exist. It actually occurs *within* the "organism" or individual or interpretant. Symbol does not point to anything, but it *becomes* the object in symbolization within the organism. Percy reverses the second arrow, drawing an entirely different metaphysical event (Fig. 5.4).

Percy illustrates this using Helen Keller's famous epiphany in the garden where she understands the American Sign Language word "water" *triadically* rather than *dyadically* when her teacher signs it into her hand. She experiences triadic symbol at that moment, even though she had been signing dyadically all along, to *get* water (and anything else she wanted). But in the garden moment, Helen already *had* the water flowing over her hand; she now realized the symbol *was* the water—a completely different epistemological experience than had been occurring with her dyadic sign-using before. She experienced a moment of joy and illumination, says Percy: "It wasn't the case that Helen had received the word 'water,' which had then directed her attention or behavior toward the water. That wasn't what happened. What happened was that she received *both*, both the sensory message from the hand Miss Sullivan was spelling into and that from the other hand, which the water was flowing over"

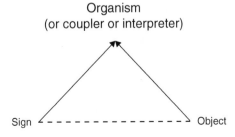

Fig. 5.4 The triadic symbolic event

(MB, p. 37). Her eager repetition of the word and eagerness to know the name of as many things as she could immediately afterward was not to receive the water, which she already had, but joy at recognizing the water, *in alio esse*, within the symbol and within her.

Symbol-mongering, a triadic activity, is not cause-effect (therefore, non-linear), and it is without matter or energy (non-energic). Symbols can't be explained by a materialistic science because language doesn't have a material substance that can be observed or examined by a dyadic paradigm. But, just like Peirce's concept of the law of gravity, freedom, and Hamlet being real but not existing, that doesn't mean language or symbol is not "real." Although non-tangible in the material world, triadic symbol, like Thirdness, is as real as any dyadic event in that it affects our life and the entire world, regardless of our wishes otherwise.

Finally, language occurs only in community. Symbol is existential *and* communal. Symbol is a social reality, not an isolated reality. Feral children, raised without humans, do not achieve language in their social isolation; we need a community of humans to attain symbolic ability.

Percy expands his triadic theory of language, adding the *tetrad*, representing the human community that is necessary for language to occur. In addition to the first three elements, that is, the signifier (word), the signified (object), and the coupler (whatever it is in the human that "couples" the word and object),[6] there is a fourth element—the receiver of the symbol, the other human. "Without the presence of another, symbolization cannot conceivably occur because there is no one from whom the word can be received or meaningful. The irreducible condition of every act of symbolization is the rendering intelligible; that is to say, the formulation of experience for a real or an implied someone else" (MB, p. 257). Percy diagrams a tetrad to represent this (Fig. 5.5).

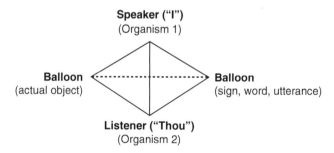

Fig. 5.5   The intersubjective tetrad

For Percy, what happens along the vertical axis, the relationship between the two human beings, defines and makes possible what happens along the horizontal axis, the dotted line between word and object, which has no real causal relations, but is merely designated so by the two humans (MB, p. 252). Percy explains, "By the very nature of symbolic meaning, there must be two 'organisms' in the meaning relation, one who gives the name and one for whom the name becomes meaningful" (MB, p. 256). In addition to the "I," or the human being who names, there must be a "thou" to whom the "I" speaks. The other human being must be conceived, not as another object in the world (Gabriel Marcel's and Martin Buber's concept of "It"), but as a co-celebrant (Marcel's and Buber's "Thou") (MB, p. 257). The other person, the "thou," understands the "I" because both have agreed upon the name for the object and understand that to be so. We say "Yes!" to the other's designation, so we say "Yes!" not only to that symbol, but to the world created by the community. We participate in community and affirm the "other." This is Percy's concept of "intersubjectivity" (MB, p. 258).

Intersubjectivity—relationships and community—also is the concrete medium in this world through which God is lived and experienced. Existentialist Gabriel Marcel's theology has implications in Percy's novels that echo his tetradic semiotic. It is through community that God is found, says Marcel.[7] While others have argued Percy's Kierkegaardian roots, understanding his connection to Marcel is more vital when contemplating Percy's semiotic. The answer to the existential crisis, for Marcel and also Percy, was not Kierkegaard's abstracted life of the monk reading and praying in isolation, eschewing the world. Percy and Marcel do not split spirit from the physical world nor mind from the body. The physical world and its people are not a fallen place to flee, but a divine arena that affirms creation, life, and love, hence Percy's, like poet Gerard Manly Hopkins', lush landscapes.[8]

While Kierkegaard's final religious stage would require the believer, like Abraham, to give up the entire world, including all earthly relationships (if asked by God), for Marcel and Percy the opposite is true. Humans need to live in the reality and presence of the physical world, with other humans, to experience the divine. By entering into a commitment of fidelity to another person and of service to a community, the believer enters into a life of the religious sphere, the life of faith and service to God—one reason is why all of Percy's novels end in marriage.[9] Percy affirms: "There's something else going on besides a love story" (MCWP, p. 62). Percy's novels end with his protagonists leaving Kierkegaard's aesthetic sphere and entering into a Marcellian world where commitment to relationships and life in the body and this world are the medium of growth (CWP, pp. 75, 204; MCWP, pp. 62, 69, 74–75, 107). Percy does not foresee his protagonists eventually abandoning community to have the ultimate union with God as Kierkegaard does. It is not the abstracted Protestant Kierkegaard, but the grounded Catholic existentialist Marcel, whose answer of community as the place where God is manifest, who most closely resembles Percy's intersubjective tetrad in the Peirce-Percy Semiotic.

Another geometric event Percy uses can be designated as *triangulation*, which is related to number symbolism, but of a slightly different character: an action, rather than a static symbol. Triangulation uses two (or more) elements, which can be seen or experienced, to determine the existence—often the location and/or presence—of a third, which cannot be seen. Naming is ultimately an *action* of triangulation: the object and symbol can be seen, though the coupler cannot be seen. We must deduce from the evidence that the coupler exists. In this sense, all symbols are acts of triangulation in that they are physically present entities that give us clues or awareness of another presence, an unseen one, including a transcendent one. Percy's characters triangulate throughout his novels from physical clues to the divine presence. Triangulation is key to Percy's triadic theory of language—the idea of the word as part of a triad and not a dyad. Triadic theory would not be possible without triangulation. The coupler cannot be seen (and as such remains an unsolved mystery), but is clearly present, as evidenced by the nature of the interaction between word and object to create a name. One of Percy's protagonists' tasks is to recognize the clues and symbols they encounter as clues to the divine through triangulation. God's presence surrounds us constantly, but is only accessible if we acknowledge and can "see" it in clues, or signposts, in a strange land.

The Peirce-Percy Semiotic in the Novels

Percy's novels illustrate the existential paradox: socially successful characters who are spiritually empty or unfulfilled; unsuccessful, ill, or otherwise struggling characters in their world who are spiritually full. His novels also show the mistaken dyadic solutions to psychological splits, engendered by current flawed anthropology and the misguided physicalist resolution of the mind-body split. Dyadic manipulators attempt to heal characters' inner rifts: by lapsometers (LR); or the right medication and dosage for sodium imbalances (SC); or chemical substances in the water causing behavioral efficiencies, on the one hand, and behavioral malfunctions, on the other hand (TS). But, for Percy, these dyadic solutions are based in an errant understanding of what a human being is and fail to create a truly "fulfilled" individual.

The correct solution is found in the triads and tetrads of the Peirce-Percy Semiotic. Though Percy never mentions it, these semiotic principles become integral to Percy's last three novels. A different number, each with semiotic roots, is emphasized in each of these novels, corresponding with differing themes. In Percy's fourth novel, L, threes and triangles correspond to protagonist Lancelot Andrewes Lamar's attempt to find some higher element within human beings besides mere physical impulses. Next, SC's fours, squares, and diamonds correspond with the love story, and the theme of community in general, of humans needing each other. And finally, TS's *Syndrome's* twos (and sixes) correspond to humans receiving chemical or physical solutions to spiritual problems or dilemmas, essentially transforming into "beasts" and losing important elements of their humanity, including their capacity for language, a dyadic result both behavioristic and diabolic.

Percy's use of number in his novels is evident in his fifth novel, SC. At first, when protagonists Will and Ally are alone and searching for some greater meaning for their lives than dyadic ones being offered to each of them, Percy uses threes and triads; however, about halfway through the novel, when they find each other, his semiotic symbols become fours, diamonds, and squares as the two together create an intersubjective community.

This book is a love story, about two lonely people who serendipitously find each other. When Williston Bibb Barrett meets his soul mate, Allie, and they connect, love and an authentic community (eventually extending beyond themselves) are created. The novel opens as Allie escapes from a mental institution and takes up residence in a greenhouse in the woods on land she inherits. Will first meets her when he stumbles off the golf course looking for his misdirected ball, but later, he falls through a cave wall into her greenhouse, and she cares for him in his unconscious state. Their love takes off, and after a series of obstacles (Will is institutionalized; Allie fights to stay in her forest home), they reunite and start a community with each other and then with others. Triads, signs of the divine, of the presence of God surround Will and Allie at first (and the other characters, who remain oblivious to the signs). These signs guide Will and Allie on a "treasure hunt" for authentic relationship with God and others. The novel itself is a treasure hunt, and the signs are clues as to where and what the treasure is. The treasure hunt is a metaphor for life; the real, authentic treasure is the tetradic diamond—the intersubjective diamond of community. Percy represents the treasure many ways—gold, light, birds, and Hopkins' nature imagery, but primarily with diamonds.

Will's threes that he encounters as the novel opens are little clues—ones that he sometimes notices, sometimes misses—that there is something "more," an intersubjective community of "fours," waiting for him. The novel's first sentence opens with a "sign": "The first sign that something had gone wrong manifested itself when he was playing golf" (SC, p. 3). From the very beginning, signs point to something beyond the golf links (a shallow society) to an authentic community and life. His ball carries a "good three hundred yards," and he uses a "three-wood" on the shot (SC, p. 5). Vance waits for his "third shot" (SC, p. 6) at the same time. The numbered wood serves double duty; the "three" refers to Percy's language theory, but also the postmodern impersonal nature brought to the game ("Now you can choose a numbered club from the back of an electric cart") when it used to be called a "spoon" (Ibid.)—an intimate sleeping position between lovers, a very personal community. When Will slices (a golfing failure) the "third ball," he sees it as a "failure at living, a minor deceit, perhaps even a sin," judging himself by the values of the world (SC, p. 45). The religious concept of sin enters with threes; the dyadic world of animals does not have this concept.

Yet that slice leads him into the woods, off the golf course toward the fulfillment he had been searching for, when no amount of conformity to contemporary values (the straight line to the hole) had ever done that. Later, Will wonders "whether he would hit the ball three feet or three hundred feet? Did it matter?" (SC, p. 65). On the golf course, which represents the shallow community, but a community nonetheless, one plays in a "foursome," (a community, but dedicated merely to a game). Symbols surround him, leading him away from that world to a more authentic one, with Allie, one that has lasting meaning and real relationships and true love.

Everywhere, Percy sprinkles divine clues of threes, leading his protagonists to the treasure of fours. It seems that threes, or signs of God calling to Allie and Will, manifest themselves even, or especially, in the midst of the least divine, most worldly, of situations: not just the golf course, but also the garage where Ewell tries to get him in on a porn movie deal. Another three-clue that Will examines are the shells from the shotgun that his father used when he shot his son. Will wonders his whole life what had happened, trying to piece the event together, examining over and over again, the "three empty Super-X shells" (SC, p. 60), shells that deafened him and almost killed him. In one moment, "holding the three-iron in both hands," as Percy repeats over and over, the truth comes to Will as he replays the event in his mind, just as he had done for "thirty years" (Ibid.). Repeating the event, holding the three-iron as if it were a magic ball or "a divining rod" (SC, p. 61), or rather, a divine rod, a three that can lead him to the answer, Will realizes what happened: "There were *four* shells" (Ibid.). Will's three-iron is a divining rod that leads him to find "four"—leading him to community. "He was watching the three iron as, held in front of him like a divining rod, it sank toward the earth. Ah, I've found it after all. The buried treasure, he thought smiling" (Ibid.). The treasure is "fours," the inter-subjective community.

Newly escaped from the mental home and amnesiac from shock treatments, Allie tries to determine both her identity and her purpose, as well as where to go. She triangulates. She looks at her driver's license, which expired *three* years ago, to find both the date and her identity. First, "[s]he looked at the calendar and the date of the expiration of her driver's license. She made a calculation" (SC, p. 24). From this, she finds the date. She triangulates again. "She gazed at the photograph on the license. She read the name. Earlier in the Gulf rest room she had looked from the photograph to the mirror then back to the photograph. The hair was shorter and darker in the photograph, the face in the mirror was thinner, but it was the same person" (Ibid.). Triangulation reveals self and the answers she seeks. Like Allie, Will triangulates, too. His identity is also at the third point in the triangle. Percy writes of Will's triangulation: "With two mirrors it is possible to see oneself briefly as a man among men rather than a self sucking everything into itself—just as you can see the back of your head in a clothier's triple mirror" (SC, p. 14).

More threes surround Allie; she gets her hair cut like the actress in *Three Days of the Condor*; she checks into the Triple-A motel. She is recreating her life based on threes. Her old life in the mental institution, she reads in her diary, does not have threes. She had written her diary after her sixth course of electroconvulsive therapy. Later, in Percy's next novel, sixes are used to represent "the beast" or man without God. Interestingly, the movie *Three Days of the Condor* was based on the novel *Six Days of the Condor*. Percy transforms its name from six into three, just as Allie has left her life of sixes for threes.

As she sits on the park bench to locate herself and her direction, she receives three choices of paths to follow: one, an abstracted proselytizer with a tract; the second, a runner offering physical health. But she takes a third solution, unique to her, and Percy's answer to how to live life, how to address the existential angst in a postmodern world, which is counter to the normal paths offered today. She charts her own path: "After marking the trail with her Scripto pencil and making an X in the blank space, she folded the map carefully with the marked trail on the outside and stuck it in the breast pocket of her shirt" (SC, p. 43). The four-pointed X—representing the intersubjective tetrad—is the greenhouse in the forest where she will reside—and eventually, though she doesn't know it yet, build an intersubjective community with Will. She keeps her treasure map—X marking the treasure—close to her heart.

Her real treasure, her life in a "stained glass" house with a cathedral of stone in an Edenic setting (SC, p. 83), is devoid of the material trappings of America's consumer society. "She meant to live with few things" (SC, p. 43). Her stained glass cathedral is the holy life she has chosen. Allie's nature setting in the woods, surrounded by life and greenery and sunlight, is God's presence in the world, with imagery from Gerard Manly Hopkins' poetry. There, Allie's work and use of tools is divine work. She has the "strength of three men" with her block and tackle (SC, p. 234). She puts "three bricks" under the door that serves as a bed for Will when she nurses him back to health (SC, p. 235). She continues "the search" just as Will does, looking for clues, marked by threes: "For one thing, she could read these books for more clues" (SC, p. 83).

Later come the intersubjective diamonds and the fours, when Will and Allie meet. The threes guide Will to Allie and along their respective, but isolated, paths in life. Threes guide them to the fours, the Marcellian community with each other in which life with God is created and manifested. In contrast, the surface conviviality of the golf links represents a shallower society, not an authentic community, but a superficial one governed by social approbation for values based on a worthless fool's goals—just as "fool's gold" is worthless (SC, p. 40).

Will's first meeting with Allie is a "four" meeting, and her need for "four" (community, relationship) awakens when she meets him. As he goes to retrieve his golf balls from the forest, she has them, a Spalding Pro-Flite and a Hogan Four:

"This one woke me up."

"What?"

"Hogan woke me up."

"Hogan woke you up?"

"It broke my window," she said, nodding towards the greenhouse .... "I was lying in my house in the sun reading that book. Then *plink, tinkle,* the glass breaks and this little ball rolls up and touches me. I felt concealed and revealed" (SC, pp. 75–76).

The "four" breaks the wall of glass surrounding her and touches her deeply and intimately. She is no longer isolated, no longer behind a barrier, just as the naming/symbolic event (represented by the Hogan Four) between one person and another creates community between the two of them. The ball acts as a naming event, as it reveals her the way the symbol does, waking her up, as the intersubjective naming event is a waking event to a whole new world. Naming is a "breakthrough" event of the human species and the breakthrough event for each individual to human divinity and community, just like Helen Keller's moment of joy and awakening upon realization that "water" was water in the garden.

However, Will doesn't recognize what he's found; he doesn't stay. Ironically, he leaves the intersubjective possibility to go on an abstracted journey in search of God: "My project is the first scientific experiment in history to settle once and for all the question of God's existence" (SC, p. 192). He enters a cave, taking pleasure in his search for God, a dyadic scientific experiment for concrete proof, at least a more meaningful endeavor than golf. However, dyadic science is not the answer to the question of God's existence; community is. As Percy also says of language, God cannot be subsumed under science—the latter is the subset of the former; mystery and relation are the bigger set. A scientific experiment will not uncover the presence of God, but love will.

Will journeys into the cave, searching for "the answer" (or, what Allie calls, the secret), and the answer is—as God's answers often are—quite unexpected. Instead of the expected sign, God gives Will a toothache, a clear rejection of the scientific path to God, driving Will out of his generalized abstraction and straight back into his body: "What kind of answer is this to an elegant scientific question?" Will wonders (SC, p. 224). He becomes too sick to look for the answer to the question; too sick to even ask the question. Will's blind journey to exit the cave then leads him through a sealed hole in the cave rock that the greenhouse juxtaposes. He falls through the hole—a free-fall headfirst through "air and color [spirit and life] brilliant greens and violet and vermilion and a blue unlike any sky" (SC, p. 226). He falls out of the scientific abstraction of the lonely cave into the physical reality of Allie's greenhouse, into love, into a life with her, into intersubjective community.

Percy writes: "*The hole was a square* [my italics]" (Ibid.). This is the start of their romance, and it begins by Will's falling through the intersubjective diamond. It was "deliverance from the cave" (Ibid.), from his isolated self, from his aloneness. God is not found abstractedly, through a Kierkegaardian rejection of the world, as Will attempted in his cave search. Will does not find God until he falls out of the cave. God is lived through world and community—the answer of Catholic Marcel and the final tetrad of the Peirce-Percy Semiotic. Will is spiritually reborn and now about to start his real journey to God and with others.

Allie bathes him in threes—in divine signs—to help him recuperate from his fall. When he is sick or unconscious, she gives him three aspirins (SC, p. 227); to lift him, she has the strength of (better than) three men with her block and tackle (SC, p. 234); she puts three bricks under the door to bathe him (SC, p. 235). But when they are together and in love, it is no longer threes, but fours and diamonds, which represent their love. As she lay next to him, she and he together are shaped like a diamond with their bodies: "When she started to climb over him, she discovered that he had moved to make room. As she turned to nest again, he held her shoulder and she came down facing him. But he was bent a little away from her. She bent too" (SC, p. 257). Together, they create Percy's intersubjective diamond with their bodies. Percy is clearer with this reference a little later: "He turned back. Their foreheads touched. Their bodies made a diamond" (SC, p. 262). These diamonds are what one finds in a treasure chest, but as Percy's intersubjective tetrad, the treasure is their loving community. When the electrical storm arrives and they are in the greenhouse: "Facets of glass flashed blue and white. It was like living inside a diamond ... Lighting struck again. The glass house glittered like a diamond trapping light" (SC, pp. 264–265). Blue, white, light—the colors that surround them are those of the divine. Their little community of love is divine, but instead of the treasure being outside of them, possessed by them, they are living inside the diamond; they *are* the diamond. They have not "found" the treasure, but they have *become* the treasure and are living it through their love and through community. The treasure is not outside of us, but within us, and in how we live our lives everyday.

Many have commented on Percy's existential wondering about what to do at four o'clock on a Wednesday afternoon (the *fourth* day of the week). Somehow the malaise just "gets" to you then. Percy's oft-noted observation of depression in the middle of the afternoon in the middle of the week seems to have been chosen for its middling nature—as in the middle of life, we wonder why we are here, what it's all about, and don't know. Here, four o'clock has a greater significance. "Imagine having you around at four o'clock in the afternoon," Allie says to Will, in amazement and joy at his presence (SC, p. 257). The time of four o'clock is not arbitrary. It is four, the time for community; the antidote to the existential depression of life is community. Even later she says it again, "Late afternoon needs another person .... What if four o'clock comes and I need another person?" (SC, p. 239). Four o'clock is the hour of community and of love, because four is the number of intersubjective community. Will wonders about Allie when it is 4:30, if she is OK, or spiraling into herself (SC, p. 310). Later, when they finally reunite, Allie says, "Now I know what was wrong with four-o'clock the afternoon" (SC, p. 341). So Allie knows when Will arrives that the existential malaise of four o'clock is solved by the presence of love and a community: "As a life of smiling ease with someone else and the sweetness for you deep in me and play and frolic and dear sweet love the livelong day, even at four o'clock in the afternoon turning the old yellow green-glade lonesomeness into a being with you at ease not a being with you at unease?" (SC, p. 329). Allie thinks later:

> Then along comes late afternoon—four o'clock? Five o'clock?—a time which she thought of as yellow spent time because if time is to be filled or spent by working, sleeping, eating, what do you do when you finish and there is time left over? ... clock time became a waiting and a length which she thought of as a longens. Only in late afternoon did she miss people ... In this longitude longens ensues in a longing if not an unbelonging (SC, pp. 237–238).

At the end of the novel, when Allie and Will are together, he comes to see her:

> I was talking to a man at St. Mark's and all of a sudden I realized it was almost four o'clock and I wanted to see you.
> You wanted to see me because you know how I feel at four o'clock in the afternoon?
> That and more (SC, p. 354).

And then, he promises more: "I will always come see you at four o'clock in the afternoon ..." (SC, p. 355), and they lay down next to the Grand Crown stove (a stove of "fours").

Allie thinks to herself: "[I]s loving you the secret, the *be-all* not *end-all* [my italics] but starting point of my very life, or is it just one of the things creatures do like eating and drinking and therefore nothing special and therefore nothing to dream about? Is loving a filling of the four o'clock gap or is it more?" (SC, p. 258). Allie's wondering if her love is like eating or drinking, is wondering if it is dyadic—a mere biologically programmed instinct for survival. Or is it a triadic/tetradic phenomenon—not of the body, but of the soul, meaning, and fulfillment? Put differently, why do Percy's protagonists spend the entire novel searching for God, only to abandon that search to settle down with a good woman in a leafy enclave? This is the end to Percy's novels. Is the community, this relationship just a distraction from the emptiness, or are they an actual authentic solution? Is it merely physical instinct that all animals, all creatures are compelled to, or is it something entirely different—a human activity solely, not a distraction, but a new human orientation, an ontological one of "being" (and hence, a "be-all" not an "end-all").

The answer is not an external goal ("end-all"), but an internal way of living a life of love ("be-all"). Allie says, "Either way would be okay but I need to know and think I know. It might be the secret because a minute ago when you held me and I came against you there were signs of coming close to it, for the first time, like the signs you recognize when you are getting near the ocean for the first time" (Ibid.). Even if it is the "secret" and a "sign" to nearing to the ocean (the transcendent), rather than merely a satisfaction of a biological need or a distraction from the malaise, Allie distinguishes between the "be-all," which it might be, and the "end-all," which it is not. The "end-all" of course is the destination, the ocean—the transcendent, or God—which human relationships can't suffice for, can't take the place of. The "be-all" however is how we must be and what we must do while we are on our journey to the ocean. Besides referring to the ontological stance instead of the biological one, "be-all" refers to Gabriel Marcel's intersubjective ontological orientation ("being") instead of functional ("doing"). Relationships are how we live out our lives while we are here in "this world" and while we are on our way to the ocean; they are also signs of the way there. They are the ground through which the eternal (God) manifests in the temporal world.

When Will is in the institution, there are no fours, only three men, Will, Mr. Arnold, and Mr. Ryan, and the fourth is the TV. "He discovered it was possible to talk to them and even for them to talk to each other, if all three watched TV. The TV was like a fourth at bridge, the dummy partner they could all watch" (SC, p. 319). The TV, the "fourth," makes possible community. But this solution is not the real answer; it is a living death, an aimless community of distraction without purpose: "So here is the giant-screen Sony projector TV and CBS day and night and some of the programs not half bad either, some the programs in fact well done and amusing, yes, especially the sports and documentaries, yes? M*A*S*H ain't bad. No? No. There was something he had to do" (SC, p. 325). The institution tries to give dyadic, physical solutions to triadic existential problems. But the existential problem is answered not by the right mixture of medicine to ratchet up certain brain chemicals, nor a delivery of Prozac, nor the distraction of TV, nor even "Episcopal decorum." The existential problem needs an existential solution: an authentic community of true love, divinely sanctioned. Allie knows that the existential misfit in society is not due to brain chemistry being off. It is due to that missing of God and of "the other"—a Thou to commune with. She says to Will, "Our lapses are not due to synapses" (SC, p. 329). "Our lapses" are the individual lapses on an everyday basis which are manifest through existential longing and attempts to solve with distractions; on a larger scale, the human race's lapse with "the Fall," a lapse which drugs cannot actually cure, only hide. Their lapses are not biological, but ontological—a need for God and community.

When Will settles down with Allie at the novel's end, escaping the hospital (institution), they build a community with his fellow patients and their cumulative skills. Mr. Arnold can build a "*four*-room house with a creek-rock chimney" (SC, p. 320), a home which is at once a part of nature (creek, rock) but also made of "four" rooms. Much to Will's surprise, the answer is not God alone, but a loving community in which God can manifest. Just as community is necessary for language to manifest—as well as art, culture, and religion—it is necessary for God's divine presence to take concrete shape. Will falls into Allie's greenhouse onto the "concrete" (SC, p. 226). He is no longer in his cave of abstractions, but in concrete reality of others' lives, and the concrete manifestation of God through helping others (as they will soon proceed to help each other, and then later, those in the institution, and create a literal community). On a larger scale, the individuals in community have complementary skills just as Will and Allie complement each other. Mr. Arnold and the other men in the institution will help Will create a community—a whole greater than the sum of its parts—for all of them. Here, Percy moves from the threes (God alone, and the protagonists alone) to fours (love, relationship, God-in-community).

Early in his career, Percy identifies modern science's inability to fully understand human beings using a dyadic methodology, and he spends the rest of his life working on the solution, the Peirce-Percy Semiotic, which shows up later in his fiction as well as in his non-fiction. Percy's fifth novel may be a love story, but it's one that is far far "more than just a love story" (MCWP, p. 62). In SC, Percy shows the intersubjective tetrad of community answering the human angst, loneliness, despair, and meaninglessness that current social sciences cannot even identify. Percy gives the existential problem a semiotic solution.

NOTES

1. See, Bell and Ketner 2006.
2. Charles Sanders Peirce uses the term "sign" varyingly, as sometimes referring to a dyadic event, other times a triadic event. Walker Percy is more consistent, using the term "sign" to indicate a dyadic event in contrast to the term "symbol" to denote a triadic event. However, sometimes for Percy, "signs" can also be "signposts," or clues to, evidence of, the divine, as in "*Signposts in a Strange Land*" or the "signs" that Will and Allie encounter in SC leading them on the path to each other.
3. Whether some species besides humans are capable of symbolic activity is debated; Percy didn't think so, while others thought that higher-level primates and even elephants, dolphins, or parrots engage in rudimentary symbolic communication or even culture activities. Percy's thesis that sign and symbol are different still stands, even if his view of animals' capacity for symbol is in error.
4. According to Percy here, that is. Her trainers say she learned 1000 signs over the years and could understand 2000 English words; her gorilla partner, Michael, could sign 600 words. Steven Pinker feels this number may be exaggerated, however. At any rate, it is exponentially less than the human child's fluency in language acquisition.
5. Meaning, not directly or absolutely, but "in another mode of existence."
6. Percy spends much time discussing what the coupler might be, but never comes to a conclusion about the essence of it, other than that he speculates it is "inside" the organism (human), and he's fairly certain it's not material.

7. Buber's theology emphasizes intersubjectivity as well. Pragmatist Josiah Royce has a similar result in his *The Problem of Christianity*, which is heavily into CSP and semeiotic; Royce was one of Peirce's few disciples.

8. Nature suffuses Percy's novels, as a kind of sacrament, a conduit to the transcendent, and Percy's appreciation of nature directly opposes Kierkegaard's "stark landscapes" (CWP, p. 123). Percy says of Hopkins, "It is as if the whole universe is filled with grace. It's not just gracious Jesus, which is so Protestant" (CWP, p. 124).

9. Except LG, although Percy says that "the implication was that Will Barrett was going back to the start, probably marry Kitty" (CWP, p. 205) (though by the time the sequel arrives, things have changed).

References

Bell, Ralph G. and Ketner, Kenneth L. 2006. *A Triadic Theory of Elementary Particle Interactions and Quantum Computing*. Lubbock: Institute for Studies in Pragmaticism.

Houser, Nathan and Christian Kloesel. 2009. *The Essential Peirce – Volume 1: Selected Philosophical Writings (1867–1893)*. Bloomington: Indiana University Press.

Lawson, Lewis A., and Victor Kramer eds. 1985. Conversations with Walker Percy. Jackson: University Press of Mississippi.

———. eds. 1993. *More Conversations with Walker Percy*. Jackson: University Press of Mississippi.

Percy, Walker. 1971. *Love in the Ruins*. New York: Farrar Straus and Giroux.

———. 1977. *Lancelot*. New York: Farrar, Straus & Giroux.

Percy, Walker. 1980. *The Second Coming*. New York: Farrar Straus and Giroux (Picador).

———. 1987. *The Thanatos Syndrome*. New York: Farrar, Straus and Giroux (Picador).

———. 1991. *Signposts in a Strange Land*, edited by Patrick Samway. New York: Farrar Straus and Giroux (Picador).

———. 2000. *The Message in the Bottle: How Queer Man Is, How Queer Language Is, and What One Has to Do with the Other*. New York: Farrar Straus and Giroux (Picador).

Samway, Patrick H. (ed.). 1995. *A Thief of Peirce: The Letters of Kenneth Laine Ketner and Walker Percy*. Jackson: University Press of Mississippi.

Tolson, Jay, ed. 1997. *The Correspondence of Shelby Foote and Walker Percy*. New York: Norton (Doubletake).

CHAPTER 6

Walker Percy's Intersubjectivity: An Existential Semiotic or 3 + 3 = 4

Rhonda R. McDonnell

In "The Delta Factor," the introductory chapter of MB, Walker Percy wrote, "Most readers will not want to read all chapters. It is hard, for example, to imagine anyone at all at the present time who would want to read the last" (MB, p. 10). With this wry observation, Percy acknowledged that he was ahead of his time. He had found during the years between his first essay publication in the 1950s and the publication of MB that the scientific community (not to mention the lay population) was not prepared for a rigorous science based upon a triadic rather than a binary model, a science which could explain "how queer man is, how queer language is, and what one has to do with the other." Further, that this science proposed by Percy is a semeiotic[1] existentialist interdisciplinary science asked his audience to combine theories not typically combined and to acknowledge gaps in their own theories which were built on a binary base. Had Percy not had strong sales as a novelist, his publisher probably would not have published a book on language, but Percy's literary star shone brightly enough to justify publishing a collection of essays espousing theories unlikely, by his own admission, to interest readers. However, Percy knew from his own experience that his

R. R. McDonnell (✉)
Scottsdale Community College, Scottsdale, AZ, USA

© The Author(s) 2018
L. Marsh (ed.), *Walker Percy, Philosopher*,
https://doi.org/10.1007/978-3-319-77968-3_6

115

method for understanding humanity by analyzing intersubjective communication works. Further, if his method is applied to the social sciences, the human psyche and the relations between humans can be diagnosed and treated in a new and more effective manner.

EXISTENTIALIST SEMIOTICS: A "NEW" MODEL?

In the preface of his monograph *Existential Semiotics* (2001), Eero Tarasti boldly declared that he was laying the groundwork for a new avenue of inquiry in the study of signs. He explained that frustration with those he terms "second-generation semioticians" (Eco, Derrida, and later works of Foucault, Barthes, and Kristeva) led him to consider new theories. "Their texts," he wrote, "reflect the conditionality of all permanent values, unbelief, the inner conflicts of postmodern man, particularly the dangers of anything 'social,' 'communal,' chaos instead of structures. After the glorious days of structuralism, no one has dared to create a new theory of semiotics" (Tarasti 2001, p. 3). As answer to these frustrations, Tarasti reflected that he had abandoned "'structuralist semiotics' in its Greimasian forms, and [had] been looking for a new basis on which to construct a theory of semiosis" (Tarasti 2001, p. 18). That theory integrates existentialist concepts with his semiotic theory, and he cited existentialists Kierkegaard, Heidegger, Jaspers, and Sartre as influences, adding to them the German philosophers such as Kant, Hegel, Schelling, and others. As a longtime student of Walker Percy, I felt a certain prickling sensation on encountering Tarasti. As part of the *Advances in Semiotics* series, Tarasti is part of a rather elite roster of semioticians, including such figures as Umberto Eco and John Deeley, both universally recognized heavy hitters in the field, not to mention series editor Thomas Sebeok, a sometime correspondent of Percy. Such positioning in itself validates Tarasti's theory of Existential Semiotics within the academic community. In later publications, such as "Existential Semiotics and Cultural Psychology," Tarasti (2012) applies his discovery to psychology, exemplifying the flexibility of Existential Semiotics as a way of studying human behavior, a very Percy-like enterprise. However, the sensation, call it a shock of recognition, I experienced on reading Tarasti was not merely due to his theory, in and of itself. Rather, it was created by my sense of familiarity with much of what Tarasti expressed, both in the combination of existentialism and Peircean semeiotic and in his critique of contemporary semiotic studies. This familiarity is not created by my own expertise with the field, but rather by my expertise in all things Walker Percy, created by over 20 years of research on Percy. For that entire time, I have been reading the very ideas that Tarasti posits as new.

While I mean in no way to discredit Tarasti's work, I am obliged to note that he was not, in fact, discovering something new, despite the novelty of the propositions he set forth to both himself and the international semiotics community. He noted the difficulty encountered when one tries to signify the self, the "crystallization of signs" (cf. SSL, pp. 134–135, 389; LC on ossification), the essentialness of transcendence in semiotics, the tension between "'being' and 'not-being,'" and the crucial role of community in semiosis (Tarasti 2001, pp. 3–16). Readers of Percy's nonfiction are likely to recognize all of these concepts Tarasti explicates as being central to Percy's philosophy, the foundations of which were laid half a century prior to the publication of *Existential Semiotics*. I can only conclude that, as often happens in science,[2] Tarasti independently arrived at realizations that Percy had first explored in the 1950s, as evidenced by Percy's publication of several essays using a combination of Peircean semeiotic and existentialism, along with an eclectic mix of theorists from other disciplines, to defend his theses, all which ultimately concern how a person might live in the world.

As a point of clarification, lest I be misunderstood, I am not asserting that Tarasti's theories are an exact replication of Percy's. Even in their influences, the two men differ. For instance, both men are strongly influenced by Charles Sanders Peirce's semeiotic, but Tarasti has been shaped and influenced by the Structuralists, while Percy harkens back to the Scholastics such as John Poinsot (John of St. Thomas). As a musicologist, Tarasti's musical education filters his perceptions, while Percy's perceptions are filtered by his medical degree. Both thinkers exhibit an affinity for psychiatric studies, but Percy also includes anthropologists of his day in equal measure. In short, because their influences, experience, and time period differ, their resultant theories have differences. However, both can be placed in the same school of thought, with Percy as the precursor. Although Percy did not use the term "Existential Semiotics" to name his theory, the "radical anthropology" (MB, p. 224) he described combined semeiotic[3] and existentialism to form a new way of understanding humanity, diagnosing certain psychological disturbances and treating our peculiar "human" predicament.

PERCY'S SEMEIOTIC

When Percy writes in "Culture: The Antinomy of the Scientific Method" that his desire is "to advance the cause of a radical anthropology, a science of man which will take account of all human realities, not merely space-time events," (Ibid) he is making three assertions: (1) human beings are different from other organisms; (2) current scientific theories are unable to account for the totality of human experience; (3) space-time events are part of what is real, but reality also includes the non-material, which are as real as concrete, observable, causal events. While parsing Percy's statement might help a bit in nailing down this anthropology of his, additional terminology will help us to move forward. Briefly, Percy's theories cannot be understood without referencing his appropriation of C. S. Peirce's Categories, specifically Secondness (dyads, dyadic) and Thirdness (triads, triadic).[4] What about Firstness? As Percy wrote to Kenneth Laine Ketner, "I've never seen much use in CSP's [Charles Sanders Peirce's] 'Firstness,' except to make the system more elegant" (Samway 1995, p. 6). On the other hand, Percy had great use for Secondness and Thirdness. He lauds Peirce in multiple places for not only identifying Secondness and Thirdness, but for being "the first to distinguish clearly between the 'dyadic' behavior of stimulus-response sequences and the 'triadic' character of symbol-use" (LC, 86n). As Percy explained to Ketner, Secondness and Thirdness, in and of themselves, were not what interested him, as much as what he believed "to be the seminal distinction between dyads and triads ... –seminal because it is precisely there that so much of present day psychology and semiotics stumbles" (Samway 1995, p. 13). Addressing that stumbling point was the focus of Percy's career, whether he approached the problem through his fiction or through his essays on philosophy, psychology, existentialism, and semeiotic. To effectively accomplish his goal, he wedded aspects of Peircean semeiotic to features of existentialism, creating something entirely new but neither unwieldy nor forcefully coupled. In fact, Ketner has argued that "pragmaticism [Peirce's philosophy as distinguished from James's Pragmatism] *is* an existentialism," (Ketner 1996, pp. 105–110, emphasis added) making semeiotic and existentialism natural bedfellows.

THE INTERDEPENDENCE OF EXISTENTIALISM AND SEMEIOTIC

Particularly in Percy's philosophy, existentialism and semeiotic are interdependent, as each is crucial to his definition of humanity. Throughout Percy's oeuvre, the human behavior of naming, particularly as exemplified by Helen Keller in the oft-referenced well scene, is his focus. A casual reader might wonder, "Why the perseveration?" Yet, as Percy himself explains in his author's note for MB, a collection of essays covering a span of 20 years, "A certain repetition is inevitable ... [and] has been preserved here [in MB], for example, the 'Helen Keller phenomenon,' if for no other reason as evidence of my curiosity and my inability to get rid of it. This particular bone ... needed worrying."[5] The centrality of the "Helen Keller phenomenon" to Percy's thought lies in Helen's moment of realization, a eureka moment in the truest sense of the term, that the combination of letters w-a-t-e-r spelled into her hand by Anne Sullivan was not a request that Helen go get water, nor was it a question inquiring if Helen wanted water, both of which would have been stimuli eliciting a response. Instead, the combination of the letters asserted the name of the wet stuff running over Helen's hand (MB, pp. 30–39). Percy interprets this moment as Keller's "breakthrough from the good responding animal which behaviorists study so successfully to the strange name-giving and sentence-uttering creature who begins by naming shoes and ships and sealing wax, and later tells jokes, curses, reads the paper, writes *La sua volontade è nostra pace*, or becomes a Hegel and composes an entire system of philosophy" (MB, p. 35).[6] In short, in that moment, by both Percy's interpretation and Keller's own, Helen Keller entered into the human community as a full participant, becoming "*Homo symbolificus*, man the symbol-monger" (MB, p. 17).

That breakthrough moment, which Percy referred to as the "Helen Keller phenomenon," identifies the entry into what Percy terms a world. Prior to the breakthrough, Keller (like all children) existed in an environment. To distinguish the difference between world and environment, Percy brought into play the notions of *Welt* and *Umwelt* as used by Ludwig Binswanger in "The Existential Analysis School of Thought" (MB, pp. 255–56). An animal lives in a dyadic environment (*Umwelt*) where it responds to stimuli from that environment. This Secondness is the animal's state, despite the triadic nature of all signs. As Percy noted, "The relation of signification is a triadic one of sign-organism-object ... This schema holds true for any significatory meaning situation. It is true of a dog responding to a buzzer by salivation; it is true of a polar bear responding to the sound of splitting ice; it is true of a man responding to a telephone bell."[7] Note that in all of Percy's examples, the subject (whether animal or human) is responding to an environmental stimulus; further, the automated response of a person reacting to a telephone bell is not qualitatively different from a dog salivating at a buzzer's sound.

Stimulus plus response equals Secondness, or a dyadic event, in Percy's theory.[8] All living organisms, even the simplest, exist at a dyadic level because they are in an environment to which they respond.

What of the interactions between organisms? Percy maintained that dyadic interactions between two organisms have no qualitative difference from the response an organism has to its environment. "The action of a dog in responding intelligently to the bark or feint of another dog—Mead's 'conversation of gesture'—is generically the same sort of meaning relation as that in which a solitary polar bear responds to the sound of splitting ice" (SSL, p. 265). Both Peirce and Percy encourage applying a scientific curiosity toward all propositions, testing the validity of said propositions prior to accepting them. Therefore, I have put Percy's theory to a test by closely observing the interactions of my two dogs with each other and the humans in my household. While I have ample evidence of them responding to stimuli—such as the rumble of thunder, the invitations for play that they extend to each other through vocalization or action, or the word "walk" uttered by any human—I have no evidence that they experience Thirdness.

While Secondness is characterized by causation, Thirdness is a different sort of phenomenon. Percy identified it as "a nonlinear nonenergic natural phenomenon (that is to say, a natural phenomenon in which energy exchanges account for some but not all of what happens)" (MB, p. 39). When a polar bear hears splitting ice and reacts by moving to a more stable surface, only two elements are involved: the stimulus and the response to the sound (S → R). However, with naming, three elements are involved: "[S]ign A is understood by organism B, not as a signal to flee or approach, but as 'meaning' or referring to another perceived segment of the environment" (LC, p. 96). Percy represents this relation as a triangle, following the model provided by Ogden and Richards (Fig. 6.1) (Ibid.)[9]: Percy, like Peirce before him, proves repeatedly that triadic relations are "irreducible" (Ketner et al. 2011, pp. 3–14).[10] Percy arrived at his conclusion of the irreducible nature of triadic relations independently of Peirce (much as Tarasti hit upon existential semiotics independently of Percy), as Peirce expert Ketner emphasized by coining the term "the Peirce-Percy Principle" (Samway 1995, pp. 256–284). While Percy acknowledged that all signification involves a triad, in his theory only symbolization results in Thirdness.

Percy insists that symbolization is, as far as we have evidence, a uniquely human behavior. At the core of human communication is symbolization, which at an elementary level is naming. Now, the importance of Helen Keller's narrative to Percy is clear. Keller's physical limitations prevented her from progressing as the majority of children do. While most children

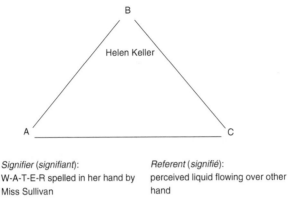

Signifier (*signifiant*):
W-A-T-E-R spelled in her hand by
Miss Sullivan

Referent (*signifié*):
perceived liquid flowing over other
hand

Fig. 6.1   Percy's Triadic Model

begin to use language within their first year, moving quickly to the naming stage as toddlers, Keller lost hearing and sight at approximately the same age that most children catch onto language. When she entered the naming stage and understood that words represented objects, people, and ideas, she was seven years old. Her advanced age allowed her the unusual ability to recognize what life was like when she only could respond to her environment as compared to her existence once she was able to symbolize. With symbolization, Keller began to fully inhabit a world as opposed to functioning in an environment. She described it as her "soul's sudden awakening" (Keller 1905). Percy returned to the passage in her autobiography describing Keller's breakthrough into symbolization in many of his writings, as Keller's recounting of the experience along with the language she used to describe that pivotal moment verified to Percy his distinction between *Welt* and *Umwelt*, world and environment. When Keller was able merely to respond to environmental stimuli or to demand that others respond to her needs, she existed in a dyadic fashion that was not observably different from the existence of a pampered pet (my dogs, for example). However, once she had the flash of understanding that linked symbol (word) to object, she became a triadic being (Thirdness), able to communicate feelings, thoughts, and ideas with other people.

In Percy's words, once she began to learn the names of things, Helen Keller had a world. "The world," according to Percy, "is simply the totality of that which is formulated through symbols" (MB, p. 202). The world is made up of all that humans can name. Accordingly, some elements of the environment that humans are unaware of are not part of their world. Prior to the discovery of atoms, for example, atoms existed in the environment, but were not in the world of humans. Additionally, things that do not exist in the environment like "*unicorn* and *boogerman* may be very much a part of a person's world" (LC, p. 102). The primary difference between world (*Welt*) and environment (*Umwelt*) is the presence or lack of gaps. In a world, "all perceived objects and actions and qualities are named. Even the gaps are named—by the word *gaps* .... The Cosmos is accounted for willy-nilly, rightly or wrongly, mythically or scientifically, its past present, and future" (LC, p. 101). The environment, however, is riddled with gaps. Dyadic organisms recognize those elements which elicit response. All else is a gap. As Percy wryly observes in *Lost in the Cosmos*, "A cat has no myths and names no real or imaginary beings. It responds to the Cosmos exactly as it has learned or been programmed to respond" (Ibid.). This distinction between *Welt* and *Umwelt* underscores, as is so powerfully exemplified by Helen Keller's experience, that the link between language and *human* (triadic) existence is requisite.

Another reason for the centrality of Helen Keller to Percy's semeiotic is not Keller, but rather, the interaction between Keller and Sullivan. Language acquisition requires a minimum of two people: the namer and the hearer. In "Semiotic and a Theory of Knowledge," Percy argues, "The presence of the two organisms is not merely a genetic requirement, a *sine qua non* of symbolization; it is rather its enduring condition, its indispensable climate. Every act of symbolization, a naming, forming an hypothesis, creating a line of poetry, perhaps even thinking implies *another* as a co-conceiver, a co-celebrant of the thing which is symbolized. Symbolization is an exercise in intersubjectivity" (MB, p. 257). A rather simplistic definition of intersubjectivity can be obtained through segmenting the word: *inter* (between) *subjects*. As with Percy's own definition of consciousness— "*Conscious* from *con-scio*, I know with" (LC, p. 106; cf. SSL, p. 124)—the word itself reveals the meaning. The terms were intimately related for Percy, as being conscious of something indicates being aware of that thing as part of one's world. Such awareness only comes through naming, and naming only happens in a communal setting. As he noted in "Naming and Being," the title of which underscores his existential semeiotic, "This is water, means that this is water *for you and for me*" (SSL, p. 133). That sharing of meaning forges the bonds of community and only can be accessed through symbolization. Based upon his own observations and Keller's narrative, Percy's assessment was that people do not become fully *human* (experience Thirdness) without a relationship with at least one other person.[11] In fact, Percy went so far as to aver, "If there were only one person in the world, symbolization could not conceivably occur (but signification [signaling] could); for my discovery of water as something derives from your telling me so, that this is water for you too" (MB, p. 281). The other person must, like Sullivan, be able to bring them into the naming stage so that, ultimately, they can name their own thoughts and feelings. "The 'you' or 'thou' is, as you see, assigned a unique position in the semiotic model. In other words, the I-you or interpersonal relation is, accordingly, not merely a desirable state of affairs, as Buber would say, but is rather the very condition of being and knowing and feeling in a human way. It, this interpersonal relation, is a major variable in all semiotic transactions and its manifestations occur in a continuum running from the I-it through the I-you-they to the I-all-of-you" (SSL, p. 127). However broad the continuum might be, the prime relationship to initiate one into triadic behavior must be an I-thou relation, where each is the "co-namer, co-discoverer, co-sustainer of [the other's] world" (LC, p. 102). Without the I-thou relation, we are condemned to be dyadic organisms responding to the environment rather than triadic organisms in a world resplendent with meaning. As previously noted, all signification is triadic, and responding to signs is not limited to humans.

When my hunting dog sees the neighbor's cat, he barks in a certain way that signals he has sighted prey. This bark does not name the cat, nor does it convey ideas about the nature of cat-ness, the differences between species, or admiration for the cat's ability to scale a wall. Instead the bark is part of the innate hunting response and is part of a causal series of events that lead to my dog trying and failing to catch and eat the cat. My dog lives in an environment and responds to that environment. When I discuss this situation with my neighbor, expressing concern for the safety of the cat (and for the structural integrity of my back door), something else is happening. I am not merely responding to the environment. Instead, I name the situation to my neighbor, using language which is inherently symbolic. In doing so, I establish myself and my neighbor as living in a world wherein all aspects of the world, including the war between my dog and the neighbor's cat, are named. Additionally, as triadic beings, my neighbor and I use symbols to discuss the situation and search for a solution rather than responding to the signals produced by the animals. Unlike our pets, my neighbor and I are engaged in intersubjective behavior.

Intersubjective Communication: A Tetradic Model

At its best, this intersubjectivity is not merely triadic; instead, Percy proposed a tetradic model of communication. As Percy explained, the triad of the symbol user (the namer) is one half of communication. "Every symbolic formulation, whether it be language, art, or even thought, requires a real or posited *someone else* for whom the symbol is intended as meaningful" (MB, p. 271). In fact, even private journals are written for an audience of the future self (MB, 200n).[12] The receiver of the symbolization (hearer or reader) likewise is a symbol user and is, therefore, part of a triad. The pairing of these triangles creates a tetrad (Fig. 6.2). When "Symbol, Consciousness, and Intersubjectivity" was published in 1958,

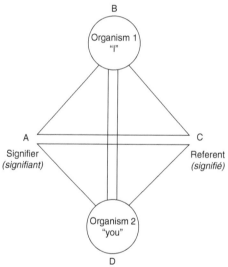

Relation AC—your giving a name to a class of objects to make a sign, and my understanding or misunderstanding of such a naming—cannot be understood as a dyadic interaction.

Relation BD—the I-you intersubjectivity of an exchange of signs—cannot be understood as a dyadic interaction.

These are two conjoined triadic events which always happen in any exchange of signs, whether in talk, looking at a painting, reading a novel, or listening to music. It allows for such peculiar properties of triadic events as understanding, misunderstanding, truth-telling, lying.

Fig. 6.2 Percy's Tetradic Model

Percy asserted that "symbolization is essentially and irreducibly a tetradic relation" (MB, p. 269). He later clarified that stance. By the mid-1970s when he republished his essays on language as MB, he explained:

> The tetrad I proposed can, if one wishes to deal with atomic rather than molecular events, be split apart along its interface between the utterer and receiver of a sentence, yielding a coupling of sentence elements by the utterer and a subsequent coupling by receiver. The tetradic model, I see now, is appropriate only in successful communication, i.e., those transactions in which the same elements are coupled by both utterer and receiver and in the same mode of coupling. Unfortunately this is not always the case.
>
> In short, in Chapter 9 I deal with the "molecular" structure of the communication process, whereas I am here dealing with the "atomic" structure (MB, 167n).

When the triad of meaning-making and the triad of meaning-receiving are linked, a sort of Fourthness is achieved, though it is tenuous and breakable. If the receiver, rather than taking the namer's (utterer's) meaning, mistakes it, the tetrad is broken into two triads, proving that tetrads are reducible to triads, but the triads remain irreducible.

The tetradic moments are more difficult to achieve as symbolic formulations gain in complexity. For the child the naming stage was called by Percy "the first Edenic world of the sign-user" (LC, p. 99). Like Adam and Eve in the Garden, the child and the other share in the joy of creating the world surrounding the child. The child learns the name of an object, such as Percy's often-used example of the ball. Later, seeing a ball, the child names it for the parent, and the parent agrees, "Yes, that is a ball." The affirmation marks the tetradic moment. "Naming or symbolization may be defined as the affirmation of the thing as being what it is under the auspices of the symbol .... But an affirmation requires two persons, the namer and the hearer .... Only a person may say yes, and he may say it only to another person" (Samway 1991, p. 133). Through naming and the affirmation of the name, "one lives authentically .... as a namer or a hearer, as an 'I' or a 'thou'—and in either case as a co-celebrant of what is" (Samway 1991, pp. 134–35). Consider then the difficulty encountered when one of the three following situations occurs: (1) a symbol loses its significance, (2) the self is unformulable, and/or (3) the receiver mistakes the meaning of the namer. In each case, a person is catapulted into an existential crisis, cast out of the Eden previously created through affirmation.

A person can experience a loss of part of the world, resulting in existential angst, when the symbol ossifies, or becomes hardened. Percy referred to the common sparrow as an example of this phenomenon. When a child first learns of sparrows, the joy of naming imbues the sparrows with a resplendence. Later, the sparrow is concealed by its symbol, rendering it invisible. "If one sees a movement in a tree and recognizes it and says it is 'only a sparrow,' one is disposing of the creature through its symbolic formulation" (Ibid.). The same semeiotic process that allows for the discovery of the world destroys the world piece by piece. The resplendence is gone and parts of the world that were once celebrated fade away. The joy is replaced by boredom. In that boredom, Percy wrote, "I exist as a nought in the center of the picture-book world of the *en soi*" (Ibid.).[13] When the being of things evaporates, leaving a person surrounded by the "simulacrum of symbol," (Ibid.) the person now inhabits an ersatz world, seeing each named object not as the glorious and individual item it once was, but as a generic, cardboard figure. For such a person, the world of the symbol user has decayed and the person falls into inauthenticity. Recovery of the world and of authentic existence is possible, Percy argued in multiple places, through ordeal. In MG, Binx Bolling discovers a dung beetle while lying wounded under a bush in Korea, and, in LG, Will Barrett is finally able to "see" a Velázquez painting after a worker crashes through a skylight in front of the painting. In moments of catastrophe, such as the above examples or another of Percy's favorites, a hurricane, the charged atmosphere restores the brilliance to objects, and the world can be inhabited once again. Such moments, however, are fleeting.

Percy's argument is clear: language is the key to *being* in the world as humans, and without language, we are no different from other organisms. However, Percy pointed out that even in that Edenic world of first language use, when one exults in the joyousness of co-celebration, that Eden "harbors its own semiotic snake in the grass" (LC, p. 107). As children develop, they reach a stage of self-awareness, a self-consciousness that results in a degree of withdrawal from the world: in short, alienation begins by about age seven (LC, 108n). What causes that particularly human dis-ease? In my informal scientific observations, I have noted that my dogs seem to experience no such feelings about themselves. The environment may cause them to become alert, perhaps even whining or barking, but such behavior is a response to outer stimulus. The same seems true of animals both wild and domestic that I have observed. People, on the other hand, are fraught with worry about themselves and their place within the world from an early age. Why is it that of all mammals, only humans seem to experience alienation? The difference, Percy maintained, between humans and animals is symbolization.

Humans, as *homo symbolificus*, know and understand their world through symbolization. Percy argued, "The whole objectizing act of the mind is to render all things *darstellbar* [representable], not 'proper' but presentable, that is, formulable" (MB, p. 283). Standing apart from all other things in the world, a person can name those things and can understand them. However, standing apart from one's self is difficult and slippery. In trying to formulate the self, the self is fragmented into social roles and personality characteristics:

> The self, that which symbolizes, will, if it perverts its native project of being conscious of something else and tries to grasp itself as a something, either fail and remain as the unformulable, a nothingness (Sartre), the aching wound of self (Marcel)—or it will fall prey to miserable unauthentic transformations (the impersonations of Marcel and Sartre, and in primitive life, the totemic transformation: In the importunate need for construing all things, the self in its terrible inscrutability is as capable of being one thing as another; I can as well "be" a parakeet as an alligator—anything at all is more tolerable than the vacuum which I am) (Ibid.).

Either the self is unable to grasp itself, is everything and nothing simultaneously, or the self is playing some role. In either case, the outcome is bad. The self is either alienated or is living inauthentically—playing a role. Our only chance of being formulated is within the gaze of the other. For Sartre, this possibility was intolerable. In *No Exit*, he consigns four characters to a hell of being captured relentlessly in each other's gaze, with no alternative distraction provided. As Sartre writes in *Being and Nothingness*, "My original fall is the existence of the Other" (Sartre 1962, p. 352). Fitting into Percy's Edenic metaphor, the fall into alienation occurs, Sartre argued, when the gaze of another pins us into place, subjects us to objectification, and reveals our inauthenticity, the bad faith of self-deception that forms our identity. The look of the other was a source of shame, according to Sartre. Percy agreed with such a possibility. Certainly, the Other could reveal our bad faith, the emptiness and inauthenticity of our existence. But in Percy's theory, much more is possible. Percy reflected, "In the exchange of stares everything is at stake. *L'enfer c'est autrui*. But so is heaven" (Sartre 1962, p. 285).[14] The affirmative joy grasped by the child in the naming stage is still possible after the irruption of self-consciousness into that state. It is gained in tetradic moments, when a person expresses a feeling, an idea, or a truth of experienced existence, and the hearer understands and affirms the expression: "Yes, it is so." In the affirmation is heaven. The same agent, the Other, who may be cause of our alienation also holds the promise of our authentic being.

When the affirmation is lacking, when the meaning is missed, a slippage of intersubjectivity is the third cause of alienation. Percy explored this concept of such slippage extensively in the correspondence he carried out with National Institute of Mental Health psychiatrist F. Gentry Harris, M.D.[15] In that correspondence, both men analyzed the family therapy sessions of schizophrenic patients, writing extensive letters and documents, some with the formality of academic papers, that were peppered with diagrams based on Percy's tetrad. Percy noted in his first analysis of one of the family therapy sessions conducted by Harris that the patient, despite describing a dismal life, was heartened when Harris named the situation correctly. The patient's experience was authenticated, thereby slightly ameliorating the patient's alienation (Percy and Harris, n.d.). More typically, though, the analysis of the family therapy sessions revealed the alienation of not just the patients diagnosed as schizophrenics but also of the family members from each other. Percy and Harris discussed at length the reasons for mistakes in meaning. For the schizophrenics, the failures in intersubjective communication often were symptomatic of their schizophrenia, as they used a private language, investing words with meanings exclusive to themselves (Ibid.). Other members of the therapy sessions were also guilty of misunderstandings or the creation of alienation through objectification. This most frequently occurred when the patient was moved into the position of an object rather than a person. In an essay he titled "Therapeutic Stasis Due to Intersubjective Slippage along a Transcendent-Immanent Scale," Percy noted that when a patient's pathology became the patient's identity, whether through the agency of the doctor or the patient, the patient then was moved from the position of co-celebrant to that of the object being named as belonging to a class of other objects, having lost sovereignty and individuality (Percy and Harris, n.d.). Role-playing also contributed to inauthenticity, as laypersons in the therapy sessions adopted the specialized language of psychiatry to describe themselves and their situations rather than using genuine language from their experience. The psychiatrists, on the other hand, had the tendency to use more prosaic language in an attempt to jar session participants into authentic behavior. Percy tended to praise the gambits made by the doctors as attempts to counter actions of bad faith by the patients.[16] In either case, though, the interactions clearly demonstrated the slippage from true intersubjectivity into alienation. Finally, bad faith was also represented by family members who minimized or attempted to positively construct negative situations (Percy and Harris, n.d.). In all cases, the slippage of intersubjectivity evidenced the inauthenticity of the persons involved. In these cases, Percy confirmed Sartre's assertion: "Hell is other people."

Despite the many ways that we might be exiled from the Eden experienced through co-celebratory language, the best chance for wholeness is through intersubjective relationships. "The look is of the order of pure intersubjectivity without the mediation of the symbol, and if it can be hatred in the exposure of my impersonation, it can also be love in the communion of selves …. The Thou is the knower, the namer, the co-inspector with me of the common thing and the authority for its name. Whatever devious constitution of self I have been able to arrive at, whatever my 'self-system,' my impersonation, it melts away before the steady gaze of another" (MB, p. 285). Worth noting is Percy's inability to conceive of the situation without language. He explained, "My vulnerability before the look derives from the aboriginal triadic communion of consciousness" (Ibid.). We cannot know anything, according to Percy, without formulating it through symbolization. Even in the moment of "pure intersubjectivity," we recognize the Other as "the namer." And what is it that we recognize, in the true intersubjective moment, that the Other can name? It is the self, formulated by the Other, that exceeds our own efforts of self-formulation. As Percy explained, "For me, certain signifiers fit you, and not others. For me, all signifiers fit me, one as well as another. I am rascal, hero, craven, brave, treacherous, loyal, at once the secret hero and asshole of the Cosmos. You are not a sign in your world" (LC, pp. 107–8). You are, however, a sign in my world, as I am in yours. In combination, two selves restore each other to their worlds, relieving the existential alienation, albeit temporarily.

As Percy's theories affirmed, language, consciousness, and existence are inextricably linked. While he was aware of this link and repeatedly made the argument, he was ahead of his time. Coming half a century prior to Tarasti's appropriation of these same means to stake out a new school of semiotics, Percy's radical anthropology was built upon the pillars of Peircean semeiotic and existentialism. Binary science at large may not have been ready for a triadic method. However, in the early 1960s, through applying his semeiotic to the analyses of family therapy sessions, Percy demonstrated the validity of existential semeiotic as a triadic method for understanding human behavior. It was Percy's hope, with his radical anthropology, to use such tools as the analysis of intersubjective relations to better understand humans, to apply a rigorous triadic science to triadic creatures. Certainly, the time has come to see that hope realized in such diverse fields as medicine, psychology, anthropology, literary theory, and philosophy.

NOTES

1. Semeiosis is Charles S. Peirce's theory of signs.
2. I use this term much as Percy does, in reference to the study of knowledge, whether the field is the physical world or that which deals with those things which are non-material but nonetheless real.
3. Percy most frequently used the term semiotic rather than semeiotic or semiotics. However, the use of Charles S. Peirce's spelling, *semeiotic*, clearly demarcates the term, lest readers believe an 's' was accidentally omitted; further, Percy's application of the term is rooted in Peirce, not in other American semioticians such as Charles Morris, so the Peircean spelling is the more logical choice.
4. Percy's appropriation of Peirce is done with modifications of Peirce's definitions of terminology, and discussion of Percy's use of Secondness and Thirdness should not be seen as reflecting a pure use of Peirce's terms.
5. Author's Note in MB.
6. *La sua volontade è nostra pace* is from Dante's *Divina Commedia: Paradiso* (3:85), translated by Longfellow as "His will is our peace."
7. Walker Percy. "Semiotic and a Theory of Knowledge." (MB, pp. 255–56).
8. Percy (SSL, pp. 120–121) uses Peirce's theory to explain the differences between dyadic and triadic events:

> Peirce believed that there are at least two kinds of natural phenomena, and by this he did not mean physical and mental phenomena. He referred to the two as dyadic and triadic events ....

> To make the distinction as briefly as possible: by dyadic events, Peirce meant nothing more or less than the phenomena studied by the conventional sciences, whether the collision of subatomic particles, or the reaction of $NaOH$ with H_2SO_4, or the response of an amoeba to a change in pH, or the performance of a rat in learning to thread a maze ....

> But there is one kind of natural phenomenon which, according to Peirce, cannot be so explained. It is man's transactions with symbols, of which, of course, the prime example is his use of language ....

Thus, language in particular and all of man's transactions with symbols in general are not dyadic but triadic behavior.

9. Percy's persistence with the triangle was a source of unending frustration for Ketner, who repeatedly argued in their correspondence that Percy should shift to Peirce's model. However, by the time Percy began corresponding with Ketner, he had been sketching triangles and tetrads for some 30 years, and he resisted Ketner's attempts to change his representations of human communication (Cf. Samway 1991, p. 30).

10. This paper references a number of recent studies that vindicate Peirce's nonreduction claims.

11. Percy sums up the importance of Keller's experience: "Unquestionably Helen's breakthrough was critical and went to the very heart of the terra incognita. Before, Helen had behaved like a good responding organism. Afterward, she acted like a rejoicing symbol-mongering human. Before, she was little more than an animal. Afterward, she became *wholly human.*" (MB, p. 38, italics added).

12. Percy's argument seems to rest upon the supposition that the future self differs from the now self to the degree that through journal writing we engage in intersubjectivity with the self. Even the process of fully formulated but unarticulated thoughts is placed in this category by Percy, suggesting that a self-distancing occurs to posit the self as being simultaneously the other. Using Samuel Pepys as an example because Pepys's journal was kept in a private code, Percy asserted that Pepys "was nevertheless formulating the experiences and so setting it at a distance for a someone else—himself."

13. *En soi*, Jean-Paul Sartre's term for being-in-itself, is used by Percy to describe those creatures living in an environment, those for whom Secondness is the only mode of being.

14. *L'enfer c'est autrui* seems to be Percy's translation into French of the English translation of the Sartre's original, which is "l'enfer, c'est les Autres." (*Huis Clos* [*No Exit*] Scene 5) Sartre's line is typically translated as "Hell is other people," though it would be more true to Sartre to translate it as "Hell is the Other," which is reflected in Percy's phrase.

15. In 1963, F. Gentry Harris, the Chief of Clinical Studies at the National Institute of Mental Health, recruited Percy as a consultant on a study involving the family therapy of schizophrenic patients. Harris reached out to Percy after reading "The Symbolic Structure of Interpersonal Process," noting in Percy a fellow follower of Peirce's semeiotic. Percy's role consisted of listening to tapes of family therapy sessions and reporting back to Harris on his analysis of the intersubjective relationships presented in those sessions. Percy and Harris continued their correspondence for some time

after the dissolution of the study, continuing to ponder and argue the application of Peirce's Categories to human behavior.

16. Percy and Harris: Such interactions are noted repeatedly throughout Percy's analyses of therapy sessions involving multiple family groups.

REFERENCES

Dante. Paradiso: Canto III. http://digitaldante.columbia.edu/dante/divinecomedy/paradiso/paradiso-3/.

Keller, Helen. 1905. *The Story of My Life. A Celebration of Women Writers*. Ed. Mary Mark Ockerbloom. New York: Doubleday, Page and Company. http://digital.library.upenn.edu/women/keller/life/life.html

Ketner, Kenneth Laine. 1996. Pragmaticism is an Existentialism? *Frontiers in American Philosophy (Volume 2)*. Eds. Robert W. Burch and Herman J. Saatkamp, Jr. College Station: Texas A & M University Press.

———. et al. 2011. Peirce's Nonreduction and Relational Completeness Claims in the Context of First-Order Predicate Logic. Interdisciplinary Seminar on Peirce. *KODIKAS* Volume 34:: 3–14.

Percy, Walker. 1984. *Lost in the Cosmos: The Last Self-Help Book*. New York: Washington Square Press.

———. 1989. *The Message in the Bottle: How Queer Man Is, How Queer Language Is, and What One Has to Do with the Other*. New York: Farrar, Strauss, and Giroux.

———. 1991. *Signposts in a Strange Land: Essays*. Ed. Patrick Samway. New York: Farrar, Straus and Giroux.

Percy, Walker and Gentry Harris. n.d. *The Walker Percy-Gentry Harris Correspondence*. Texas Tech University Institute for Studies in Pragmaticism. Item 0000027.

Samway, Patrick J., S. J. (ed.). 1995. *A Thief of Peirce: The Letters of Kenneth Laine Ketner and Walker Percy*. Jackson: University Press of Mississippi.

Sartre, Jean-Paul 1962. *Being and Nothingness*. Trans. Hazel E. Barnes. New York: Washington Square Press.

Tarasti, Eero. 2001. *Existential Semiotics*. Bloomington: Indiana University Press.

———. 2012. Existential Semiotics and Cultural Psychology. In: The Oxford Handbook of Culture and Psychology. Ed. Jean Valsiner. Oxford: Oxford University Press.

To Take the Writer's Meaning: An Unpublished Manuscript on "Peirce and Modern Semiotic" by Walker Percy

Kenneth Laine Ketner

Section One

A Hard Fact of Life

I really miss Walker Percy. You also probably became accustomed to anticipating another novel from his hand, or another essay, or another self-help book, or another surprising insight into human nature. Many of his readers know the experience of peering through the telescope he focused deeply inside the mists of life. But there will be no more. So we have to make the most of what we have.

With that principle in mind, if we experience Percy using an unnecessarily limited set of optics, we might misperceive the images he wanted us to consider. There are various filters of this kind currently used by some readers: Southern writer, Roman Catholic intellectual, Existentialist. He was openly hostile about the first, although some critics persist in using it. He seemed ambivalent about the second, yet he didn't reject it. And both

K. L. Ketner (✉)
Institute for Studies in Pragmaticism, Texas Tech University, Lubbock, TX, USA
e-mail: Kenneth.Ketner@ttu.edu

© The Author(s) 2018
L. Marsh (ed.), *Walker Percy, Philosopher*,
https://doi.org/10.1007/978-3-319-77968-3_7

133

he and his readers agree the third is important. But there are at least two more principal lenses available that we neglect at the price of serious loss in understanding his work. The fourth is the strong influence of Charles Sanders Peirce (1839–1914), and the fifth is Percy's deep familiarity with laboratory science as well as mid-twentieth century philosophical research. Almost no commentators on Percy's writing touch on those two essential facets; readers without access to these lenses risk missing important parts of the image in Percy's scope. One value of this essay is Percy's own demonstration that the fourth factor (my present main focus) is as strong as any other.

Indeed, "Peirce and Modern Semiotic," located near the start of his writing career (1950s), clearly announced that its author understood and defended Peirce's scientific theory of Semeiosis. (A useful outline of Peirce's Semeiotic is found in *Das Bild zwischen Kognition und Kreativität*, p. 375 f.) Of course, writing this essay in 1959, Percy did not possess the Peirce scholarship of the next 50 years—a period of explosive growth in newly published writings by and about Peirce. Despite that factor, Percy's piece stands up well, precisely because he was *correct* in the approach he took. Later study vindicated him.

But you, good reader, probably do not want a set of scholar's notes about the essay. Your instincts are sound, so I offer a sketch of this terrain sufficient to confirm that Percy was right on track, that Peirce was a major influence on his writing.

And, no, the word *semiotic* in Percy's title was not misspelled. Percy was not discussing semiotics here, but semiotic that is Peirce's description of *semeiosis*. There is no equivalency relation between semeiotic (Peirce's preferred spelling was *semeiotic* or *semiotic*, pronounced "see-my-OH-tick") and contemporary semiotics. That confusion has led some to think of Peirce as an early post-modernist, which he definitely wasn't. As a career physicist for the U.S. government and member of the National Academy of Sciences since 1876, Peirce held strongly to the role of reality and discoverable objective truth in human knowledge (Ketner 1998). Neither was Peirce located in the other extreme: scientism. This also, Percy saw clearly (Ketner 1999). In Peirce's work, the middle held, no doubt another reason Percy admired him.

While discussing the important topic of terminology, an interpretative hypothesis I propose might, if correct, aid us in appreciating Percy's essay. The *modern semiotic* he speaks of is in effect contemporary semiotics. Other phrases in the essay, such as *current semiotic*, or *behavioral semiotic*, seem equivalent. As Percy discerned, avoiding ambiguous terminology is a vital scientific virtue. One should ponder the careful terminology of medicine or biology or chemistry, and the reasons for taking such care. As a scientist, Percy knew these features intimately, and knew what kind of disasters sloppy terminology could promote in medicine. That factor appears in the basis of one of Percy's central claims: C. W. Morris took Peirce's carefully delineated term, *semeiotic*, and misused it, hence Percy's need for qualifiers such as *modern* or *current* or *behavioral* to distinguish Peirce's realistic semeiotic from Morris's nominalistic semiotics. That is, Percy clearly grasped that there are deep theoretical differences between Peirce and Morris, hence the need to distinguish the two hypotheses involves more than some silly preference for spelling. Percy also knew that the diagnostic tradition of the medical world had roots in the semeiotic (a doctrine concerning disease symptoms/signs/indexical-semeioses) developed by physicians in ancient times.

Another chief point concerns the phenomenon of interpreting: in Percy's exceptional and robust phrase, we *take the meaning* of another person. He argued that this was an event one could observe as a scientist, as real as any other event in a laboratory. His patient devastation here of behavioristic reductions of such events foreshadows his more detailed later discussions of the same topic—most notably in MB (Chaps. 1 and 11). Those later essays are sometimes unspecific in their attribution to Peirce, but here that aspect is strong and clear: Peirce's *semeiotic* is the antidote to the behavioral reductionist extremism of Morris or Skinner or contemporary semiotics. Percy found a remedy—*Professor Peirce's Noble Elixir*—that he prescribed liberally in his later essays and novels. "Peirce and Modern Semiotic" gives interested persons a window into that channel of influence.

The principal flaw of Morris and friends then, and now, in semiotics lies in a typical assumption that dyadic relations will accomplish all the tasks required within a theory of semeiosis, or within an account of human nature. Independent and dependent variables, cause and effect, stimulus-and-response are relations basically structurally similar and basically dyadic. Using Peirce's tools, Percy clearly saw, and clearly demonstrated in this essay, the impossibility of dealing effectively with meaning using only dyadic resources. No one denies the importance or usefulness of causes or stimuli or reflexes. The trouble comes when—as Morris and Skinner and their contemporary friends propose—an explainer self-limits explanatory resources to dyadic items only. Percy argued successfully that triadic relations, meaning-events, or semeioses (sign actions) are equally as real as causal relations (dynamic actions), and are equally observable. In effect, said Percy the Peirce expert, Morris violated a basic principle of logic by attempting to reduce triadic relations to only dyadic relations. Morris committed a logical *faux pas* (Unspecified authors, 2015).[1] Despite his lack of enthusiasm for formal logic, Percy, the sharp-eyed diagnostician, clearly discerned the truth of the NonReduction Theorem, chiefly by carefully tracing the unhappy consequences of its serious denial as a way of living a fully human life. Such is his strategy in the essay at hand.

This is the "hard fact of life," Percy's magnificently ironic description of a shortcoming of Morris, aspiring arch-scientist, who looked right past a profound and ubiquitous laboratory truth because his own neopositivist ideology (and perhaps his wish to be accepted by his like-minded colleagues) gained improper control of his judgment as a working scientist. Percy's last major comment, his 1989 Jefferson Lecture for the National Endowment for the Humanities (reprinted in SSL, and as an earlier draft in *A Thief of Peirce*), returned to Peirce and this same theme, but now with a lifetime of further consideration to add to the evidence. A few months after that lecture, and 30 years after writing "Peirce and Modern Semiotic," Percy commented about Milton Singer's Peircean Anthropology (Singer 1984)[2] in a letter to me: "P. S. Only place Singer is wrong is listing Charles Morris as a proper heir of CSP. Morris is a dyadic subverter of CSP." The full details of the subversion are given in Gene Halton's recent book *Meaning and Modernity*, but Percy knew the basics of this subversion by 1959.

Is all this nothing but a quibble among theorists, this talk of meaning and triadic relations? I think the answer is a strong "NO!" It is in effect an important part of the battle for understanding the human soul in our age. If human nature in this most sensitive area of meaning can be fully captured and explained through dyadic or robotic or algorithmic relationships, what is left over besides material items and their wiggles, squirts, causal interbumpings, or unswerving routines? The physicalist or follower of scientism says, in effect, "Nothing is left over."

A good scientist will not attempt to force a preconceived answer to this question. If we do not dictate, but look around with an open mind, there is plenty of scientific evidence that the physicalist hypothesis is wrong. There are other realities besides clunks of stuff and their mutual thumpings or zappings or robotic routines. Indeed, quantum physicists of today may be about to show us just how exceptionally essential real triadic relations are at the level even of so-called basic particles (Beil and Ketner 2003).[3]

Percy had a remarkable talent for showing a nonspecialist audience what was important about the work of some deep specialist. Clearly he performed that magic with Kierkegaard, with Heidegger, with Buber, with Marcel. (Also there may be important relevant connections between existentialism and pragmaticism as noted in Samway 1995, pp. 288–295.) The message in this particular bottle is that Percy did the same with Charley Peirce.

Perhaps you agree as far as Percy's essays go, but you might ask, "What about his fiction?" Some examples can be readily displayed.

The general theme of Percy's TS is announced when Dr. More, the outstanding diagnostician, detects robotic or hyperdyadic behavior in his wife and many other citizens. (Here we should remember that a prominent ancient name for medical diagnosis was the Theory of Signs, or Semeiotic—symptomology is one important subset of semeiosis.) He discovers that some social engineering physicians have "doctored" the water supply of an entire region, results being that the denizens lose interpreting capacity and begin acting like docile and robotic (dyadic) creatures. The final comic shootout, supervised by the local sheriff, is a skirmish between the controller physicians and More's small Peircean patrol. After the water is normalized, residents resume displaying typical triadic activities. This work is also a study in Peircean ethics of science, contrasting the deficient scientific community of would-be controllers—whose practices are ruining health—with the smaller, more genuinely scientific group around Dr. More (but still a community functioning as Peircean "Scientific Intelligences") striving to diagnose and restore health. One of the chief bad guys is lampooned as a practitioner of Morrisean semiotics. In many ways, this novel is a fictional embodiment—or case study—of the essay we are considering here.

Allie within SC is a classic study in semeiotic. Her slow recovery of language is virtually a fictionalized transcendental deduction of the essential components of language and communication (a prominent form of semeiosis). Another Peircean theme, arising from Peirce's classic essay "Questions Concerning Certain Faculties Claimed for Man" (Peirce 1932, Volume 5), is found in the manner in which she reconstructs her very self almost from nothing, following Peirce's analysis of how each human self is formed at an early age through processes of semeiosis.

Examples from all of Percy's fiction could be multiplied, but I leave the balance of the fun to you, good reader.

As we Choctaw Taoists say out here in the post-oak shinnery woods of Oklahoma, "Ol' Walker was one of a kind." I think his work can only increase in worth over the years as more people learn to think as he and Peirce did, in a nonreductive manner that gives full value to observable real relations that constitute the inner heart of our lives as meaning-mongering creatures.

And do enjoy Walker's voice one more time. (Does that unique voice instantiate his "bed-side manner" as he "treats" readers of his novels?)

SECTION TWO

"Peirce and Modern Semiotic" by Walker Percy

I

Charles Peirce is generally acknowledged to be, if not the father, at least a major progenitor of current semiotic. The fact is, however, that while Peirce's general scheme of sign-behavior, the "meaning" triad of sign-interpretant-object, has proved extremely useful, not much attention has been paid to the careful distinction Peirce drew between different kinds of signs, distinctions to which Peirce himself attached great importance.

One reason for the neglect of much of Peirce's work on signs is clear enough. Current semiotic is frankly behavioral in its orientation. In the words of Charles Morris, "the basic terms of semiotic are all formulable in terms applicable to behavior as it occurs in an environment."[4] This is as it should be, it seems to me. A great deal of Peirce's writings on signs, on the other hand, appears to be ancillary to his metaphysics of Firstness, Secondness and Thirdness. His classification of signs, in fact, is derived from metaphysical categories and not, on the face of it at least, from an empirical study of the behavior of organisms. For this reason, no doubt, Peirce's semiotic has not recommended itself, in detail, to contemporary theorists.

It shall be the contention of this paper, however, that whatever the merits of Peirce's metaphysics, and whatever the relevance of metaphysics to positive science, the fact is that Peirce did draw a radical behavioral distinction between signs, and that, further, this distinction is of the utmost importance to a broad semiotic and can only be passed over with the most grievous consequences.

For brevity's sake, I shall deal with only two writers and one topic. The second writer is Charles Morris. If Charles Peirce is the father of modern semiotic, Charles Morris is certainly its current guiding spirit. It is his [Morris] notable contribution, as Sellars has pointed out,[5] to have seen the limitations of the logical empiricism of Neurath and Carnap and to have extended it into the dimensions of semantics and pragmatics.

The single topic I shall be concerned with is the nature of semiosis, or meaning-event, as it is understood by the two men. Since Morris has explicitly subscribed to Peirce's view,[6] adducing recent experimental work in support of Peirce's semiosis,[7] it is open to us to re-examine Peirce's views toward the end of determining whether the two men are talking about the same thing or whether the likeness is attained only through an ambiguous use of Peirce's terminology.

As a self-appointed spokesman of the absent Peirce, I shall attempt to say at least one thing Peirce would almost certainly say and, in doing so, to lay bare what looks to me like a serious misconstruction of his notion of semiosis. The misconstruction amounts to nothing else than this: the triadic structure of semiosis, "meaning," which Peirce was at such great pains and with typical Peircean crotchet to set forth as a prime and irreducible relation—irreducible to "dyadic relations"—this triad has been adopted as the basic scheme of current semiotic under the strict condition that it *is* in fact reducible to dyadic relations.

It shall remain then only to raise the question of whether Peirce's triadic semiosis is a dispensable byproduct of his metaphysic of Thirdness, or whether it is one of the hard facts of life that must sooner or later be confronted by a natural science of meaning.

II

Morris defines semiosis as "the process by which something functions as a sign."[8] A sign is defined as follows: "If something, A, controls behavior in a way similar to (but not necessarily identical with) the way something else, B, would control behavior with respect to that goal in a situation in which it were observed, then A is a sign."[9] In another place Morris gives a similar definition, but one that makes use of a more explicitly behavioristic language, using terms like *preparatory-stimulus, stimulus-object, response-sequence, behavior-family,* etc.[10]

Both definitions are clear enough. They are written in a language at once familiar to anyone who has some knowledge of the behavioral sciences and of the fruitful notion of organism-in-an-environment.

Peirce wrote of semiosis as follows: "It is important to understand what I mean by *semiosis*. All dynamical action, or action of brute force, physical or psychical, either takes place between two subjects ... or at any rate is a resultant of such action between pairs. But by 'semiosis' I mean, on the contrary, an action, or influence, which is, or involves, a coöperation of *three* subjects, such as a sign, its object, and its interpretant, this tri-relative influence not being in any way resolvable into actions between pairs.... My definition confers on anything that so acts the title of a 'sign.'"[11]

Morris agrees. The buzzer is the sign, operating in place of the sight and smell of food; the interpretant is the disposition of the dog to respond in a certain way; the food is the object or designatum. The triad is applicable to human language behavior. Person A, driving along a road to a certain town, is stopped by another person B and told that the road is blocked by a landslide, whereupon person A turns off the road and reaches his destination by a detour. The sign is the warning given by person B, in place of the sight of the landslide; the interpretant is the disposition of the driver to respond appropriately; the goal is the town.[12]

Peirce's triad also serves as the framework for the classification of the three branches or "dimensions" of current semiotic.[13] The relation between one sign and another establishes the dimension of syntactics. The relation of signs to objects establishes the dimension of semantics. The natural science of all three elements yields the dimension of pragmatics.[14]

But long before now, Peirce would almost certainly have called a halt. Hold on a minute, semiotical friend, he might well say. Much as I appreciate your cordial reception of my triad, it strikes me that you somewhat underestimate what I had in mind; that, to tell the truth, what you have is not a triad at all.

It must be determined (1) whether Peirce's semiosis differs from Morris's semiosis, and (2) if it does, whether Peirce's triadic meaning-event has any validity as a datum in a behavioral science of signs.

Every genuine triadic relation involves meaning, according to Peirce, and is not reducible to dyadic relations.[15] To illustrate the difference between a genuine triad and a pseudo-triad, he cites two examples. A gives B to C: a genuine triad. A throws B away and B happens to hit C in the eye: a pair of linked dyads.

No doubt these examples raise more questions than they answer. Words like "giving," "accidentally," "transfer of the right of property," bristle with ambiguities and begged questions. The issue is better joined when Peirce gets down to the same cases that interest Morris: sign-transactions between organisms. Peirce classified signs by three trichotomies and derived therefrom ten classes of signs with numerous subdivisions. I shall be concerned with only two kinds of signs and one distinction. But it is a distinction that is both radical in Peirce's thought and relevant to current behavioral semiotic.

There would, presumably, be no difference between Morris and Peirce as to the nature of what Morris calls a signal[16] and what Peirce called an index. An index is an actual existent that is in a dynamical (including spatial) connection with the object.[17] The connection between an index (signal) and its object exists whether there is an interpreter or not.[18] A low barometer is an index of rain whether the meteorologist looks at it or not.[19] A deer's scent is an index of the deer whether the lion smells it or not.

The trouble starts when we come to consider the language symbol: what is called by Morris comsigns or comsymbols and families thereof, and by Peirce, symbols and legisigns and replicas thereof.

At first it seems that there is substantial agreement here too, since Morris subscribes to Peirce's formula: "To determine the meaning of any sign we have only to determine what habit it produces."[20] It soon becomes evident, however, that the word *habit* is not used in an ordinary univocal sense. By *habit* Morris clearly means a "disposition to behavior," that is, a congenital or acquired inclination of the organism to respond to a kind of stimulus in a certain way.[21] But in the places where Peirce speaks of habit, it looks as if he meant something quite different. Of course the whole evolutionary-pragmatic revolution in the behavioral sciences intervened between the two, and a semioticist might reasonably maintain that a Peirce living today would speak a language as behavioristic as Morris and Bloomfield. Yet the question still remains: are Peirce and Morris really talking about the same thing? A symbol, according to Peirce, is a "habit," or "an acquired law," or a "convention" or "contract," by which men agree to call a certain class of objects by a certain name.[22]

The use of the word *habit* is at least ambiguous and perhaps equivocal when it is applied to both signal behavior and symbol behavior, for the following reasons. There would be general agreement as to what is meant by the word *habit* when it is applied to the disposition of the dog to respond to the buzzer by seeking food. *Habit* here is surely synonymous with the physico-physiological state of the organism, a state that has to a degree been brought about by previous conditioning. But it is far from clear what *habit* means when it is applied to a solitary man reading a book

about Alaska, to [use] Morris's example. Morris's behavioristic interpretation of *habit* as the reader's disposition to respond at a later date to a given
environment[23] does not seem to have much to do with the here-and-now
event, the reading, the here-and-now capacity of the reader to understand
the printed symbols, *to take the writer's meaning.*

One must in all fairness, however, remember Morris's methodological
objective, which is not to rule out an aspect of sign-phenomena because it
is "meaningless" but "simply to advance semiotic as a science."[24]

No one can take exception to Morris's setting forth the problem as a
methodological one. What must be settled is whether the method proposed allows one to take account of the realities observed.

Our suspicion that something has been left out of behavioristic semiotic
is confirmed by the discovery that this same something is treated promi-
nently in formal semiotic. Giving names to things, for example, is the
subject matter of the formal discipline of semantics, which abstracts from
the name-giver. The assumption is apparently made that name-giving,
while it is a real event in the world, can only be treated by formal science.[25]
This assumption is particularly apparent in the semioticist's inveterate
habit of speaking in two tongues about the same event in the world without making it clear how one tongue is translatable into the other. As a
natural scientist, the semioticist speaks of organisms responding to environments. But in the next breath he has put on a semantical-syntactical
cap and is speaking of assigning names, making rules, deducing theorems.
Or saying in the same breath that animals respond to signs and men too,
but that men also put signs together to make sentences that correspond to
"an actual state of affairs"[26]—as though one had not jumped an abyss in
the middle of the sentence that is deep enough to make ordinary men
dizzy. If it is clear to behaviorists, semanticists and logical empiricists how
it is that "giving names to things" is continuous *even in principle* with
"responding to an environment," so clear that it goes without saying, it is
far from clear to me.

Morris agrees that "something has been left out" of behavioral semiotic, a lot of things, in fact: all mental entities like ideas, thoughts and
images.[27] They have to be left out because there is no way to control by
observation-statements the mentalist's explanation of sign-events. I agree:
it advances semiotic not at all to say that a sign gives rise to an "idea" in
the interpreter's "mind" and causes him to "think" of something. But the
problem has nothing to do with mentalism. The problem is how a behavioral scientist can give an account of observable symbolic and assertory

behavior: giving names to things, making assertions about things. A pragmatic semioticist is not dispensed from this duty by regularly beating up the mentalist straw man.

Morris cites Peirce's meaning-triad in support of current behavioristic semiotic. Yet this same semiotic cannot give an account of what Peirce considered the prime meaning-event in symbol-behavior.

III

It will perhaps be most fruitful to re-examine Peirce's concepts of an *index* and a *symbol*. Index and symbol occur in Peirce's second trichotomy: the classification of signs in the light of the relation between a sign and its object.[28]

Peirce distinguishes here between an index and a symbol, a distinction that is comparable to Morris's distinction between a signal and a symbol.[29]

An index is a sign that refers to its object "because it is in dynamical (including spatial) connection with the individual object, on the one hand, and with the senses or memory of the person for whom it serves as a sign, on the other hand."[30]

"A symbol is a sign which refers to the object that it denotes by virtue of a law...."[31]

An example will make clear in what sense an index differs from a symbol. In using the example, taken from Peirce, let us be careful to stipulate in what dimension of current semiotic we choose to operate. Let us stipulate here and now that we shall take the perspective of natural scientists who are observing events (or reflecting upon some events all of us have observed). We are concerned with the entire sign-event and are therefore not in this instance semanticists (who abstract from sign-users) or syntacticists (who abstract from both sign-users and objects). We are, in short, pragmaticists, not in this instance laboratory pragmaticists, but rather reflective pragmaticists as Mead and Morris are reflective pragmaticists when they write about what is going on between sign-using animals.

A man walking with a child points to an object and says: "There is a balloon."[32] The child understands the giving of the name and asks: "What is a balloon?" Then they talk about balloons.

What does Peirce make of this event? First there are indexical elements, the man's pointing and the word *there*—here-and-now events that direct the boy's attention to a here-and-now object. So far, no difficulties between a Peircean semiotic and a Morrisian semiotic. But what about the word *balloon*? What sort of a sign is it? Both Peirce and Morris say it is a symbol (Morris would call it a designative comsymbol). But what Peirce understands to be going on in the event itself is quite different from what Morris understands to be going on.

According to Peirce, the actual utterance of the man, the never-to-be-repeated little howling sound "balloon," is not the symbol but its replica. The symbol is the English language word *balloon*, which is a law or contract or convention by which it is understood among English-speaking people that they will throw together (συμβαλλημ, symballein) this kind of sound with this kind of rubbery inflatable thing.[33]

Now there is no question about the spatio-temporal existence of the sound "balloon" that was uttered by the man. It exists in the same sense as a particular buzz of the buzzer in a learning experiment. But in what sense may we say that there "is" a word *balloon* in the English language? In this sense according to Peirce: the word *balloon* has no "existence" and its entire "being" consists in the fact *that existent replicas of it will conform to it*. The word *balloon* is a law.

The "Thirdness" or irreducibly triadic character of the symbol-event consists in this: that the connection between the word and the object depends altogether on the *symballein* or throwing together of *symbol* (a family of sounds) and a *designatum* through a convention and by a *thrower* or symbolizer.[34]

By contrast the connection between thunder and rain does not require the presence of a sentient organism. So also will the buzzer be followed by food, even though the dog may have dropped dead without the psychologist's knowledge.

Morris allows that a symbol is a kind of sign that is distinct from a signal. He defines a symbol as "a sign produced by its interpretant that acts as a substitute for some sign with which it is synonymous."[35] Thus a symbol might operate in a dog's behavior. "The symbol could take the place in the control of the dog's behavior which the buzzer formerly exercised: hunger cramps for instance might themselves come to be a sign (that is, a symbol) of food at the customary place."[36]

What we must determine is in what sense, if any, one may apply the term *symbol* to both the behavioral sequence in Morris's example and the contractual interpersonal event described by Peirce. Fully aware of Morris's anxiety to save continuity for the sake of a unified science of meaning, we must nevertheless recognize that continuity cannot be saved by the equivocal use of words to signify utterly different happenings.

Different as appears Peirce's symbol-triad from Morris's hunger cramps, Morris nevertheless endorses Peirce's semiosis and adduces recent experimental work in support of it.[37] It is particularly instructive to see how Peirce's triad is construed in terms of neobehavioristic psychology.

Morris concedes that Peirce would not accept a behavioristic psychology that attempted to reduce behavior to a two-term relation between stimuli and responses. He adds, however, that recent formulations of behavior theory have in their own way accepted Peirce's position in so far as they recognize that the conditioning of one's response to a stimulus that previously produced another response is mediated by a third factor: a reinforcing state of affairs in which a need of the animal is reduced or satisfied. "In Peirce's sense, such conditioning is then triadic, and the reinforcing state of affairs is the factor of mediation."[38]

But is such conditioning triadic in Peirce's sense? Morris is saying that a simple stimulus-and-response, a blow of the reflex hammer followed by a knee jerk, is a dyadic relation, but that a stimulus-and-response-and-reinforcement fulfill the conditions of Peirce's triad. That is to say, when the conditioned dog hears the buzzer and goes to look for food, the food is to be regarded as a mediating third factor.

It is hard to see, from Peirce's point of view, how Morris could have chosen a relation more readily resolvable into dyads. As a reducible triad, Peirce cites the example of A throwing B up in the air and B happening to hit C in the eye. The action may be understood as a sequence of space-time events or energy exchanges. So also may the response-sequence: buzzer stimulates organism, organism goes to look for food. Space-time sequences or energy exchanges may be understood as twos in a functional relation:

$$a = f(b).$$

But a symbol meaning-event may not be so understood. Naming takes three. The relation between name and thing is not a space-time relation but one intended by the namer. The behavioristic "triad" of buzzer-dog-food answers nicely to Peirce's criteria of Secondness, namely, a sequence of hitting, of "matter" in interaction. Indeed, such "Secondness" is precisely the sort of reality allowed by [Morris].

If the neobehaviorist protests at this juncture that he can't see any sense in counting "terms" and "relations" in the first place, that the dog's behavior is neither "dyadic" nor "triadic" but is rather an on-going adaptive interaction between an organism and an environment—I heartily agree. I only seek grounds of comparison between Peirce's doctrine of symbol and current semiotic. The point is that whether one uses as criteria terms or relations or generic kinds of behavior, symbol-behavior is different from signal behavior and is not to be reduced to it.

The determination of semioticists to unite symbol and signal behavior by the univocal application of a stimulus-response language leads to characteristic ambiguities in the meaning of terms. A good example is the way Morris translates Peirce's distinction between a *symbol* and its *replica* into pragmatical language. Only replicas of symbols exist in the world, particular utterances spoken at a particular time and place. The English word *balloon* does not exist at all in the space-time continuum: "Its being consists in the fact that existents will conform to it."[39]

Morris draws a similar distinction between symbols and families of symbols.[40] Just as the word *house* is a general sign and the many utterances of the word members of the same sign family, so do the many individual buzzes of the buzzer belong to the same family.

It will be noted that there is here a considerable ambiguity in the attribution of the term "general sign" to the two cases. The individual buzzes of the buzzer are no more instances of a "general buzz" than are the droplets of HCl falling on a stack of NaOH instances of a "general droplet"—though the NaOH "responds" in the same way to each. A chemist can get along very well without speaking of a "general droplet"; a psychologist can get along very well without mentioning a general buzz of the buzzer. But it is impossible to say the first thing about symbolic activity, language for example, without mentioning symbols, words, of which specific utterances are the instances.[41]

IV

It is my contention that there does not presently exist a natural science of symbolic behavior *as such*. There exist formal sciences: semantics and syntactics. There exist descriptive and comparative sciences in linguistics. There exist natural sciences at a sub-symbolic level, acoustics for example. There exist natural applied sciences of symbolic behavior, psychiatry for example. But I am not aware of a discipline that undertakes the study, classification, and analysis of symbolic behavior as such, the modes of assertory behavior, the status of the intersubjective bond between producer and receiver of the symbol; the modes, magic and otherwise, in which symbol and thing are thrown together and interpenetrated by each other.

It is much as if biologists were content to describe the various kinds of mitosis that occur in the gametes of various organisms but had not thought to study the nature of mitosis itself.

Yes, there are studies of symbolic behavior, in which examples are selected that lend themselves to the response sequences of learning psychology. Malinowski liked to talk about the language behavior of Trobriand Islanders engaged in a fishing expedition: "Fish here!" "A little more to the left!" "Lower your nets!" etc. Morris talks about the driver getting directions and turning off the road. Mead gives examples like a man crying "Fire!" in a theater, or me asking you to get up and get the visitor a chair. But what I would like to know is what is going on when Malinowski's islanders come home and sit down and listen to somebody tell a story—or what is going on here and now when the reader reads a book about Alaska, not what he is going to do later when he goes to Alaska. I should particularly like to hear what a pragmaticist [like Morris] has to say about the behavior of a syntacticist who is sitting at his desk erecting a postulational-deductive system. When a neobehaviorist reads a scientific paper written by another neobehaviorist, he might indeed *respond*, by rage or mirth or gooseflesh, and later perhaps by getting up and going into his laboratory and doing some experiments suggested by the paper. But apart from motor and glandular activity, he also understands the paper, *takes its meaning*. And this is an event.

One must be content here to raise a question which, I, for one, cannot answer. If it is true that symbolic behavior is a kind of event that cannot be understood by a space-time scheme of stimulus-response-goal, then by what canon can it be understood? In professing ignorance, however, I am quite confident that such a science is possible, and that the alternative to behaviorism is not the mentalist straw man the semioticists have been beating all these years. I would only note here that there is a public observable realm of meaning quite apart from response sequences. Symbolic behavior is observable. When we see a man point to a balloon and say "There is a balloon," we are observing a *symballein* or throwing together of symbol and object by a thrower, a triadic relation that is not a response sequence.[42] We observe an assertory event. There is no need to resort to ideas and thoughts. To raise the question of mentalism only serves to distract attention from the problem: that of laying a groundwork for an adequate [science of symbols].[43]

NOTES

1. Since the 1950s, considerable work in logic has come to establish that Peirce's NonReduction Theorem is indeed an implicit principle of First-Order Logic of Relations. This history is introduced and summarized in Ketner et al. (2011); See also *His Glassy Essence* and articles collected in Samway 1995.
2. See the chapter "For a Semiotic Anthropology."
3. See also their U.S. Patent 6,819,474 *Quantum Switches and Circuits.*
4. Morris 1946, p. 19.
5. Sellars 1948, p. 94.
6. Op. cit., p. v.
7. Ibid., p. 288.
8. Neurath et al. 1955, p. 81.
9. Op. cit., p. 7.
10. Ibid., p. 10.
11. Peirce 1932, 5.484 (as quoted by Morris). Hereafter CP, with volume number and paragraph number, thus: CP 5.484 [meaning Volume 5, paragraph 484].
12. Op. cit., p. 6.
13. *Encyc.*, op. cit., pp. 84–85.
14. There is some ambiguity about the word pragmatics, since it is used both in the sense of a "metascience" and so limited to the study of scientists and their signs and objects (ibid., p. 70), and in the sense of a natural science co-ordinate with other natural sciences, hence as the name of the general behavioral science of signs and their users (ibid., pp. 80, 108.). It is in the second sense that I use it here.
15. CP 1.345.
16. I shall use Morris's terminology: *sign* as the general term, *signal* and *symbol* as species of signs.
17. CP 2.305.
18. CP 2.299.
19. CP 2.286.
20. Op. cit., p. v.
21. Ibid., p. 348.
22. CP 2.293.
23. Op. cit., p. 14.
24. Ibid., p. 28.
25. Carnap, it is true, distinguishes between *pure* (formal) *semantics*, the construction and analysis of semantical systems, and *descriptive semantics*, the study of historical languages. But a natural science of meaning, besides describing the structure of historical languages, must also make clear exactly in what sense it uses the word "giving" when it says that Germans

"give" the word *Mond* to the moon. Is this "giving" a kind of response? If it isn't, what is it?

26. Reichenbach 1956, p. 265.
27. Op. cit., p. 28.
28. CP 2.247.
29. I omit the first of the three signs, the icon, as being least relevant to a behavioral semiotic.
30. CP 2.305.
31. CP 2.249.
32. CP 2.293.
33. *Symbol* is regarded by Peirce as a particularly apt word, since its root meaning, throw together, was early and often used by the Greeks to mean a convention or contract.
34. CP 2.293. The symbol in use, according to Peirce, *denotes* that particular balloon and *signifies* a character (that of balloons in general).
35. Op. cit., p. 25.
36. Ibid., p. 25.
37. Ibid., p. 288.
38. Ibid., p. 288.
39. CP 2.292.
40. Op. cit., p. 35.
41. Thus Peirce was not discontent with Ockham's slogan that universals are nothing but words, since he, Peirce, believed the words were as good universals as any (CP 2.301).
42. Stepping out of the role of Peirce's spokesman, I would suggest that the symbol-relation is actually tetradic, since a convention, and intersubjectivity, requires two people. See W. Percy, "Symbol, Consciousness, and Intersubjectivity," this *Journal*, Vol. LV (1958) pp. 631–641. [KLK: "this *Journal*" was *The Journal of Philosophy*, see MB, essay number 12. That remark indicates Percy was planning to submit "Peirce and Modern Semiotic" to *The Journal of Philosophy*.]
43. [KLK: There is no last page in the manuscript (number 101, Percy Archive, University of North Carolina Chapel Hill). This is my conjectured ending; just these three words offer a proper closing.]

REFERENCES

Beil, Ralph G., and Kenneth Laine Ketner. 2003. Peirce, Clifford, and Quantum Theory. *International Journal of Theoretical Physics* 42 (9): 1957–1972.

Ketner, Kenneth Laine. 1998. *His Glassy Essence: An Autobiography of Charles Sanders Peirce*. Nashville: Vanderbilt University Press.

150   K. L. KETNER

———. 1999. Rescuing Science from Scientism: The Achievement of Walker Percy. *The Intercollegiate Review* Fall 1999: 22–27.

———. et al. 2011. Peirce's Nonreduction and Relational Completeness Claims in the Context of First-Order Predicate Logic. Interdisciplinary Seminar on Peirce. *KODIKAS* 34: 3–14.

Morris, Charles. 1946. *Signs, Language and Behavior.* New York: Prentice-Hall.

Neurath, Otto, Charles Morris, and Rudolf Carnap. 1955. Foundations of the Theory of Signs. In: *International Encyclopedia of Unified Science*, 81. Chicago: University of Chicago Press.

Peirce, Charles Sanders. 1932. *Collected Papers of Charles Sanders Peirce.* Ed. Charles Hartshorne and Paul Weiss. Cambridge, MA: Harvard University Press.

Reichenbach, Hans. 1956. *The Rise of Scientific Philosophy.* Berkeley: University of California Press.

Samway, Patrick J., S. J., ed. 1995. *A Thief of Peirce: The Letters of Kenneth Laine Ketner and Walker Percy.* Jackson: University Press of Mississippi.

Sellars, Roy Wood. 1949. Materialism and Human Knowing. In *Philosophy for the Future.* New York: Macmillan.

Singer, Milton. 1984. *Man's Glassy Essence: Explorations in Semiotic Anthropology.* Bloomington: Indiana University Press.

CHAPTER 8

An Attempt Toward a Natural/Unnatural History of The Lay-Scientific Interface or How Walker Percy Got on the Way to Becoming a Radical (Anthropologist)

Scott R. Cunningham

Walker Percy devoted a great portion of his life trying to understand the structure of symbolic behavior, what he called one of the "essential features of symbolic knowing (Percy 1950–1980)." Percy sought understanding of the nature of the symbol in the disciplines of linguistics, sociology, philosophy, theology, and anthropology. All of these he tried and found them wanting.

In a letter to Kenneth Ketner, Percy writes that he had "been at some pains to sketch out an 'anthropology,' a theory of man" (Ketner 1995, p. 131) and that he hoped to use "CSP's [Charles Sanders Peirce's] 'ontology'[1] of Secondness and Thirdness (not Firstness)[2] as the ground for a more or less scientific introduction to a philosophical anthropology."

In "Culture: The Antinomy of the Scientific Method" Percy predesignated an important question, "But may we not require of anthropology, the science of man, some assessment of that creature himself who makes

S. R. Cunningham (✉)
Institute for Studies in Pragmaticism, Texas Tech University, Lubbock, TX, USA
e-mail: scott.cunningham@ttu.edu

© The Author(s) 2018
L. Marsh (ed.), *Walker Percy, Philosopher*,
https://doi.org/10.1007/978-3-319-77968-3_8

culture possible? The question which can not be put off forever is not what is the nature of culture and what are the laws of culture, but what is the ontological nature of the creature who makes the assertions of culture?" (Percy 1958a, p. 478).

It is clear that Percy had "been at some pains" for roughly 30 years[3] to sketch out a scientific philosophical anthropology in order to answer his question about the ontological nature of the creature. Yet among his writings there does not appear to be a singular work containing such a sketch.

Taking Percy at his word that he had been working on such a project and finding no one work of the sort suggests that its components are to be found throughout his writing. With this in mind the purpose of this essay is not to provide an account of the entirety of his sketch but instead to examine one clear major component of that sketch, "The Lay-Scientific Interface."

"The Lay-Scientific Interface," a phenomenon discovered by Walker Percy, is able to be observed when individuals with two distinct sets of linguistic symbols and sentences attempt to communicate. In examining his concept of this phenomenon evidence will be offered that it was fairly well developed, and served an integral purpose in providing him a laboratory where he could make observations that prove foundational for his sketch of a scientific philosophical anthropology.

What Was Percy Doing? Not Philosophy but Philosophical Work[4]

Percy is sometimes referred to as a novelist, sometimes a philosopher, and sometimes both. It is true that he wrote novels and did philosophy.[5] However, it is important to understand that while he did do philosophy, he did not do it in the ordinary, usually understood way. Philosophy is often thought of as existing somewhere along a continuum between extremes. One end of the continuum consists of the banal generalities that comprise pleasant, over-caffeinated coffee shop chit-chat, with the other being the over-serious consideration of collections of absurd questions.[6]

Percy is practicing philosophy nowhere along this continuum. He is instead practicing philosophy in Peirce's sense of philosophy in that "philosophy is (or could easily become) a science that is embedded within a context of other sciences or presuppositions of science; ..." (Stuhr 1987, p. 15). Instead of asking "Is Percy a novelist or philosopher?", a better question might be: "Is Percy practicing novel science,[7] that is, writing a radical anthropology, or both?" (Percy 1958a).[8]

PERCY'S PHILOSOPHICAL WORK ON "THE LAY-SCIENTIFIC INTERFACE": THE RADICAL ANTHROPOLOGICAL INQUIRY BEGINS

Percy, writing in a lengthy unpublished manuscript, gives a summary of his philosophical work to that point,

> I have tried in the last two chapters to do three things: (1) to delineate the essential features of pure symbolic knowing, as it can be arrived at through an examination of one's figuration[9] of linguistic symbols and sentences; (2) to examine some of the more obvious traits of primitive cognition for what light the "a priori categories of pure symbolic knowing" may throw upon them; (3) having established a rough conception of the formal conditions under which "magic cognition" occurs in primitive society, to turn again to modern life in order to determine whether or not under analogous conditions, magic cognition may not also occur (Percy 1950–80).

In the two chapters to which Percy refers inquiry is begun by attempting "to delineate the essential features of pure symbolic knowing"[10] by reasoning in the abductive mode, a state that Charles Peirce would call musement:

> There is no kind of reasoning that I should wish to discourage in Musement; and I should lament to find anybody confining it to a method of such moderate fertility as logical analysis. Only, the Player should bear in mind that the higher weapons in the arsenal of thought are not playthings but edgetools. In any mere Play they can be used by way of exercise alone; while logical analysis can be put to its full efficiency in Musement. So, continuing the counsels that had been asked of me, I should say, "Enter your skiff of Musement, push off into the lake of thought, and leave the breath of heaven to swell your sail. With your eyes open, awake to what is about or within you, and open conversation with yourself; for such is all meditation." It is, however, not a conversation in words alone, but is illustrated, like a lecture, with diagrams and with experiments (Peirce 1908, pp. 94–95).[11]

Out of Percy's musement on "the essential features of symbolic knowing" come three things of note for the examination and study of "The
Lay-Scientific Interface." First is the recognition and identification of at
least two distinct groups involved in the phenomenon clearly demar-
cated, according to Percy, by "two entirely different and even mutually
exclusive points of view" (Percy 1950–80) through which they conceive
human beings. These two default conceptions, or points of view, he
argues are consequences of the "failure to recognize the all-pervasive,
all-construing life of the symbolic-imagination" (Ibid.) Percy gives these
distinct, individual conceptions of man the names "Object Man" and
"Subject Man." The former thought of "as an organism adapting to an
environment and the later thought of as a symbol-mongerer dealing in
propositions" (Ibid.). Man as "Object Man" is conceived "as a biological unit, equipped with highly-organized neurological equipment to be
sure, but reacting according to the universal canons of adaptation and
instrumentality" (Ibid.). Man as "Subject Man," if spoken about by
scientists, is just as likely to be spoken about "in terms of highly abstract
formulae which bear a truth-falsehood relation to the world" (Ibid.).
Second, Percy posits[12] man as "organism" (LC, p. 88; see also Peirce
1868a, b). Once man is posited as organism the inquiry turns to
musement about "organisms" and their interactions with "worlds,"
"environments," and "cultures" (Percy 1958a, pp. 443–475; 1985,
pp. 98–102; Samway 1995, pp. 6–7).[13] Finally, at this early point in his
inquiry, while Percy does not specifically define what he will eventually
term the "Lay" and "Scientific" sub-cultures, he does offer some descrip-
tors of them. The "Lay" he says, are "at some remotion from the action"
and "outside a particular technical specialty" (Percy 1950–80).[14] It
would appear then that the "Scientific" are at least more near the action
(whatever action it is that Percy has in mind) and inside a particular technical specialty. Percy, now being aware of certain vague properties of
"The Lay-Scientific Interface," makes further, more determinate, observations of the phenomenon, resulting in some assertions pertaining to
the way this phenomenon might present.[15]

THE LAY-SCIENTIFIC INTERFACE PRESENTS

The phenomenon of "The Lay-Scientific Interface" offered Percy the
opportunity to identify a situation within which, given its concomitant
properties and characteristics, he might have the opportunity to observe

symbolic behavior (and its results) both within and between organisms in vivo. This phenomenon occurs when representative users of the two distinct groups, the "Lay" and the "Scientific," each using their distinct sets of linguistic symbols and sentences, attempt to communicate. In this phenomenon each representative's efforts to communicate, *to take the other's meaning*, result in the manifestation of a measurable, observational object[16] amenable to scientific study.

BEARING DOWN AND CLOSING IN: OBSERVATIONS OF "THE LAY-SCIENTIFIC INTERFACE": WHERE CAN IT BE FOUND?[17]

"The Lay-Scientific Interface" can be found throughout both Percy's fiction and non-fiction. Major portions of his inquiry into "The Lay-Scientific Interface" can be found in the following publications: "Semiotic and a Theory of Knowledge," "Metaphor as Mistake," "Naming and Being," "The Symbolic Structure of Interpersonal Process," "Toward a Triadic Theory of Meaning," and also "A Semiotic Primer of the Self" (the self described "intermezzo of forty pages") found in the middle of LC. Other pieces can be found in documents produced by Percy during his participation in a research project at the National Institutes of Mental Health (NIMH) directed by F. Gentry Harris, M.D.[18]

Percy's novels could be thought of as laboratories, experimental settings for the testing of hypotheses, "as a tool for aiding readers to construct mental (or non-mental) diagrams. These models would then be available to readers who can perhaps learn something about (have an insight about – an IN-sight!) an area of relative ignorance within their persons (within their personal self-knowledge, in the Socratic or Gnostic sense) by exploring the relations that are partially understood within the world (the diagram, the relational patterns) of a novel" (Ketner 1993, pp. 53–54).

Encounters and engagements between representatives of the "Lay" and the "Scientific" occur in Percy's fiction almost continuously. "The Lay-Scientific Interface" can be found and seen most explicitly in his depictions of therapeutic encounters.[19] One example of the clinical setting variety that comes quickly to mind is the therapeutic encounter involving Will Barrett and Dr. Gamow in LG.[20]

Percy begins inquiry into "The Lay-Scientific Interface" in each of his non-fiction publications[21] by asking some specific question about the general nature of communication events. The results of those inquiries provide

Percy with the resources that he fully deploys in "The Symbolic Structure of Interpersonal Process," where he directly addresses "The Lay-Scientific Interface." Let us digress for a moment to examine a few of the questions Percy poses.

In "Symbol as Need" (Percy 1954, pp. 381, 389–390) Percy uses the occasion of reviewing Susan Langer's *Feeling and Form* to consider the nature of what kind of human need is the "basic need of symbolization" (Ibid.). Percy's next paper "Semiotic and a Theory of Knowledge" is a piece not of speculation but of speculative rhetoric/methodeutic,[22] as he (like Peirce) is interested in "a correct account of the nature and function of methods that permit the discovery of truth" (Samway 1995, p. 226).[23] In this paper Percy attempts to observe the results of a true "semiotic", "an open 'semiotical'[24] analysis of symbolization—that is, one undertaken without theoretical presuppositions," and encountered two metaphysical relations: the cognitive relation of identity (Veatch 1952, pp. 8–10, 24–27, 37–38) and the relation of intersubjectivity. "Culture: The Antinomy of the Scientific Method" is a continuation of his study of methodeutic, as it relates to the process of symbolization. Specifically, Percy says he will, first, examine the "remarkable difference between the sort of reality the scientific method is and the sort of reality it understands its data to be" and, second, that he wishes to investigate "the state of affairs which comes when the scientific method is applied to this very activity of which it is itself a mode: the assertory phenomena of culture" (Percy 1958a, p. 444). Percy writes in "Metaphor as Mistake" (Percy 1958b) that "[i]t might be useful to look into the workings of these accidental stumblings into poetic meaning, because they exhibit in a striking fashion that particular feature of metaphor which has most troubled philosophers: that it is 'wrong'—it asserts of one thing that it is something else—and further, that its beauty often seems proportionate to its wrongness or outlandishness" (Ibid.).[25] As the paper closes Percy writes that the examination of these instances of accidental blunderings into meaning is useful for the understanding they give as to how communication (Ketner 1993, p. 35)[26] can go awry.

In "The Symbolic Structure of Interpersonal Process" (Percy 1961) the results of Percy's inquiry of the previous four papers coalesces and is brought to bear on "The Lay-Scientific Interface" as observed in the therapist-patient relationship. The question of this paper is whether psychiatry as an empirical science can progress given that its understanding of intersubjective communication events and the explanatory resources about those events are of a strictly causal-functional nature. With this as background let us now return to Percy's concept of "The Lay-Scientific Interface."

In "Semiotic and a Theory of Knowledge" (Percy 1957) Percy clearly no longer wishes to be inured by the fact "that a man engaged in the business of building a logical calculus is doing a very different sort of thing from an animal (or man) responding to a sign," and that the difference cannot be "conjured away ... as though there were no epistemological abyss in between" (Ibid.; MB, pp. 77–87). Here he makes the claim that manifested behaviors resulting from at least certain types of cognitive activity are different from other observed behaviors. The difference lay in their not being able to be fully explained or understood if seen only as the result of an ordinarily understood Pavlovian stimulus-response sequence.[27]

In his second philosophical paper "Semiotic and a Theory of Knowledge," the inquiry takes on a quite different style. His diction and tone here change to match the level of analysis attempted. Here[28] Percy writes,

> I think it will be possible to show (1) that the "unified science"[29] of semi-otic[30] is a spurious unity conferred by a deliberate equivocation of the word "sign" to designate two generically different meaning-situations (the sign-relation and the symbol-relation) and (2) that an open "semiotical"[31] analysis of symbolization–that is, one undertaken without theoretical presuppositions–will encounter and shed light upon two metaphysical relations: the first, the cognitive relation of identity[32] by which a concept, a "formal sign," comes to contain within itself *in alio esse*[33] the thing signified; the second, the relation of intersubjectivity, one of the favorite themes of modern existentialists.[34]

Why would Percy be interested in showing these two things? (1a) That contemporary, dyadic semiotics equivocates in its use of the word "sign," using it dyadically to represent a triadic event, and (1b) that a correct understanding of the "sign" event, which is triadic in nature, is one of identity, not stimulus-response; and (2) that "symbol" (also of a triadic nature) is intersubjective; that is, it occurs in community? First, he would want to show that the "unified science" project of Morris et al. is doomed to failure. Second, for there to be a difference between "signal using" and "sign using," (Percy 1958a, pp. 443–475)[35] "something"[36] must occur both within and between sign users and this "something" that does and must occur cannot be accounted for by either exclusive dyadic causality or by bad semiotic as (semiotics) understood by the "unified science" crowd.

His third semiotic reflection "Metaphor as Mistake" (Percy 1958b) must be read carefully when being considered as a contribution to Percy's inquiry into "The Lay-Scientific Interface." In "Metaphor as Mistake" Percy writes that given common, accepted misnomers for scientific names, such as "blue dollar hawk' for "blue-darter hawk" or mishearings such as "Seabird" record player for "Seeburg" record player, "[i]t might be useful to look into the workings of these accidental stumblings into poetic meaning, because they exhibit in a striking fashion that particular feature of metaphor which has most troubled philosophers; that it is 'wrong'–it asserts of one thing that it is something else–and further, that its beauty often seems proportionate to its wrongness or outlandishness" (Ibid.). Here Percy's words encourage a misreading of "Metaphor as Mistake" as being *only* an exploration of a certain kind of literary counter-intuitiveness. With focus being placed on looking at these accidental types of poetic meaning, it then becomes difficult to see the connection to, and the relation of, this portion as contributing to Percy's inquiry into "The Lay-Scientific Interface." To make clear the connection and to have the possible suggestion of another understanding of "Metaphor as Mistake," we must look slightly ahead to his fifth philosophical paper "The Symbolic Structure of Interpersonal Process."

In this paper Percy appears to be completely finished with the hand-waving dismissal and inability of behavioristic theories to account for the difference between "signal using" and "sign using." "It is the thesis of this paper that this ambiguity in both psychiatry and social psychology can be traced to an equivocation of behavioral terms such as *sign, stimulus, interaction*, and so forth, in which they are applied to two generically different communication events. It is further proposed (1) to call into question the behavioristic or sign theory of interpersonal process, (2) to outline the generic structure of symbolic behavior, and (3) to examine briefly its relevance for the therapist-patient relation" (Percy 1961, p. 39).

Here can be seen a connection with, and return to, Percy's complaint of the equivocation referred to in "Semiotic and a Theory of Knowledge" (Percy 1957). It now becomes clear why Percy is so deeply concerned, a twofold concern, with this equivocation. First, if the equivocation is allowed to hold, then the behavioristic theory of interpersonal process and the explanations it produces will remain. Second, if the behavioristic theory is left intact, then an antinomy occurs,[37] resulting in the impossibility of there being assertory events. If there can be no assertory events, with culture being understood by Percy as largely "a tissue of assertions," (Ketner 1993, p. 34) then the potential for the understanding of cultural realities, and even culture itself, is greatly diminished, if not eliminated altogether. "For [then] cultural realities are inexplicable solely in terms of functional or causal information" (Ibid.). With these observations, let us return for a moment to "Metaphor as Mistake" and its connection to the "The Lay-Scientific Interface" that is now seemingly apparent.

Percy begins "Metaphor as Mistake" by saying, "Four of the five examples given above are mistakes: misnamings, misunderstandings, or misrememberings" (Percy 1958a). This writing is, as he says, "a look into the workings of these accidental stumblings into poetic meaning," but it turns out to be much more.

In the later portions of his inquiry Percy's initial vague musings about the essential features of symbolic knowing become more determinate[38] through his intense focus on a specific feature of symbolic knowing: symbolic behavior. Also, the focus of his inquiry is specifically directed toward observations and analysis of the intersubjective therapist-patient relation.[39]

WHERE FIGURATIONS[40] MIGHT BE OBSERVED

In the therapist-patient relation[41] Percy sees an opportunity to observe what happens when the two groups, the two sub-cultures, the "Lay" and the "Scientific" engage one another in a clinical "field of interaction" (Percy 1961, p. 39).

Percy's analysis of the therapist-patient relationship[42] in "The Symbolic Structure of Interpersonal Process" makes it quite clear that something "unusual" happens when the "Lay" and the "Scientific" "interface" and attempt communication. Percy observes that communication does not go well. He points out that "mistakes" in taking each other's meaning occur as they "interface" though the use of language across the interactive field.[43]

The connection of "Metaphor as Mistake" to his inquiry can now clearly be seen. "Metaphor as Mistake" is an attempt to study and understand what the nature of making a "mistake" might be and what a "mistake" might look like when these two groups, two sub-cultures, attempt to interface (communicate).

Based on evidence gathered from his observations of "The Lay-Scientific Interface," what conclusion does Percy reach about what happens when these two sub-cultures interface? He reaches the same conclusion in both "Metaphor as Mistake" (a folksy, ordinary interface account) and "The Symbolic Structure of Interpersonal Process" (Percy 1958b, p. 93; 1961; Eisenstadt 1992, pp. 29–87) (a formal clinical interface account). "Intersubjectivity fails."

Why, according to Percy, does this failure occur between these two sub-cultures? It isn't the case that one is signal[44]-using and the other is symbol (sign)-using. In the therapist-patient relation both are symbol-users. Percy's hypothesis is that in spite of both being symbol-users they each have a "being-in-the-world" wholly different from each other. This different "being-in-the world" comes from the fact that the "Scientist" has directly adopted his/her so-called objective viewpoint, while the "Lay" has adopted it, more or less out of some unspecified feeling of necessity, secondhand. "His (the Lay's) problem is not, as is the scientist's, *What sense can I make of the data before me?*, but is instead, *How can I live in a world which I have disposed of theoretically?*" (Percy 1961, p. 51; Veatch 1969, pp. 26–41, 126–144).

In "Toward a Triadic Theory of Meaning," the sixth and last major paper, the understanding of the connection and contribution of "Metaphor as Meaning" to the inquiry is deepened and its vital importance to it realized. "Metaphor as Meaning" can now be seen and understood as a deep and extended musement on the nature of meaning that provide Percy basic details concerning the nature of communication events across the interface and how they can go terribly and horribly wrong.

In "Toward a Triadic Theory of Meaning" Percy tells us several things of great interest and importance to understanding his inquiry into "The Lay-Scientific Interface." He begins by stating that he is not offering the psychiatrist an adequate and whole theory of language but that instead he is offering "a sample of another way of looking at things." Looking at what things? What psychiatrists do, Percy notes, can be described as "listening-and-talking" and in connection mentions his observation, "Yet if there exists a basic science of listening-and-talking I have not heard of it."[45]

He hopes that what he offers in this paper "might either stimulate or irritate behavioral scientists toward the end that they will devise operational means of confirming or disconfirming these statements—or perhaps even launch more fruitful studies than this very tentative investigation" (Percy 1972, p. 2).

RADICAL ANTHROPOLOGICAL TALK

What is Percy saying here? He is saying something radical. Why do I say "radical"? In a short piece, (Lewontin and Levins 2002) its authors claimed that Gould's work could be characterized as having a consistent radicalism. They remark that the word *radical* has become synonymous with *extreme* in our everyday usage. However, they point out that a quick look at the *Oxford English Dictionary* reminds us that the root of the word radical comes from *radix*, the Latin word for *root*. To be radical, they say, is to consider things from their very root, from square one, to examine one's actions and ideas and ask if they could, in fact, be reconstructed from first principles. "The impulse to be radical is the impulse to ask, 'How do I know that?' and 'Why am I following this course rather than another?' " One could say of Percy's writing that it too exhibits a consistent radicalism and can be read as a constant call to examine the myriad connections between one's first principles, actions, and ideas.

WHY IS PERCY FOLLOWING THIS RADICAL COURSE?

If Percy's suggestion of taking a "radical," an alternative way of looking at things, in this case the "things" being the phenomenon of the listening-and-talking of psychiatrists with their patients (one place where The Lay-Scientific Interface can be observed), is considered, then other possibilities of inquiry (and understanding) might become available. The first possibility is that his thoughts might serve as a springboard for further inquiry along the lines of his suggestions. Second, and this is certainly the more interesting and exciting of the two possibilities, that his suggestions might result in work (the production of operational definitions) that would enable the testing (confirming or disconfirming) of his statements (hypotheses) by experimentation (means).

Percy asks: What has behavioral science, a science that interests itself in the overt behavior of other organisms, made of observable behaviors that cannot be understood as exclusively dyadic energy transactions? He writes that behavioral science has admitted that there is such a thing as "symbol-mongering" (e.g. naming things and uttering sentences) and that such activities are natural phenomena open to scientific investigation. But, Percy points out, instead of conducting scientific investigation into the phenomena, there has been instead a hand-waving dismissal of the problem of symbolic activity, a work-around arrived at "by treating the products of symbol-mongering formally,"[46] which results in no account of symbolic activity.

Percy's great radical insight is gained as the result of the question he poses in "Toward a Triadic Theory of Meaning." He asks, "If triadic activity is overt behavior and as such is the proper object of investigation of a factual behavioral science and is not formulable by the postulates and laws of conventional behaviorism, what manner of 'postulates' and 'laws,' would be suitable for such a science?" (Percy 1972, p. 3). Where might behavioral science look for an alternative way of looking at things (Veatch 1969, pp. 125–144) containing the possibility of fruitful, suitable postulates and laws?

Percy Suggests Looking to Peirce

Percy writes at the beginning of "Toward a Triadic Theory of Meaning" that "although Peirce is recognized as the founder of semiotic,[47] the theory of signs, modern behavioral scientists have not been made aware of the *radical character* [my italics] of his ideas about language" (Percy 1972). Percy continues by suggesting consideration of Peirce's theory of language[48] "as a natural phenomenon, i.e., not as logic or a formal structure but as overt behavior open to scientific inquiry" (Percy 1972, p. 2). Percy's suggestions take the form of loose postulates and definitions "which I take to be implied by Peirce's triadic theory of signs," (Ibid.) that they "are empirical statements which are more or less self-evident" (Ibid.) and which he takes as "suitable for a behavioral schema of symbol use" (Ibid.)

What then are the postulates Percy claims as suitable for a behavioral schema of symbol use implied by the consideration of symbolic events as triadic events[49] in Peirce's theory of language? First, that the basic unit of language behavior is the sentence and, second, that the receiver of a sentence can take or mistake the meaning of the sentence.[50]

Noted earlier: that Percy is interested in showing two things. First, he is interested in showing that the "unified science" project of Morris et al. is doomed to failure and, second, for there to be a difference between "signal using" and "sign using," "something" must occur both within and between sign users and that this "something" that does and must occur cannot be accounted for by either exclusive dyadic causality or by semiotic as dyadic semiotics as understood by the "unified science" crowd. Where two or more gather together might there be a "third" and if so what kind of something might this "third" be? Percy called it "the coupler."

Coupling and the Coupler

In his correspondence with Ketner, Percy asked questions about the coupler (Ketner 1995, p. 13),[51] the coupling process, what pictures of that sort of thing happening in the brain might look like, pictures of what an interpretant might be, and many other questions along the same lines

(Ketner 1995, pp. 13, 42). It is safe to say that Percy was never satisfied with his understanding of the "coupler" and "coupling."

Percy's understanding and explication of "coupling"[52] and how and why it can go terribly awry in "Toward a Triadic Theory of Meaning" will prove important to understanding the "The Lay-Scientific Interface" and in his continuing his sketch of a scientific philosophical anthropology. It will be important because apparently Percy thought this "coupling," no matter what it is, no matter where it occurs, no matter its manner of manifestation, held the secret to understanding the connection between the symbol and the object symbolized. The quest for this understanding is what set him on the road to becoming a radical anthropologist.

CONCLUSION

With his pen and voice Walker Percy (1958a, p. 240) proposed and tested the hypothesis that:

> [t]he functional method of the sciences is a non-radical method of knowing because, while it recognizes only functional linkages, it presupposes other kinds of reality, the intersubjectivity of scientists and their assertions neither of which are space-time linkages and neither of which can be grasped by the functional method. Therefore, when the functional method is elevated to a total organon of reality and other cognitive claims denied, the consequence must be an antinomy, for a non-radical instrument is being required to construe the more radical reality which it presupposes but does not understand.

If we read Percy as seriously considering this hypothesis, what might we come to hear and understand? Might Percy's sketch of a scientific philosophical anthropology provide access to the radical instrument that enables us to construe the necessarily presupposed radical reality and through it might we interpret and translate aloud an understanding? If we unceasingly participate in his deep and continual inquiry with the same dedication, devotion, and persistence he put into his inquiry of "The Lay-Scientific Interface," we might understand the phenomenon more fully. And if we do acquire these understandings we just might realize Percy's hope and find ourselves with "a theory of man by virtue of which he is understood to be by his very nature open to the kerygma and 'news'" (Samway 1995, p. 131).

NOTES

1. The theory of being; that branch of metaphysics which investigates the nature of being and the essence of things, both substances and accidents (Peirce 1900, pp. 141–162; See also Gerhart and Russell 1984, pp. 141–162).
2. "Firstness," "Secondness," and "Thirdness" refer to Peirce's Categories.
3. The sketch, as sustained inquiry, at least in its written form, began sometime around the late 1950s and ended sometime around the early-to-mid 1980s.
4. There is a difference between doing philosophy and doing philosophical work. For a quick understanding of this difference see Stuhr 1987, pp. 14–15.
5. When thinking of Percy as philosopher it is more correct to think of him as a natural philosopher as understood in the nineteenth century.
6. For a description and consideration of a scientific option for doing philosophy see Scott 2006.
7. For an understanding of "Novel Science" see Ketner 1993, pp. 33–59.
8. Especially pp. 469–475.
9. In general, the visible or tangible form of anything, but also a mystical type; an antecedent symbol or emblem; that which prefigures or represents a coming reality. See Peirce 1900, p. 2209.
10. This word is not being used here as nor is it to be understood as a denigration of the nature of the text. It is in fact used to indicate exactly the opposite. See Peirce 1908, especially pp. 92–98.
11. Musement can also be thought of as a certain kind of scientific philosophical consideration of the question at hand.
12. This is an interesting "posit," as later in the story, the ideas of "placement" and "being placed" become very important. What this might mean is that the later discussions of "placement" might become discussions of "placements of places" or "placements of placings."
13. Environment (signal-user)—"those elements of the Cosmos which affect the organism significantly (Saturn does not) and to which the organism either is genetically coded to respond or has learned to respond." World (sign-user)—"is segmented and named by language. All perceived objects and actions and qualities are named." Culture—"the main elements of cultural activity are in their most characteristic moments also assertory in nature. The central acts of language, of worship, of myth-making, of storytelling, of art, as well as of science are assertions." "An environment, in his [Percy's] sense, is a setting in which only efficient causal relations are to be found. A world, on the other hand, along with environmental factors, also includes significance, meaning, interpretation, understanding, and selves. … Or worlds are not reducible to environments.

14. The "Lay" here have backed away from or are at a remove from the world in that they have disposed of it theoretically.
15. "Present" here is to be understood as it is used in medicine, to appear for examination.
16. With the object consisting of the extent to which each is able to take each other's meaning as indicated by observable behaviors toward each other. See Ketner (Chap. 7) in this volume.
17. I believe a thorough and complete account of Percy's conception of "The Lay-Scientific Interface" could be constituted using several complete articles, along with a few selected passages and documents.
18. A case could be made that the opportunity to explore and analyze "The Lay-Scientific Interface" in a formal clinical setting was certainly a, if not the, major factor in Percy's agreeing to participate in Harris's research project. For a brief account of Percy's participation in this project see Cunningham 2004.
19. Encounters between characters that embody the mutually exclusive "Lay" and "Scientific" conceptions of man can also be found in dialog not occurring in clinical therapeutic settings. I say "clinical therapeutic settings" in that there are certainly encounters between characters in Percy's novels under ordinary, everyday conditions that are therapeutic.
20. An interesting discussion of the exchange between Barrett and Gamow can be found in Lawson 1996, pp. 180–194. No doubt at least one great tome could be written on the occurrences of "The Lay-Scientific Interface" in Percy's novels. However, the purpose of this essay is to show from his non-fiction that "The Lay-Scientific Interface" provides a foundation for his sketch of a scientific philosophical anthropology.
21. Argument could be made that Percy experimented with and attempted to observe "The Lay-Scientific Interface" phenomenon in nearly all of his writing.
22. Methodeutic—this shows how to conduct an inquiry.
23. Argument could be made that Percy experimented with and attempted to observe "The Lay-Scientific Interface" phenomenon in nearly all of his writing.
24. That is, more realist and Peircean than Morris; see Ketner (Chap. 7) in this volume, Percy's terminology was still not clear in his mind at this early moment.
25. It is interesting to note that on the offprint Percy sent to his friend F. Gentry Harris, M.D., Percy typed "An early approach to the artistic employment of the tetrad."
26. "Therefore, intersubjective communication is not a strictly causal matter."
27. A continuation of inquiry into this claim can be found in Bisanz et al. 2011, and McLaughlin et al. 2015.

28. In this article Percy puts forward his tetrad as a revision of the sign triad.

29. Percy's use of "unified science" here refers to doctrines found in 20 introductory monographs bound as Neurath et al. 1955.

30. That is, bad Morrissean semiotics.

31. That is, more realist and Peircean than Morris; see Ketner in this volume, Percy's terminology was still not clear in his mind at this early moment.

32. See Veatch 1952, pp. 8–10, 24–27, 37–38.

33. "in another mode of existence."

34. Percy 1957, pp. 227–228.

35. Signal using is a dyadic relation.

36. This "something" Percy called "coupling."

37. Antinomy—contradiction ... a paradox

38. In logic this is to explain or limit by adding differences. I am using Peirce's sense of "determine" here. See Peirce 1868a. There are also helpful passages regarding the meaning of "determined" in Samway 1995, pp. 35–36. Also as with the use of the word "musement," the use of the word "vague" is not meant to be seen as being derogatory. To understand the idea of vagueness see Brock 1969 and 1979.

39. The therapist-patient relation, either directly experienced by or recalled by characters, is a regular occurrence in Percy's novels.

40. A mystical type; an antecedent symbol or emblem; that which prefigures or represents a coming reality.

41. F. Gentry Harris recommended the reading of Pilisuk 1963 to Percy. This article might be of interest to those interested in what sources might have contributed to Percy's understanding of the patient-therapist relationship.

42. Percy had sent F. Gentry Harris, M.D. an offprint of "Symbolic Structure." At the bottom of the page in the offprint where Percy was writing about the therapist-patient interaction Harris wrote, "If I understand rightly, a much better example, + one much more useful + less precious, is H. Kaiser," *Psychiatry* 18: 205–211, 1955. I was able to ask Harris about this and if he had made the comment to Percy. Harris said, "Yes" and laughed. Intrigued by his laughter, and thinking it possibly had something to do with how Percy responded, I asked him if Percy had replied. Harris said, "Yes, he told me to f_ _k off."

43. Four years later while working with F. Gentry Harris, M.D. on a project at NIMH in one of the project documents in which Percy is analyzing the therapist-patient interaction, he draws a diagram of the interactive field and denotes a line within it as "the membrane."

44. Signal—a dyadic relation.

45. It is interesting to note that this was written in 1961 shortly before Percy began to work with F. Gentry Harris, M.D. on a project at NIMH. In this Percy writes, "In the study of a spoken language-event, a written transcript

is, of course, wholly unacceptable. All phonetics and modifiers are omitted. Even a tape recording is inadequate since it does not transmit gestures." While working on the project at NIMH transcripts and tape recordings were all the materials with which Percy had to work.

46. Percy 1972, p. 3. This is interesting. This could mean, "in the formal ways known to Walker Percy," whereas other formal ways such as semeiotic might be able to pull it off.

47. Semeiotic—an experimental and observational science in which scientific intelligences (semioticists) observe and experiment upon the activities of other scientific intelligences in order to achieve a natural philosophy of the semiosis of scientific intelligence. Semiotic is composed of Speculative Grammar, Critic, and Methodeutic.

48. It is clear from his comments that Percy does not intend this piece as hagiography. His intent is "to disentangle from (Peirce's) metaphysic those insights germane to a view of language as behavior."

49. Percy points out that Peirce's distinction between dyadic and triadic behavior has been noted before, but, as for example with the "unified science" crowd (i.e. Neurath et al.), that the triadic relation is recognized as understood as an unorganized collection of dyads.

50. To prevent the disruption of reading the definitions contained in the multiple subsections of the two postulates have been placed in an appendix. These are included because "The Lay-Scientific Interface" is mentioned several times in the subsections.

51. Percy also referred to this as "asserter."

52. If you are interested in the concept of coupling and its relation to "The Lay-Scientific Interface," it is highly recommended that you read Percy's definitions and commentary about the two postulates. The definitions and commentary generally fall into two groups: observations pertaining to the coupling relation both within and between representatives of the two groups and observations on "The Lay-Scientific Interface" phenomenon itself.

REFERENCES

Bisanz, E., et al. 2011. Peirce's NonReduction and Relational Completeness Claims in the Context of First-Order Predicate Logic. *KODIKAS /CODE, Ars Semiotica* 34: 1–2.

Brock, Jarrett. 1969. *C. S. Peirce's Logic of Vagueness*. Doctoral dissertation. Retrieved from ProQuest/DAI, (287941332/7013254).

———. 1979. Principal Themes in Peirce's Logic of Vagueness. In: *Peirce Studies Number 1, Studies in Peirce's Semiotic: A Symposium by Members of the Institute for Studies in Pragmaticism*, 41–49. Lubbock: Institute for Studies in Pragmaticism.

Cunningham, Scott. 2004. *Walker Percy at the NIMH: A Story You May Not Have Heard.* Unpublished Manuscript. On file at the Institute for Studies in Pragmaticism, Texas Tech University, Lubbock.

Eisenstadt, Shmuel Noah, ed. 1992. *Martin Buber: On Intersubjectivity and Cultural Creativity.* Chicago and London: The University of Chicago Press.

Gerhart, Mary, and Allan Melvin Russell. 1984. *Metaphoric Process: The Creation of Scientific and Religious Understanding.* Fort Worth: Texas Christian University Press.

Ketner, Kenneth Laine. 1993. Novel Science: Or How Contemporary Social Science Is Not Well and Why Literature and Semiotic Provide a Cure. *Semiotica* 93 (1993): 33–59.

———. 1995. *Charles Sanders Peirce: Physicist and Non-Philosopher.* Invited Paper Read for the American Physical Society, Texas, Unpublished Manuscript. On file at the Institute for Studies in Pragmaticism, Texas Tech University, Lubbock.

Kierkegaard, Søren. 1962. *The Present Age and of the Difference Between a Genius and an Apostle.* Trans. Alexander Dru. New York and Evanston: Harper and Row.

Lawson, Lewis A. 1996. Will Barrett's Psychoanalysis. In: *Still Following Percy,* 180–194. Jackson: University Press of Mississippi.

Lewontin, Richard, and Richard Levins. 2002. Stephen Jay Gould—What Does It Mean To Be a Radical? *Monthly Review* 54 (06).

McLaughlin, T., et al. 2015. "Betagraphic": An Alternative Formulation of Predicate Calculus. *Transactions of the Charles S. Peirce Society* 51 (2): 137–172.

Neurath, Otto, Charles Morris, and Rudolf Carnap. 1955. Foundations of the Theory of Signs. *International Encyclopedia of Unified Science.* Chicago: University of Chicago Press.

Peirce, Charles Sanders. 1868a-1. Letter to the Editor of *The Journal of Speculative Philosophy* Whose Purpose was to Clarify What He Meant by "Determined" (Vol. 2, pp. 190–191).

———. Some Consequences of Four Incapacities. In: Peirce 1984, 140–157.

———. 1984. *Writings of Charles S. Peirce: A Chronological Edition, Volume 2.* Letter to the Editor of *Journal of Speculative Philosophy.* pp. 190–191.

———. Some Consequences of Four Incapacities. In: The Century Dictionary: An Encyclopedic Lexicon of the English Language, ed. William Dwight Whitney et al. New York: The Century Co.

———. Some Consequences of Four Incapacities. In Peirce 1908–1909. A Neglected Argument for the Reality of God. *The Hibbert Journal* VII: 90–112. But especially pp. 92–98.

Percy, Walker. 1950–1980. [unpublished manuscript]. Walker Percy Papers (4294). Southern Historical Collection, Louis Round Wilson Special Collections Library, University of North Carolina, Chapel Hill.

———. 1954. Symbol as Need. *Thought* xxix (Autumn): 381–390.

————. 1955. Unpublished manuscripts held at The Percy Archives. Chapel Hill: University of North Carolina.

————. 1957. Semiotic and a Theory of Knowledge. *Modern Schoolman* xxxiv: 23–246.

————. 1958a. Culture: The Antinomy of the Scientific Method. *New Scholasticism* XXXII: 443–475.

————. 1958b. Metaphor as Mistake. *Sewanee Review* 66: 79–99.

————. 1959. The Message in the Bottle. *Thought* 34: 405–433.

————. 1961. The Symbolic Structure of Interpersonal Process. *Psychiatry* 24 (1): 39–52.

————. 1971. Walter M. Miller Jr.'s A Canticle for Leibowitz: A Rediscovery. *The Southern Review* 7: 572–578.

————. 1972. Toward a Triadic Theory of Meaning. *Psychiatry* 35: 1–19.

————. 1983. *Lost in the Cosmos*. New York: The Noonday Press, Farrar, Straus and Giroux.

————. 1985. *Diagnosing the Modern Malaise*. New Orleans: Faust Publishing.

————. 1989. The Fateful Rift: The San Andreas Fault in the Modern Mind. Excerpted as "The Divided Creature". *The Wilson Quarterly* 13: 77–87. (Unpublished in final form).

Pilisuk, Marc. 1963. Cognitive Balance, Primary Groups, and the Patient-Therapist Relationship. *Behavioral Science* 8 (2): 137–145.

Samway, Patrick, S. J., ed. 1995. *A Thief of Peirce: The Letters of Kenneth Laine Ketner and Walker Percy*. Jackson: University Press of Mississippi.

Scott, Frances Williams. 2006. *C. S. Peirce's System of Science: Life as a Laboratory*. *Peirce Studies Number Seven*. Lubbock: ArisbeBooks.

Stuhr, John J. 1987. *Classical American Philosophy*. New York and Oxford: Oxford University Press.

Unspecified Authors. 2015. "Betagraphic": An Alternative Formulation of Predicate Calculus. Interdisciplinary Seminar on Peirce. *Transactions of the Charles S. Peirce Society* 51 (2): 137–172.

Veatch, Henry Babcock. 1952. *Intentional Logic: A Logic Based on Philosophical Realism*. New Haven: Yale University Press.

————. 1969. *Two Logics: The Conflict Between Classical and Neo-Analytic Philosophy*. Evanston: Northwestern University Press.

CHAPTER 9

Percy's Poetics of Dwelling: The Dialogical Self and the Ethics of Reentry in *The Last Gentleman* and *Lost in the Cosmos*

Christopher Yates

Walker Percy's LG (1966) and LC (1983) have borne that awkward fate of texts that enjoin their publics to identify in themselves the same predicament undergone by the protagonists. After all, the texts in different ways summon us to terrific self-examination while disarming us of certain default clarities. In LG Will Barrett lives within the ongoing decision for immanent and intersubjective meaning over the illusions of mere self-assertion or epistemic finality. In LC we are all implicated in a satirical "quiz" that diagnoses the self-alienation and deceptions of modernity, then positions us on the fraught threshold of "reentry" into wagers of genuine self-awareness and responsibility. It is tempting, though misguided, to read the former as an inward and surrealist exploration, and the latter as an outward and moralistic venting against a culture that was not up to the task. Alternatively, if we appreciate the texts as one collaborative project, then we are better positioned to undergo their pronounced interplay of diagnosis and remedy regarding the very displacement from which

C. Yates (✉)
Institute for Doctoral Studies in the Visual Arts, Portland, ME, USA
e-mail: cyates@idsva.edu

© The Author(s) 2018
L. Marsh (ed.), *Walker Percy, Philosopher*,
https://doi.org/10.1007/978-3-319-77968-3_9

we live and read. Divided into two main sections, this chapter will argue that LG and LC alike center on the predicament of human finitude in terms of three constitutive phenomena: (1) the dialogical unfolding of subjectivity and truth, (2) the ethical summons of alterity, and (3) the resituating of human inauthenticity within the art of reflective dwelling. But to properly discern these elements we must establish links between the literary terrain and corollary concerns in three twentieth-century philosophers: Mikhail Bakhtin, Emmanuel Levinas, and Martin Heidegger. While there is some precedence for linking Percy's oeuvre with such "existentialist" itineraries, we have yet to involve them pointedly in our interpretations. Although Percy himself, excepting some mentions of Heidegger, seldom engages such projects directly, to intertextualize them with the place (in the sense of *topos*) and the reasoning (in the sense of *logos*) of his narrative world will do well to secure the interrogative arc between LG and LC, and also allow us to understand the way in which his works enliven (more than simply illustrate) these phenomenological focal points.

Truth and Alterity in *The Last Gentleman*

In his 1966 review of Percy's LG critic Frederick Crews (1966) observes that Percy's "attention is fixed on the absoluteness of death and the impossibility of genuine intimacy". His work bears the traces of a chilling realist style, though one punctuated by "heavyhanded symbolism" regarding our modern condition and a failure "to inspect [his protagonist's] conflicts at close range or to understand them ... more clearly than [the hero] does himself" (Crews 1966). Percy tracks in Will Barrett a "passive pilgrimage" of disillusionment through which one learns that "the thing to do is to find a convenient way of blotting out the truth" (Crews 1966). This view seems as plausible and tempting now as it was upon the novel's release; certainly the style shows a realist quality and a passage into disillusionment. But to attribute passivity and a grim epistemological resolve to Will's journey, together with a failure in Percy to treat his main character from "close range," is to miss the point. Instead, the novel asks to be read through a scope of intimacy that increases with the same pace as Will's own evolving self-awareness and reconfiguration. And though the hero may at first appear calcified in a blithe passivity, he is very active from start to finish and in no way arrives at the kind of disillusionment that would resist the apparent truth of subjective or ontological dispossession. What Percy performs by drawing us into what Will endures and discovers is a deconstruction of detached and tautological inwardness for the sake of revealing and engaging an immanent mode of intersubjective becoming and thinking. Will is ever self-aware, even in a resolute way, but what emerges is a traction of self-awareness furnished decisively by mounting experiences of what I call dialogical truth and the ethics of alterity. But to trace this arc we must join him (and his author) in jettisoning any default assumptions we may have about how self-awareness should amount to full and final self-actualization. The point, instead, is to enter into a certain threshold of becoming that involves an increasing practice of "yielding"— one that in turn allows human agency to be reconstituted by otherness, responsibility, and the kind of knowledge that happens on their basis. To account for such yielding we now turn to two central poles in the story: the self of possibility and obscurity, and the self of intersubjectivity and truth. In both cases the term "of" denotes a genitival situation per Will—his "topological" horizon—and the agitations of human agency therein.

The Self of Possibility and Obscurity

The primary condition that Percy reveals and sustains within the plane of Will's personal self-relation and the cultural predicament under which this obtains is the paralysis of living within pure possibility and its attendant obscurity. Existential modes of dislocation and homelessness distill this condition. I say "primary" not so much because it is a static place of passivity to be overcome by a linear movement toward the full accomplishments of agency and revelation. Rather, the qualities spiral through the action even as they shed some of their grip. The dynamic likewise shows a situation that must be undergone and unfolded as self-awareness finds its introspective and actively social concretization. The generative point, then, is to join with Will in his experience of the very precise and layered threshold between paralysis and performative action—something akin to the Kierkegaardian conception of passing from the aesthetic stage of self-involvement through to the ethical and religious stages of choice and faith. Four points of reference evidence this point.

First, at the outset of the novel we learn that, having discovered the telescope in Central Park, Will understands that his life had hitherto been "lived in a state of pure possibility, not knowing what sort of man he was or what he must do, and supposing therefore that he must be all men and do everything. But after this morning's incident his life took a turn in a particular direction" (LG, p. 4). The epiphanic "turn" is, we learn, a turn toward that variable and stuttering "direction" of which "pure possibility" remains a persistent coefficient—one that Will must encounter in deepening manifestations. Within two pages Percy steps back to describe both the cultural frame for unsteady possibility and the way this is lodged in Will's subjectivity: "Often nowadays people do not know what to do and so live their lives as if they were waiting for some sign or another. This young man was such a person" (LG, p. 6). The narrative voice implies that although Will's "turn" may seem decisive for him, it is more nominative than predicative—even more so than he at first realizes. Again: "Like many young men in the South, he became overly subtle and had trouble ruling out the possible. ... What happens to a man to whom all things seem possible and every course of action open? Nothing of course. Except war" (LG, p. 10). The statement hints that Will still has more to endure, and that his overcoming of the predicament will need to entail something other than war—possibly, instead, it will be a making of love on several levels, and a making of the kind of responsibility and devotion that fill the abyss of possibility.

Second, by page 81 it seems some progress has been made, for, upon a lament of self-regret from Mr. Vaught, Will takes comfort in the self-measuring thought that "he had lived a life of pure possibility" (LG, p. 81) as if he were already wise to its misadventures. But Will's confidence is merely theoretical. Going forward, his factical experiences will show a resurgence of the dislocation that cycles back upon this haunting structure of possibility. When Will meets David Ross, servant to the Vaught family, the young man seems to act without the trappings of possibility's vulnerabilities (LG, pp. 196–98). Will is perplexed by this, and shortly thereafter regresses into feelings of "serious dislocation" in his initial experiences of university life, and must again resolve to "be what I am no matter what potential I am" (LG, pp. 202, 214). Thus, his assertions against possibility are not yet through. And his categorical resolve also signals that he is still waging this campaign on the problematic terms of default self-mastery. Percy indeed prepared us for this unsteadiness when, at the beginning of Chap. 4, he says that Will's "homelessness was much worse in the South because he expected to find himself at home there" (LG, p. 186). The point is cautionary: the persistence of the vacuous "pure" is something of which Will has become mindful, but overcoming it remains a goal more than an accomplishment.

Third, there is a feature that runs through these first two and will mark a specific site of pivot through their obstacles, though not one that ever triumphs over them in full: the agency of internal and external perception. Early on we hear Will perceive how "New York is full of people from small towns who are quite content to live obscure lives in some out-of-the-way corner of the city" (LG, p. 9). That is a generalization that sounds like a criticism, and is made in a direction away from Will's own self. It issues from Will's own background as "a watcher and a listener and a wanderer. He could not get enough of watching" (LG, p. 10). The statements suggest that he is prone to observe the condition of obscurity in others, wonder at it, and also inhabit it himself. After all, "[m]ost of this young man's life was a gap. .. [He was] hardly aware of his own name" (LG, p. 12). That the outward and categorical perception is also a personal predicament is evident in Will's own isolating YMCA lodgings and in the related point that "[h]is trouble still came from groups" (LG, pp. 18–19). His first steps through this perception that is afoot within the obscurities attached to the pure-possibility problem are faltering and hold him at a telling distance in his epistemic and interpersonal engagements. He plays the part of an Ohioan (LG, pp. 21–22) in his speech, style, and gestures, and he tries to "eavesdrop" his way into conversations that, in a small way, suggest the overcoming of obscurity among others (LG, p. 64). Later on, when at the Georgia motel, Will identifies in himself a longing for the omniscient sort of knowledge that might rid him of obscurity, yet opts again for perception by way of eavesdropping, the compulsion of which is: "He had to know without being known" (LG, p. 170).

As a further specification of this, a fourth motif shows how the possibility—obscurity problem, specified in his practices of perception—brings Will to the near side of a threshold into the kind of knowing and being that happens on the grounds of intersubjective experience. I have in mind the movement from the detached objectivism befitting an "engineer" to the kind of truth-telling that is born of empathy and the unique freedom that comes from a letting-be, a yielding (what in German philosophical theology is termed *Gelassenheit*). Early on at the Metropolitan Museum of Art Will hides and notices that the people studying the artworks are "afflicted in their happiness. ... In they came, smiling, and out they went, their eyes glazed over" (LG, p. 27). He perceives the deceptive, numbing quality of objectivist perception in others, but he is caught in the same clutches. Percy reports: "Though he took pride in his 'objectivity' and his 'evidence,' what evidence there was, was evidence of his own deteriorating condition" (LG, p. 28). His excitement over the Tetzlar telescope symbolizes this. Will "prided himself on his scientific outlook and set great store by precision instruments. ... They penetrated to the heart of things" (LG, p. 29). He will have to undergo the deconstruction of this pretension, and his steps toward this unraveling can be seen in two later moments. While in his garage apartment, he overhears an exchange between Sutter and Val and, says Percy, "[t]he old itch for omniscience came upon him—lost as he was in his own potentiality … but he resisted the impulse to eavesdrop. I will not overhear nor will I oversee, he said" (LG, p. 214). Be it seeing or hearing, Will's modes of perception must be reconfigured inwardly and outwardly. Soon after, when lost in a trance-like memory of his Father, he encounters the sense of an "individual quanta of light pulsing from the filament" (LG, p. 237). The telescope has been exchanged for memory, detached mastery for receptive illumination. When Will awakes "[a] square of moonlight lay across his knees" (LG, p. 238). What is notable is that the subtle shift in perception is something that happens "to" Will, not something he, so to speak, engineers.

Taken together, these four threads show the following: (1) That the isolating weight of pure possibility first inclines one to seek release on terms that simply sustain it. (2) That the resolve to press through the related predicament of homelessness does happen in concert with increasing self-awareness, but remains naively assertive (not yet active on basis of yielding). (3) That undergoing a more genuine conversion from pure possibility and gnawing dislocation is specifically a matter of letting one's private perceptual agency surrender its own normative terms. (4) That the precise nature of this perceptual dispossession obtains in the crossing from an epistemic hermeneutic (via seeing and hearing) to an involvement in more tacit and non-categorical modes of knowing and being. I have focused especially on the agency within Will's perception in order to locate the conditions for the possibility of what becomes his shift into the agency of intersubjectivity. The link allows us to see how the overcoming of the pure-possibility problem consists not so much in a shift from the inward to the outward, but in a shift *in* Will's internal practice of knowing and relating that is increasingly intertwined in an oscillating way with a shift on the level of his outward actions. The relationship between both planes is what will overtake the operation in which pure possibility is the coefficient running across his troubled and variable selfhood. Again, this is a matter of the reconfiguration and relocation, not of triumphant disburdening or more resolute passivity.

Here we may underscore this reading by drawing upon the kind of bracketing that occurs in Bakhtin's account of dialogical selfhood and truth, and Levinas' account of the primacy of ethics over individualism and declarative reason. In his study of Dostoevsky's poetics, Bakhtin (1984) holds that an author's investment in his main character ought not be a case of finding the hero's self-consciousness objectively fixed, but as situated and underway. The hero "interests Dostoevsky as a *particular point of view on the world and on oneself.* ...What is important ... is not how his hero appears in the world but first and foremost how the world appears to his hero, and how the hero appears to himself" (Bakhtin 1984, p. 47). Continuing: "Dostoevsky sought a hero who would be occupied primarily with the task of becoming conscious" (Bakhtin 1984, p. 50), that is, whose introspection and self-consciousness are permitted to unfold to the degree that the author stays bound to the "inner logic" of his character (Bakhtin 1984, pp. 64–65, 90). This respect for unfinalizability on the side of authorial design extends also to the function of "ideas" or "points of view" intersecting in and around his characters. Here what is true of Dostoevsky may be applied to Percy: "Dostoevsky ... created images of ideas found, heard, sometimes divined by him *in reality itself,* that is, ideas already living or entering life as idea-forces. [He] possessed an extraordinary gift for ... hearing his epoch as a great dialogue, for detecting in it not only individual voices, but precisely and predominantly the *dialogic relationship* among voices, their dialogic *interaction*" (Bakhtin 1984, p. 90).

Notice how this treatment of the hero is really a treatment of the polyphonic situation in which he is embedded—and how this requires a distinct effort on the part of the author, for "the author's consciousness does not transform others' consciousnesses ... into objects, ... [Instead]. ... it senses others' equally valid consciousnesses, just as infinite and open-ended as itself. It reflects ... precisely these other consciousnesses with their worlds, re-creates them in their authentic *unfinalizability*" (Bakhtin 1984, p. 68). The author must work by way of respecting in storied form how "[h]uman thought becomes genuine thought ... only under conditions of living contact with another and alien thought, a thought embodied in someone else's voice" (Bakhtin 1984, pp. 87–88). Bakhtin is making a philosophical point as well as an endorsement of authorial care. He later stresses: "Truth is not born nor is it to be found inside the head of an individual person, it is born *between people* collectively searching for truth, in the process of their dialogic interaction" (Bakhtin 1984, p. 110). Herein ideas must be tested, points of view engaged, and the positions and voices of others embraced as the constituent elements of one's own. Percy, one could say, must enable this kind of thing to unfold in and around Will, and Will himself must learn (consciously or not) to let it unfold in a way that concretizes his own becoming.

What Levinas (1991) does to extend Bakhtin's focus can serve the dual purpose of illuminating what we have seen so far in the story and preparing us for our next series of considerations. Levinas does not work on the level of literary poetics, but on the level of human experience that can be concealed by monological "authorship" (broadly construed). Levinas holds that the condition of thought is a moral consciousness—an exterior charge of responsibility that "marks my very presence in the world" (Levinas 1991, p. 17). The notion is counter-intuitive: "Thought begins with the possibility of conceiving a freedom exterior to my own. ... The world of perception shows a face" and specifically a face through which "I am commanded, that is, recognized as capable of a work" (Levinas 1991, pp. 17, 35). The point affirms that I am only able to be an "I" on the basis of being summoned to care for my Other, and that such a relationship to the "speech" of the "face" is in fact "an event of ... collectivity" where "the other, being unique, does not undergo [my] judgment; he takes precedence over me from the start; I am under allegiance to him" (Levinas 1991, pp. 10, 202). What this point opposes is the assumption that projects of self-awareness and knowledge must start from one's private subjective position, and only then reach out to the Other (and his ideas) along the conceptual agenda of an "objectifying gaze" (Levinas 1991, pp. 193–94). That would be a "scandal of indifference" (Levinas 1991, p. 192) to one's interlocutors and, by extension, to the integrity of genuine knowledge.

Understood in concert, one could say that Levinas adds the ethical underpinnings of subjectivity and knowledge to Bakhtin's stress on the dialogical constitution of self and truth. And just as the primary signification inhering in the Face must be reawakened, so too the self-yielding design of the Author can carry this out within the course of character self-consciousness and intersubjectivity across a novel. The trappings of monological thought and agency are undone by a phenomenological event on the one hand, and by a storied event on the other. My view is that, in the way Percy shepherd's Will's predicament and the movement of perception therein, we as readers are invited into the traversal of both points.

The Self of Intersubjectivity and Truth

Returning to the novel, what we now need to explore is the way this relocation into the threshold of dialogism and alterity is, for Will, ultimately indwelled such that possibility and obscurity are converted to the actions of a better homewardness. Here I will focus on Will's interactions with Sutter and Val, and with Jamie in an implied mediator position.

By late in the story Will's heightening exchanges with Sutter have replaced his prior romanticism with Kitty, and his nascent sense of home-wardness within the Vaught collective slides to the side such that he will struggle to press on through the distilled obscurity of ethico-existential dynamics into the plane of moral commitment and connectedness. We do not have space to go into the nuances of Sutter's worldview, but we do need to observe that Sutter, in his introspective decisiveness, exhibits an intensification of the same qualities Will had shown in the first half of the story. Sutter's scientific bent supports his analysis of the crisis of the world's apparent nihilism, and also sources the program he has set for mending this very affliction in himself. But where Will has learned to surrender detached observation and step away from the throes of pure possibility, Sutter wants to turn pure possibility into a new currency so to come to terms with the impossibility of immanent grounding. The "wayfarer" condition that he ascribes to man should, eventually, yield the conclusion that "[w]e are doomed to the transcendence of abstraction and I choose the only reentry into the world which remains to us" (LG, p. 354). One notices a marked difference from Will: where Sutter speaks of suicide—of death—as "the very condition of recovering oneself" (LG, p. 372), Will's path of self-recovery has obtained as a flight from the violence of death in his lineage. But the deeper point is that here in this moment Will must face in Sutter the radicalized and deconstructive inversion of his homeward course. When Will marvel's at his own "being here" (LG, p. 381), the marvel is that he, who once lived and moved and thought from the detached position of an "engineer," is now fully present in the "here" of a very personal engage-ment with a man who is taking an opposite (more categorical) course across the abyss of pure possibility. This "marveling" is also a desperate mode of "action" with his Other—as seen when, after leaving the dying Jamie, Will races to catch up to Sutter on the path to the ranch. The sense is that Sutter is going to kill himself. "Dr. Vaught, don't leave me," Will begs. "Dr. Vaught, I want you to come back with me." "Dr. Vaught, I need you. I, Will Barrett ... need you and want you to come back" (LG, p. 409). This is a refrain that is almost liturgical in its cadence and repetition. It is Levinasian. And it is one Will could only speak after crossing into the threshold of intersubjective and moral action as the grounding of selfhood. The plea "to come back" says: come back from the rim of pure possibility and its alluring release. And why does Will "need" this of Sutter? Applying Bakhtin, it is because the path of resistance cannot be taken alone; it requires the companionship of even those who seem most determined in their resentment toward it. Note further that as Will runs after Sutter's car, yelling for him to remain, Percy writes: "The Edsel paused, sighed, and stopped ... The Edsel waited for him" (LG, p. 409). Personifying Sutter through his car, Percy suggests that he is in his own way reciprocating the intersubjective principle and action. Perhaps Sutter, too, amid his own simmering resolve and despair, is drawn into Will's "yielding" and there held back from the retreat into pure possibility.

This interpretation gains support if we realize that the condition for the possibility of this ethical and dialogical moment happened in an earlier scene with Val. When Will meets Val he is holding Sutter's casebook—the very object he returns to several times in his ongoing effort to reckon with the ideas through which Sutter lives. With Val he wants to know not just what she knows but also what she senses about himself. "*Tell me what is tugging at me*," he wants to say (LG, p. 296). In effect the desire says: show me that I am not autonomous in my subjectivity; speak of me as though you are involved in my becoming, and I in yours. Contextualized within the Levinasian encounter with the Face of the Other, there is also a Bakhtinian valence to the moment. Will remains with Val because he feels a desire to give her his attention (his perception, recalling our third point of reference above): "He knew how to listen and he knew how to get at that most secret and aggrieved enterprise upon which almost everyone is embarked. He'd give her the use of his radar" (LG, p. 299). Percy allows the characters to discuss the nature of language, what for Bakhtin is the link between our dialogical and polyphonic situatedness (of self and of truth) and the *heteroglossia* obtaining on the level of literary speech. Of her ministry work in the South, Val remarks: "I think I stayed not so much out of charity as from fascination with a linguistic phenomenon" (LG, p. 301). Here we glimpse the way modes of signification are threaded to one's (topological) position amid ethical and spiritual commitments and practices. Perhaps this mirrors the way Will will "stay" with Sutter in the interchange between his articulations of ideas and positioning in life. That the fascination with language overlaps with the practice of dialogical interaction and ethical commitment is a phenomenon evident in Val's spiritual commitment to Will: "'I'll pray for you,' she said absently. 'Will you pray for me to receive sufficient grace in order not to hate the guts of some people, however much they deserve it?' 'Certainly,'" Will agrees. Here we note that prayer is itself a form of language, and one notably planted in a context of sought-for intersubjectivity—reliance upon one another for the sake of being who one is and practicing what one intends.

To see how what is demonstrated in the Val encounter and attempted in the Sutter encounter together reflect the shift to the dialogical and polyphonic character of Will's intersubjective threshold, we must remark briefly on the final desert hospital scene between the Priest, Jamie, Will, and Sutter. The situation involves them all in matters of life, death, and faith. Between the monological positions of Sutter and the priest, and the position of Jamie's final "becoming," Will is stationed as a mediator of the participating voices and the points of view they reflect. The priest is asking Jamie to make a ceremonial confession of his faith. But he "looked not at Jamie but sideways at the wall" (LG, p. 402), as if in a state of disengagement from the Face of his Other. Will translates Jamie's plaintive responses, which are earnest questions. Sutter is on the other side of Will and is angered, impatient with the solemn trial. As the priest delivers his blessing upon Jamie, his words issue a formalistic repetition of the plea of prayer that Val had issued to Will. Referring Jamie to the "our Blessed Lord and Savior" and to "Our Lady" (LG, p. 406), the priest continues: "I ask you to pray to them for me and for your brother here and for your friend who loves you" (Ibid.). One would expect the charge to be uttered in sincerity and compassion, but the priest remains merely a functionary and he looks "blank-eyed" to Will for a translation of Jamie's response (Ibid.). What Will reports is more grounded in genuine listening and vision: "He said, 'Don't let me go' ... He means his hand, the hand there" (Ibid.). Jamie's words convey a very concrete plea for the same kind of fellowship Will has learned to beg of others, and which he will echo moments later when he catches up to Sutter on the trail. We can also observe that Percy has not settled for a finalizing resolution by way of spiritual declaration. Instead, he has shown how the matter of faith is something to be lived in the sacrament of relationships, and how the question of truth is to be sought in the practice of faith.

Still, does all this close textual attention sufficiently point, in Will, to what I want to term a dialogical poetics of dwelling? Has Percy not simply charted a path of unsteady existential entropy in his Princeton engineer? The inadequacy of this challenge can be shown if, finally, we pass the above narrative moments and philosophical lenses back through an unresolved statement that occurs at least four times across the story: Will (as "the engineer") is said to be a person who "always tells the truth" (cf. LG, pp. 111, 165, 213, 320). It is tempting to take the statement as something indicative of a constancy, a fixed characterization of some monologically subjective judgment-capacity in Will, or else as an increasingly ironic gesture (perhaps both are implied in Crews' interpretation noted earlier). But both interpretations overlook something crucial. The phrase is placed in moments where Will is interacting with another person, where the interaction has him feeling pressed back upon his own shifting self-awareness and pressed forward into small steps of development. In each instance, moreover, Will is speaking from a very personal position. And here the word "tells" stresses the agency of voice. What is "telling" in the voice is that it is something underway. Likewise the "truth" that is in the voice is not a factual truth but an evolving one, one finding its way into the threshold between the subjective and the intersubjective, isolation and action. We may thus say that the "voice" and the "truth" are together reflections on Will's formative movements into the dialogical and ethical realms of human experience and knowledge. Neither "voice" nor "truth" belongs privately to Will, but to the situations into which he is entering, as though they constitute the structures of unfinalizable human becoming.

What we have accounted for thus far consists in two interlaced lessons dramatized in a protagonist who proves to be "last" in the sense of a teleological point of departure, not a hermetic closure of lament over the travails of human finitude. Will Barrett's retrieval of the dialogical unfolding of subjectivity and truth and the ethical summons of alterity is meant to inspire our own. Dispossessed of the polished certainties of an engineer's calculative fact-finding, his course of possibility through the porous and constitutive interactions of intersubjective responsibility stands on the more stable footing of a faithful agency. Through Will, Percy brings to his popular readership what Bakhtin and Levinas brought to their philosophical publics. But suppose Will's way forward proves fraught and further agitated, encountering an increasingly stubborn world in which the hubris of transcendent self-assertion plays counterweight to the humility of immanent social restoration? Suppose the topological horizon of Will's society further proves, as our own seems to manifest, too ironically fatalistic in the finalizing course of a conquering cosmic escape? These are the worries that appear to sharpen in Percy as his own world sheds those convictions that should otherwise bring it, with Will, into the realm of more authentic human dwelling. And these are the worries that, as we will now consider, prompt Percy to place us, and not just Will, directly in question.

LOST IN THE COSMOS AS PERCY'S HEIDEGGERIAN REJOINDER TO THE SCIENCE OF INAUTHENTICITY

In 1927 philosopher Martin Heidegger makes an aside that in many ways Percy, as we have seen, performs. "Creative literature," says Heidegger, "is nothing but the elementary emergence into words, the becoming-uncovered, of existence as being-in-the-world" (Heidegger 1988, pp. 171–72). If we hear this term "elementary" as signifying something grounding or fundamental, then we have reason to surmise he believes literature to possess a revealing capacity which parallels his own early philosophical project: the disclosure of existence as being-in-the-world. I hope to have by now shown that Percy has nursed along such an "emergence" by personifying it within the world of Will Barrett. We have seen this move across the novel's action and themes, but we have also (more subtly) noted it within the story's events of language—a phenomenon echoing something Percy elsewhere remarks: "[A]s soon as one scratches the surface of the familiar and comes face to face with the nature of language, one also finds himself face to face with the nature of man" (MB, p. 150). There is, then, an uncovering of existence that happens in collaboration with the uncoverings of language. This revealing afoot within philosophy, creative literature, and the signifying operations of language is something, after all, that Percy both shows and tells. He writes: "The existentialists have taught us that what man is cannot be grasped by the sciences of man. ... [The person] is, in Heidegger's words, that being in the world whose calling it is to find a name for being, to give testimony to it, and to provide for it a clearing" (MB, p. 158). We must not overlook how the recovery of such a calling is the assignment Percy takes on in the significations that belong to the novelistic mode of creative literature as well as (and remarkably so) in those that belong to the storied experience of Socratic questions, their thought experiments, and the "clearing" of self-awareness these together catalyze. Both modes of creative agency exercise what existentialist philosophy would call the deconstructive bracketing of those concealing attitudes through which we normally live and form meaning. That Will undergoes the bracketing of "the native attitude of the modern mind" (MB, p. 152) turns out to be a performative prelude to the very same at a more direct, disarming, hilarious yet intensified pitch. Percy's path of "creative emergence" takes a lateral move in genre, but he remains devoted to a similar project of "uncovering," and he is dead serious about it.

Nearly 60 years after Heidegger, Percy reports in his interrogative epistle to the human species: "The Self since the time of Descartes has been stranded, split off from everything else in the LC, a mind which professes to understand bodies and galaxies but is by the very act of understanding marooned in the LC, with which it has no connection" (LC, p. 44). The writer is identifying our terrible distance from the phenomenon the philosopher wants revealed. The personal detachment symbolized in Will Barrett's telescope now applies directly to the engineering epistemology and abyssal paradigm of a broader social landscape. Marooned in the LC with a misguided facility for "understanding" and a need for reassurance that may take vulnerable forms, Percy now finds a broader self who in fact spins and vectors at a paralyzing remove from its being-in-the-world. Western culture has not learned Will's lesson. It has instead fallen rather steadily into Sutter's convictions, though without the "doctor's" grimly self-conscious resolve. The intersection in which the philosopher and the novelist meet thus amounts to a peculiar necessity, in *Cosmos*, to venture the "elementary emergence" while at the same time making a case for anything "elemental" whatsoever.

Percy, we know, was reading Heidegger at least as early as the authorship of MG. Twice in *Cosmos* he points specifically to themes developed in Heidegger's 1927 work, *Being and Time*. The first reference concerns Heidegger's use of the term *Welt*—the deeper sense of the *world* into which the human self is "thrown" as a fundamental matter of existence. The second gestures toward the features of what Heidegger terms *existentiala*, which Percy summarizes as "the inauthentic ways in which *Dasein*, or self, inserts itself into its world" (LC, 113n). Both are annotations that run beneath Percy's discussion of our immanent modes of signification, as if to situate the surface of his inquiry within a parallel philosophical discourse. My aim in this section, as a step toward securing the continuation of the possibility—obscurity and intersubjectivity—truth lessons of the first, is to speculate as to how exactly Heidegger's thought might be coursing through the sensibilities of *Cosmos*. To do so I must specifically show how a Heideggerian reading reveals an insightful coherence afoot in several central *Cosmos* elements that might otherwise remain a puzzle: the displacement of the real, the objectivist lay-perception as an obstacle to regaining the self, and the purpose of the rather fantastic space odyssey experiment in the book's closing sections. As in the account of LG, then, our intertextual case for the unified project spanning both texts must be made by way of a close reading of the second (and at first seemingly discreet) one.

Diagnostic Correspondences

For most of his text Percy does not so much name as show the problem of authenticity to be his guiding concern. There is the attribution of the self as a "voracious" and "singular" "nought" (LC, pp. 21, 32–33) that feeds its own nothingness yet intuits the very void of this enterprise. There is the ironic "displacement of the real" (LC, p. 43) which welcomes, or dovetails with, the reduction of all "human relationships" into a grounding "sub-stratum" (LC, p. 60) of promiscuity that even Phil Donahue's guest (the Cosmic Stranger) interprets as "a symptom of a more important disorder" (LC, p. 54). There is, as well, the genealogy of Cartesian isolation in which the kind of attentive thinking otherwise native to significations and social relations finds no real means of integration—no consciousness (LC, p. 105). Thus noughted, displaced, and disordered by causes more experienced than elected, the self is, as Percy's Question 18 announces, "demoniac." The word is rather jolting, as if a thing necessarily overstated. But it is here that Percy explicitly names the contrast between the "authentic" and "inauthentic." He appears to hesitate over the terms, placing them in single quotes and qualifying the "criteria of authenticity" as "not necessarily objective" (LC, p. 181). He then immediately characterizes the "demoniac" phenomenon in something as mundane as "recreational modes" (Ibid.)—such as *travel*. Why name the concern so forcefully then hasten this apparent moderation?

The authenticity problem, to be sure, is sited not just in his themes, but in the style of Percy's discourse. That LC parodies a self-help book is obvious. But the reason is more than whimsy. The interrogative nature of the text consents to work from within the field of that problem it wants to sound—a culture of self-deception and displacement. His decision to address his subject by way of addressing his readers honors the very predicament he wishes to illuminate. Traditional argumentation, at least, simply will not do. Our epistemic standing is one planted between the habits of fact-minded scientific objectivism, on the one hand, and the sense in which something like "myth" might "be true in another sense" (LC, p. 165). The situation recalls Will Barrett's initial faith in "precision instruments" that ostensibly "penetrated to the heart of things" (LG, p. 29), then the tempting resettlement of this scientific outlook within the cosmological determinateness of Sutter's escapist program. *Cosmos'* quiz cuts through this strange middle. And Percy's decision for a descriptive diagnosis likewise reveals a methodological shift that Heidegger, in a different milieu, undertook under the banner of phenomenology. Be it a survey or an "existential analytic," both thinkers guide their imagined interlocutors toward that kind of self-examination that brackets common opinion in the interest of a more genuine understanding. We saw this path performed in LG as a matter of one attaining to a position of marvel at "being here" (LG, p. 381)—we might say a position of "scratching the surface of the familiar" and residing in-the-world on the brink of truth's "clearing" rather than man's abyssal possibility.

When, in LC, Percy permits himself the categorical distinction between the "polarities" of the "authentic" vs. the "inauthentic," he is indulging an analytic distinction. He hesitates because such moves are known to indicate some determinative distance from their subject matter. But when he assigns such polarities to "recreational modes" he is renewing his devotion to a phenomenal analytic, not diffusing the point. *Travel,* one such mode, is the self's hopeful wager that, in getting "into the right new place, I can become a new person" (LC, p. 183). For Will, the mode consisted first in his travels around Central Park and later in his adventures in eavesdropping; both, he intuitively believed, would sanctify the projections of his "objectivity" and "evidentialist" wagers. When the two part Space Odyssey section appears like a fantastic interruption in *Cosmos* we do well to remember Percy's deconstructive declaration regarding Will: "[W]hat evidence there was, was evidence of his own deteriorating condition" (LG, p. 28). But first we must let the space odyssey imagine for us an intensified "mode" of *our* unresolved oscillation between the authentic and the inauthentic.

To return now to Heidegger involves a shift in registers, but not a terrific difference in theme. Conceived under the name "fundamental ontology," Heidegger's early philosophy is also an attempt to formulate the right *questions* for his audience, namely: "[W]hat is the meaning of Being?" The problem, as he sees it, is that the question has never been posed from within the context of distinctive human experience, but rather from a kind of cosmos that presumes to determine Being on the basis of mapping correspondences between objects and higher epistemic categories. Fundamental ontology, one could say, asks the world to drop Will's Tetzlar and wager on a mode of vision that lets-be the meaning of Being. What is "fundamental" as opposed to scientifically "objective" involves a decision to approach the meaning of Being through the very entity for whom Being is a natural preoccupation: the being of the human being, what he calls "Dasein"—literally *there-being*. He explains: "We shall proceed towards the concept of Being by way of an Interpretation of a certain special entity, *Dasein*, in which we shall arrive at the horizon for the under-standing of Being and for the possibility of interpreting it" (Heidegger 1972, p. 63). Perhaps we could say that Percy's "last gentleman" had enacted this very procession. Ever preparatory, Heidegger's course is more immanent than transcendent, more invested in the "how" of Being's meaning as it emerges through our being-in-the-world than the "what" of Being's meaning as it is pinned to the board of metaphysical explanations. The methodology that accomplishes fundamental ontology is, then, the "existential analytic" of *Dasein*—a descriptive attention to the way we comport ourselves in world, and there *in* relation to the ways in which Being "means" in the immanent world.[1]

Where Percy alerts us to the self in the condition of being noughted, displaced, and disordered, Heidegger observes how the revelatory rela-tionship between our being-in-the-world and the meaning of Being is bedeviled by an "everydayness" that attenuates our fundamental mode of what he terms "Care." He is reporting on *Dasein* specifically, but he has in mind the person whom, not unlike Percy's *self*, is understood as "a per-former of intentional acts which are bound together by the unity of mean-ing" (Heidegger 1972, p. 73). Heidegger's analytic tone is less desperate than Percy's, but anticipates it. Care, Heidegger explains, is the intended structure of our being-in-the-world—the possibility and project-based assignments we bring to our dealings with other basic entities and oppor-tunities, and through which we convert our possibilities into constitutive sources of meaningful existence (*Existenz*) across the scope of our hands-on "existentiality." (Such ventures precisely become the indicative site of our displacement and nought-ing in Percy's self.) Possibility may at first seem "pure," but is only itself when concretized, particularized. For Heidegger, the task of moving toward "a science *of Being as such*" (Heidegger 1972, p. 232), then, involves allowing an ontic relation to reveal the ontological ground which it already intuits and enjoys, but can-not and should not circumscribe as a "what."

So far, Heidegger's project mostly concerns the *constitutive*—how meaning obtains between beings and Being—whereas Percy starts from the concern that things have *gone awry*. But both are working descriptively from the immanent plane of situated personhood. For Heidegger, the wager of meaning in our being-in-the-world becomes problematic when an element meant to be productive of our Care grows disoriented: *anxiety*. In one sense, anxiety is an indefinite mode of feeling "uncanny" (not-at-home) in the face of the worldly entities in which *Dasein* is inevitably absorbed (Heidegger 1972, p. 189). But anxiety is also revelatory, for it discloses the "*world as world*" and summons us to act upon our possibilities in a desire for existential "authenticity" (Heidegger 1972, p. 232). *Dasein* is "anxious in the very depths of its Being" (Heidegger 1972, p. 234). And anxiety, says Heidegger, "makes manifest in *Dasein* its *Being towards* its ownmost potentiality-for-Being ... its *Being-free for* the freedom of choosing itself and taking hold of itself. Anxiety brings *Dasein* face to face with its *Being free for (propensio in)* the authenticity of its Being, and for this authenticity as a possibility which always is" (Heidegger 1972, p. 232). It may seem as though this treatment of the anxiety—possibility dynamic simply reinstates the obscurity—possibility dynamic we saw Will Barrett struggle to overcome. However, it is more accurate to say that Percy's Will is an exact specification of Heidegger's *Dasein* in terms of both the perils and the promise of the anxiety dynamic. Anxiety should be more of a spur toward Care in the exercise of one's possibilities than a flight from responsibility via endless and paralyzing flirtations with the seemingly "pure" scope of possibility. Will, over time, learns the lesson that Heidegger wants *Dasein* to realize. He manages to let his own "noxious particles" of the uncanny attune him toward a more authentic embrace of possibility. But neither Percy nor Heidegger take this notion of Anxiety-as-call-to-Care to be a simple leap of self-determination. Both know that anxiety is terribly hard to manage, and that we often allow ourselves to take refuge in the at-home modes of being rendered available to us by the familiarity of what Heidegger calls "publicness" (Heidegger 1972, p. 234). As one small example, we met an approximation of this habit in the stuttering modes of "perception" through which Will Barrett initially sought to mete out his sense of a personal "turn in a particular direction" yet faltered back into feelings of "serious dislocation" (LG, p. 202). Everything depends upon the quality of care in the turn, and the relational context that shapes it.

They-Perception and Lay-Perception

Let us stay within the Heideggerian register for a moment, then turn to its parallel in LC. According to Heidegger, Care falters into average everydayness as *Dasein* is "sucked into the turbulence of the 'they's' inauthenticity" (Heidegger 1972, p. 223). Heidegger's term is *das Man*, which translates awkwardly as "theyness." It recalls Plato's worries about *doxa* (common opinion) and obtains as something of a pacifying, though misguided, shelter for one's sense of truth and self. When Percy speaks of being lost in the *cosmos* he is echoing Heidegger's concern about being lost amid the *everyday* of herd-like principles and practices. The condition is one of being misplaced by the momentum of our public existence. Even the more genuine experience of anxiety (noted above) is smothered by false assurances and trivial anxieties. Overwhelmed by theyness, the fundamental burden of choosing *Dasein*'s potentiality-for-Being stands unrealized. The "they," says Heidegger, "has always kept *Dasein* from taking hold of these possibilities for Being...[and] it remains indefinite who has 'really' done the choosing" (Heidegger 1972, p. 312). Explicitly conscious of it or not, our *Dasein* struggles to assume responsibility for itself, and for the meaning of its being when stationed in the "turbulence" of everyday assumptions about meaning and truth.

Percy too has his turbulence, and he names it the "displacement of the real." Here the parallel to Heideggerian "theyness" is the *lay-perception* that derives from the paradigm of prevailing scientific objectivism. I should note that for neither thinker is the phenomenon of inauthenticity reducible to a simple cause/effect relationship between intellectual advance and personal retreat, nor a mere matter of "actualizing" our precious possibilities. The problem is more subtle and has to do with the position of *Dasein* and the Self under the sway of what is a structural inevitability yet manifests as a qualitative pressure: *das Man*. Percy's tack is more epistemological than ontological on the surface, but the two intersect in the experience of the resulting predicament—finding oneself and one's meaningfulness not-at-home and then ostensibly at-home in a misguided public residency. Standing before "the overwhelming credentials of science" and "the technological transformation of the very world itself" (LC, pp. 178–79), the position of the layperson is caught up in the wake of "unprecedented" advance yet unable to recalibrate the gage of self-awareness and understanding accordingly. As productive as "the physicist's quest" (LC, p. 43) may be where the secrets of nature are concerned, such a recipe for progress becomes incongruous when it conceives of man as simply "a locus of his bio-physico-sociological needs and drives" (LC, p. 82). Bereft of God, consciousness, or other "traditional resources of the self" (LC, p. 113), we layman are "apt to assign omniscience" to the scientific princes of the age.[2] But Percy is also alert to the problems that manifest when we try to eject from this public paradigm, such as the transcendence options in art and science and their affiliated problems of "reentry."[3] In Heideggerian terms, the tension concerns how the recovery of resolve and care in our own existential constitution would require the strength to carry us out of our displacement amid the cultural mineshaft (LC, p. 120). But the very strength itself, Percy worries, propels us too far beyond a better being-in-the-world; even the remedy for displacement lands us in orbit around the real. We *do* need to place ourselves in the immanence of the "they" as a *mit-Dasein* (Heidegger would say) of relational possibilities, but the plausibility structures of lay-perception are precisely the problem.

Percy, I believe, is engaged in an effort to test Heidegger's analytic by mapping our predicament of displacement upon the coordinates of his fundamental ontology. *Lay-perception* aligns with theyness, the *noughted self* with our inauthenticity, and *reentry* with the question of care. No doubt there is a difference of intensity. Where Heidegger could find *Dasein* situated within an underlying relationship to the meaning of Being, the being-there of Percy's Self is already so unstable as to look no further than its own malaise. Where Heidegger locates transcendence in the seizing of ownmost possibilities, Percy has posed the question as to whether such possibilities can be recovered at all without abstracting too far from our immanent situation. But differences of degree do not imply discordant concerns. Both authors are committed to traversing the full scope of inauthenticity in the interests of sounding a kind of immanent call to renewal. What I want now to suggest is that Heidegger's remedy for this predicament is, as it were, a thing Percy endeavors to perform in his closing sections of LC.

The Call of Conscience and the Question of Consciousness

Embedded as we are within the inauthentic modes of the they-self, Heidegger (1972) holds that something specific is needed to allow *anxiety* to turn us back toward our own agency. The problem is not first that it is detached from "transcendent" referents, but that it is detached from its own intrinsic relationship to Being (and thus itself). The remedy is also a structural existential feature, but one that must be enabled or, as it were, heard. To recover our bearing as creatures of possibility, against the backdrop of a Being that somehow *means* in terms of our Care, is to undergo what Heidegger terms the "call of conscience." Such a call would attest to *Dasein*'s "burden of explicitly choosing" the tasks and standards which mark its being-in-the-world. Without escaping the world, *Dasein* must "*find* itself ... it must be 'shown' to itself in its possible authenticity," and this occurs through the manner in which the "*voice of conscience*" attests to *Dasein*'s potentiality-for-Being-its-Self (Heidegger 1972, p. 313). In LG we saw Will practice a kind of counterfeit to such hearing in his practice of eavesdropping, but then also the rending of this screen as he inched empathetically into the Bakhtinian realm of listening to—and being shaped by—the polyphony of voices and viewpoints directing those around him.

Though Heidegger does not mean conscience in a moral sense, the phenomenon has everything to do with our ontological response-ability. The "call" is in fact issued *from* the self and *to* the self, an appeal we make from the depths of our potential being to the surface of our being amid the they-self (Heidegger 1972, pp. 313–14). Conscience passes over the "they" and summons the *Dasein* to own up to its possibilities in order to recover in us a "resoluteness" (Heidegger 1972, pp. 318, 315) to reclaim our role in performing our being-in-the-world. The call, says Heidegger, "comes *from* me and yet *from beyond me and over me*" (Heidegger 1972, p. 320). It allows us to recognize our uncanniness for what it is, to stem the tide of our everyday theyness and our becoming a "nullity" amid the momentum of our existential thrownness (Heidegger 1972, p. 330). All told, conscience places *Dasein* back in the possibility of its Being, where it must "bring itself back to itself from its lostness in the 'they'" (Heidegger 1972, p. 333). *Dasein* remains ever in the "they" (since it is a structural feature of who we are and how we live), but now according to a solicitude which summons Others to being-their-Selves in their own resoluteness.[4] Conscience, then, is a specific way of allowing anxiety to unveil the nullity that haunts *Dasein*'s thrownness and then "take action" on behalf of our "basic possibilities" (Heidegger 1972, pp. 357–58). Again, none of this is meant as a celebration of human determination—another temptation with which Will Barrett had flirted then forsook. Rather, the accomplishment is that it repairs a breach between our individual being and a more primordial Being, thereby recovering an essential wholeness meant to take shape across the pregnant temporality of our finitude.

Percy imagines a transmission from space but, as a thought experiment after all, it is still perhaps a call from ourselves (via his pen). The appearance of the two Space Odyssey sections in the book's final stretch performs the problem of reentry ascribed to the transcendence-immanence tension. Percy invites us to imagine this voyage and "its mission to establish communication with extraterrestrial intelligence and civilizations" (LC, p. 201) as if to indulge our lay appetite for scientific objectivism and yet stress the "marooned" character of our displacement from the real (a broader manifestation of the dislocation and homelessness cycling so often back upon Will Barrett). But the search for communication is already something different than the exercise of epistemic command, and the meaning of an odyssey (recalling Homer) in fact concerns a return *home*. That said, here we must admit that the same question Levinas might pose to Heidegger could well be a question LG poses to LC: Is not the corrective to this odyssey, in large part, the ethics of alterity that marks one's reentry into the realm of the intersubjective and its more authentic truths? Though the hyperbole of the cosmic odyssey may at first glance cloud this grounding principle, I believe we do find it signaled (quite literally) here in the deconstruction of the voyagers'—and especially Captain Schuyler's— solipsistic consciousness.

When, on the first voyage, the crew locates "communication" at what is called the Proxima Centauri "checkpoint," the issue that troubles the alien hosts is Consciousness. Essentially: Identify yourself. What kind of Consciousness are you? The interrogative nature of the engagement mirrors what Percy has been doing all along in his Quiz, and something he even preemptively asked for in an earnest vein, on our behalf, in Will's desire for Val to "*Tell me what is tugging at me*" (LG, p. 296). In LC we, who have been addressed by questions, get to observe our representatives coming under a kind of scrutiny in space. The episode is also a continuance of Percy's suggestion (much earlier) that the Cartesian revolution in objective identity and knowing failed to recognize how "no such isolated individual as he described can be conscious" (LC, p. 105). But why "Consciousness"? Let us allow two senses of this term in order to appreciate how this encounter advances the question of authentic selfhood. First, it speaks somewhat ironically to the objectivist way of capturing human identity. Second, following Heidegger, it signals that field of intentionality through which *Dasein* discovers and assumes its existential projects. Between these two senses rests the lacuna that the inquiring categorization of the C1, C2, and C3 levels tries to traverse. Working categorically, the unseen hosts interpret the earthly selves in terms befitting the "displacement" and "nought" we have noted: "It has something to do with the discovery of the self and the incapacity to deal with it ... not even knowing what the self is, and so ending by being that which it is not" (LC, p. 210). What such a consciousness needs is to be stirred by anxiety—to desire some conceptual grammar of self-awareness other than reductive symbolizing, for "it cannot be conceived under the auspices of a symbol" (LC, p. 211–12n). The predicament seems a specified way of echoing Heidegger's observations about our falleness amid *das Man* as opposed to our self-constitution in the mode of Care. In this case the otherwise productive habits of symbolic reduction spell a misadventure when applied to our own existential character. A different type of consciousness, alternatively, would have "managed by assistance from something other than self to recover itself from this mobility, through auspices other than symbolic conception, and knows itself for what it is" (LC, 212n). I do not think it too much of a stretch to read Heidegger's "call of conscience" in this dynamic. The question, of course, is how otherwise this "something other" must be. One might say that for Will Barrett the charge ultimately came in Jaime's dying plea, "Don't let me go" (LG, p. 406)—a statement that asks and begs as the same time. For Heidegger, the "something other" is not quite the Levinasian "face" of the other person, but the self calling to itself from its own depths. Still, as far as the receptivity to an other-voiced interruption in our monological myths of transcendent becoming goes, the function is the same. The problem, in LC, is that Percy's crew remains in the grip of that self-deception that lay-perception sustains: "We are the triumphant emerging species on our planet," the height of "scientific and technological and artistic achievements" (LC, p. 215). So it is that the earthly self identifies itself in terms of its modes of alleged transcendence even without pausing to demonstrate an awareness of, much less anxiety over, its immanent predicament. The earthly self is a more optimistic version of the Sutter-self, though bent ultimately on the same apparent ends.

Captain Schuyler, leader of the second odyssey, knows better than the lay-perception would have him believe, but does he exhibit a receptive resolve to heed the call to his own constitutive possibilities for care? As a parallel, we might here ask whether Schuyler's spacecraft will hesitate in the way of Sutter's Edsel—will it pause, sigh, and stop (LG, p. 409) within the iterations of the call? Percy suggests Schuyler has allowed a momentum of alleged transcendence to carry him aloft: "Accelerating toward the speed of light as he exits his world, he was never more successfully and triumphantly in his world" (LC, p. 235). When the bewitching transmission that spurs his quest proves false (LC, p. 237), Schuyler must return to his actual world and face the fallout wrought by the self-deceptive culture he departed. Here, one could say, Percy's depiction of the teeming "silence" (LC, p. 238) of the earth and the odd community of holdouts in the Bonneville desert comprise the very ontic chamber in which the ontological call to one's possibilities for personal and collective authenticity could, so to speak, finally transmit. The silence is broken by a question that requires a decision, as though the crew is situated afresh within the possibilities of Sutter's closing hesitation before Will's plea—and here to perhaps imagine with Sutter's sardonic mind what the immanent possibilities might be. There are two rival plans for resettlement offered by eccentric earthly pilgrims: A "Jones" touts the continued zeal of science and progress, thus essentially pledging the group once again to the lay-perception in its most acute ambitions. A "Liebowitz" proposes a more religious and Edenic renewal of human community in a mountain dwelling dubbed Lost Cove (LC, p. 252f). Both plans are evidently "preposterous." According to the Heideggerian analytic, we could say that Jones vies for a resolute theyness, and Liebowitz a *mit-Dasein* newly conceived according to the "possibilities" of faith. But neither choice is self-evident, for the call of conscience would necessarily seem preposterous when heard from within "the preposterous predicament of the human self" (LC, p. 254). The decision put to Captain Schuyler is, of course (and as with Jamie's call to Will, and Will's call to Sutter), ultimately put to the reader—the question sounded by the mysterious transmission from space, then specified at Bonneville, finally converges with the interrogative journey of the larger quiz. And the fact that only one answer is allowed—"(check one)" (LC, p. 254)—confirms how this culminating intersection of the fantastic and the existential is a site of necessary decision. The stakes are not as spiritual as Val's more personal question to Will— "Will you pray for me... ?" (LG, p. 303)—but the weight hanging on the answer (no matter how scaled) is the same. To answer the insistence of either question is to begin to pattern a constitutive response-ability back into our lives.

Whatever Percy intends in his closing to LC, it is not playful. To face the imagined future of our theyness with a call that demands a response is not simply an appeal to volitional responsibility; it is to reinstate us in our world. A decision requires a context, a plane of consequence, a being-in. We might not be able to answer the closing question, "Do you know who you are?" (LC, p. 262), just as Will Barrett may not have been able to chart the exact course for his own further becoming. Finalizability is not requisite for navigating the plane of immanence. What matters is that, having learned to hear the question and to live out a response, we find Percy has achieved a placement for us. With this lesson Percy is likely more Heideggerian than he knows. In his final Freiburg lecture course of 1944–45 Heidegger identifies the aim of philosophizing as a decision for reflective *dwelling*. Genuine reflection, he argues, is to become aware of one's homelessness amid determinate thinking and speaking, and then live *in* the "questioning" of our historical moment. The "task of thinking," then, is also a path of homewardness in which our thinking takes residence in a "more genuine" way—a "native sojourning in the realms in which the human belongs." Heidegger continues: "[A] guide [*Anleitung*] is required in order for humans to become more at home [*zuhause*] and to learn genuine dwelling where they always already sojourn, although ineptly and unadvisedly" (Heidegger 1944–45, p. 11). The wonder of LC, like the LG before it, is that it places us on this path without entertaining the shortcuts or destinations of formal argumentation, and without overlooking the hardships of staying the course.

These notions of placement and sojourn give us a fitting way to take stock of what we have explored in this chapter. Primarily, they speak to the existential situation I believe Percy has sought to diagnose, empathize with, and instruct in LG and LC. As well, I hope to have shown that they speak to Percy's own literary and philosophical effort—his own placement and sojourn—in the writing of these texts. My argument has been that the themes pulsing through the journey of Will Barrett are also those that, by a different means and a broader layer, are again specified and addressed in still more interrogative fashion in the experience of his later work. Though I have not accounted for his other texts—which may be treated as further storied and scholarly stages placed within this deliberate sojourn—I have offered an account of the arc of concern to which we must attune ourselves in order to not risk overlooking this underlying kinship between two texts that might otherwise appear distinct. Will Barrett's experience prepares us for our own in LC, and likewise LC offers us a retrospective means to underscore the decisive currents that Will navigates in his journey through modern homelessness to immanent dwelling. The "last" gentleman and the "last" self-help book together sound an alarm that awakens us into all that must be "first" in our collective self-examination. Along the way I have focused on the dialogical shape of subjectivity and truth, the ethical summons of alterity, and the renewal offered through the conversion of inauthenticity into reflective dwelling. The philosophical projects of Bakhtin, Levinas, and Heidegger—diversely hewn in their own ways—have given us the lenses we need in order to identify and experience these phenomena. But Percy, as philosopher, has animated these principles in a remarkably original and inspiring way. If we are going to speak of a "realism" in his style and message, it certainly is not one that concedes to some final disillusionment or paralyzing passivity. It is an invitation to resist those cultural and personal currents that so often tend to draw thought and agency to a contented halt, precisely at the place where they ought to go further.

NOTES

1. Heidegger explains: "The kind of Being which belongs to *Dasein* is ... such that, in understanding its own Being, it has a tendency to do so in terms of that entity toward which it comports itself proximally and in a way which is essentially constant—in terms of the 'world.' In *Dasein* itself and therefore in its own understanding of Being, the way the world is understood is, as we shall show, reflected back ontologically upon the way in which *Dasein* itself gets interpreted" (Heidegger 1972, pp. 36–37).

2. Percy explains: "The powers attributed to *them*, the scientists ... are as magical as those of the old gods" (LC, p. 119).

3. A Kafka, for example, might wean us from our lay-perceptions of scientific transcendence, but then the artist's own reentry predicament struggles to resolve itself in a world where "self-deception" forestalls our placement under "the exigency of truth" (LC, pp. 121, 125).

4. Resoluteness, says Heidegger, "does not withdraw itself from 'actuality,' but first discovers what is factically possible" (Heidegger 1972, p. 346).

REFERENCES

Bakhtin, Mikhail. [1929] 1984. *Problems of Dostoevky's Poetics*. Ed. and Trans. Caryl Emerson. Minneapolis: University of Minnesota Press.

Crews, Frederick C. 1966. The Hero as 'Case': *The Last Gentleman*, by Walker Percy. Commentary Magazine, September. https://www.commentarymagazine.com/articles/the-last-gentleman-by-walker-percy/. Accessed 15 Oct 2016

Heidegger, Martin. [1927] 1972. *Being and Time*. Trans. John Macquarrie and Edward Robinson. San Francisco: Harper.

———. [1927] 1988. *The Basic Problems of Phenomenology*. Trans. Albert Hofstadter. Bloomington/Indianapolis: Indiana University Press.

———. [1944–45] 2011. *Introduction to Philosophy—Thinking and Poetizing*. Trans. Phillip Jacques Braunstein. Bloomington/Indianapolis: Indiana University Press.

Levinas, Emmanuel. [1991] 1998. *Entre-Nous: Thinking-of-the-Other*. Trans. Michael B. Smith and Barbara Harshaw. New York: Columbia University Press.

Percy, Walker. 1966. *The Last Gentleman*. New York: Picador.

———. 1975. *The Message in the Bottle: How Queer Man Is, How Queer Language Is, and What One Has to Do with the Other*. New York: Farrar, Straus and Giroux.

———. 1983. *Lost in the Cosmos: The Lase Self-Help Book*. New York: Picador.

CHAPTER 10

"There Must Be a Place": Walker Percy and the Philosophy of Place

Patrick L. Connelly

Nearly a year to the day prior to his death, Walker Percy was in Washington D.C. to deliver the 1989 Jefferson Lecture in the Humanities. The content of his speech represented the culmination of a lifetime's philosophical preoccupations and intersections with the fields of science, linguistics, and religion. Percy's address explored the problem of modern science's "three-hundred-year-old dualism" of mind and matter, for which he held René Descartes responsible and found Charles Sanders Peirce helpful in resolving. "It is," Percy wrote, "as if we lived in a California house straddling the San Andreas Fault, a crack very narrow but deep, which has, however, become as familiar as an old shoe" (SSL, pp. 274, 283). This vivid image gave Percy the title of his talk: "The Fateful Rift: The San Andreas Fault in the Modern Mind." It is unsurprising that Percy reached for a metaphor of place in naming his lecture, given the significance of place in both his life and writings—fiction and nonfiction alike. Percy's works underscore the importance of place as an indispensable repository of ideas, values, and experiences. "Why not do what the French philosophers often do and Americans almost never—novelize philosophy,

P. L. Connelly (✉)
Mississippi College, Clinton, MS, USA
e-mail: plconnelly@mc.edu

© The Author(s) 2018
L. Marsh (ed.), *Walker Percy, Philosopher*,
https://doi.org/10.1007/978-3-319-77968-3_10

incarnate ideas in a person and a place," Percy once told an interviewer (Abádi-Nagy 1987, pp. 63–64).

While Percy cited the examples of writers such as Jean-Paul Sartre and Albert Camus, his own correlation of ideas, persons, and places puts him in a philosophical discourse stretching from ancient to contemporary sources. The relation of philosophy to place has been directly or indirectly considered for millennia, including recent explorations in geographic thought and phenomenology. Richard Hartshorne, David Harvey, Henri Lefebvre, Gaston Bachelard, and Maurice Merleau-Ponty are just a few of the geographers and philosophers whose works amplify the significance of place beyond coordinates on a map (Hartshorne 1939; Harvey 1969; Lefebvre 1991; Bachelard 1994; Merleau-Ponty 2002). They have validated in a variety of ways J. E. Malpas's assertion that people have a uniquely human capacity to shape places to reflect "our very needs, our hopes, our preoccupations and dreams" (Malpas 1999, p. 1). Edward S. Casey's work has been particularly instructive and imaginative in articulating the "deeply constitutive" nature of place, a belief evident in Walker Percy's novels and essays as well. For both authors, place is not a mere "cartographic location" but is a source of meaning, a context for community, and terra firma for selfhood. (Casey 1999, pp. 21, 23). Place becomes the determinative milieu of who we are, who we are becoming, and how we orient ourselves to others and the natural world. The loss of place can be a source of disorientation and exile, though for Percy and Casey pilgrimage can be a means to a recovery of place. Percy adds an additional wrinkle with his musings on the virtues of nonplace, which he distinguishes from placelessness.

The prominence of place-thinking in Percy's works merits serious consideration of his contributions to this philosophical discourse. Places, Casey asserts, serve as "lasting scenes of experience, reflection and memory" for human beings. Their centrality to human life corresponds to the importance of the body. The directionality and dimensionality of the body cultivate its reciprocal relationship with places, resulting in "a larger world of burgeoning experience" for ourselves and others. These experiences occur in homes, gardens, cities, and even wilderness, places where the intertangling of nature and culture occurs. Casey describes this intertwining in the case of wilderness as "thickening" or "the coalescence of cultural practices and natural givens" (Casey 1999, pp. xiii, 111, 253).

The concept of thickening can be applied to a variety of places, however, given that the mutually influencing interaction of nature and culture frame how lived bodies perceive, experience, and shape these places. Places do more that collect and contain natural resources and cultural products. They hold together "our sense of an ordered arrangement of things" despite their inherent complexities and conflicts. Places keep their inhabitants and make them manifest while holding not just their bodies but also gathering their "experiences, histories, even languages, and thoughts." The particularity of places enriches the gathering process and roots it in "local knowledge." As Casey notes about the impact of revisiting his hometown, the memories it keeps appear to "belong as much to the place as to my brain or body." The qualities of places and the role humans play in negotiating, substantiating, and shaping them are reminders that places are not "static sites." Places are dynamic, elastic, and yet coherent contexts for the embodied experience of time and history (Casey 1999, pp. 327, 328, 346, 347).

The vitality and multidimensionality of places are central to the embodied experience of time and history in Walker Percy's writings. Cellars, basements, attics, caves, greenhouses, parks, suburbs, laboratories, movie theaters, historic homes, shotgun cottages, slave quarters, fire towers, chain hotels, large urban centers, small towns, wilderness, islands, trains, and the cosmos itself are some of the places that mediate Percy's probing of the mysteries and complexities of the human condition. Mark Johnson, writing in 1975 at a time when Percy had only published three of his six novels, identified three major uses of place by Percy. First, places were "vehicles of his philosophy" with special emphasis given to Søren Kierkegaard. Next, places were "illustrations of artificial as opposed to authentic environments." Finally, places were metaphors "for the mode of existence of the protagonist and the condition of his society" (Johnson 1989, p. 140). These analytical categories remain surprisingly durable, despite not engaging three subsequent Percy novels and much of his nonfiction.

Consulting the full Percy canon reveals many uses of place, but five overlapping categories are particularly instructive. First, Percy's phenomenology of place is sensitive to the ways in which the lived body experiences time and space, processes memory, and understands the historical dynamism of particular locations. Secondly, Percy introduces the concept of a nonplace, which on occasion has negative connotations but predominantly is itself a type of place distinct from placelessness. Thirdly, Percy uses places for the purpose of what biographer Jay Tolson describes as "locational pathology," which involves using place to diagnose what ails individuals and societies (Tolson 1992, p. 153). Fourthly, place becomes the strategic context or symbol to recover authentic selfhood. Finally, places facilitate the possibilities of re-placement—an end frequently accomplished in varying degrees by means such as pilgrimage and reentry.

It is possible that Percy's phenomenological sense of place gets over-shadowed by other philosophical concerns. But a passage from MG reveals how Percy and his characters are attuned to the significance of place for embodied experience, an appreciation for mystery, and the search for meaning. Binx Bolling, the novel's protagonist, is in a laboratory with his friend Harry Stern from Pittsburgh in a scene with phenomenological overtones. Sunlight streams through the window on a summer afternoon. Binx observes the sounds of a building ticking and creaking in the summer heat and of a game of touch football being played outside by students. Binx notes: "I became bewitched by the presence of the building; for min-utes at a stretch I sat on the floor and watched the motes rise and fall in the sunlight." Binx tries to get Harry to pay attention to the phenome-non, but Harry is uninterested as one who is "absolutely unaffected by the singularities of time and place." He could be, Binx observes, carrying out scientific work in New Orleans or Transylvania without it making much difference. Binx decides he would not trade places with him even if he "discovered the cause and cure of cancer," for Harry lacked awareness of "the mystery which surrounds him" (MG, pp. 51–52).

Interviewer Bradley R. Dewey noted that Percy consistently demon-strates that awareness in his descriptions of the natural world. Combined with his characterizations of the unique qualities of cities like New Orleans, Chicago, and New York, Dewey observed, Percy captures "'the wonder' of the world that surrounds us" (CWP, p. 123). An example of this atten-tion to the wonder evoked by places is seen in what on the surface appears to be an insignificant description of a bayou in TS. The protagonist Dr. Tom More is on a boat in Pontchatolawa with Dr. John Van Dorn, who proves to be one of the villains of the novel due to his involvement in a conspiracy to control nature for nefarious ends. Pontchatolawa is a place "unspoiled," one that resides peacefully past country clubs and other signs of human development. More turns off the motor and notes the sudden silence in a place that "hasn't changed since the Choctaws named it." He observes shafts of sunlight, fish jumping, cicadas singing, and the sturdy presence of large cypress trees—all in stark contrast to the abuse of nature being perpetrated by his passenger in the boat (TS, p. 57).

It is not just purely natural settings that conjure a sense of wonder but also those places where nature and culture intermingle. When Binx Bolling sits in a suburban school playground close to his home, he observes the beauty of the school building "in the last golden light of day." Binx continues:

> Everything is so spic-and-span: the aluminum sashes fitted into the brick wall and gilded in the sunset, the pretty terrazzo floors and the desks molded like wings. Suspended by wires above the door is a schematic sort of bird, the Holy Ghost I suppose. It gives me a pleasant sense of the goodness of creation to think of the brick and the glass and the aluminum being extracted from common dirt—though no doubt it is less a religious sentiment than a financial one, since I own a few shares of Alcoa. How smooth and well-fitted and thrifty the aluminum feels! (MG, p. 10).

Even with his self-deprecating questioning of motive, Binx's appreciation for how nature and culture blend together to create a place of beauty reveals the extent to which wonder is found in Percy's world. Wonder is not purely contained in the natural world but also experienced through the cultural molding of its resources. Even the old, worn plywood seats of movie theaters could arouse the wonder in Binx. Revisiting a theater after a 14-year absence, he expresses "a secret sense of wonder about the enduring" of those seats even during "rainy summer nights" and the early hours of the morning with no one present. "The enduring," he concludes, "is something which must be accounted for. One cannot simply shrug it off" (MG, p. 80).

Percy's created places in fiction and actual places reminisced over in essays evoke not just their sense of wonder but their meaningful and memorable particularity. A 1984 reflection on his Uncle Will's house recalled in intricate detail the architecture and décor of his guardian and cousin William Alexander Percy's home. What made the house memorable was not only the physical details but the people who visited. The house became a place when embodiment and experience met in a locale. The pantry, "a large room with bar," was a place within a place, where "the traffic was heaviest and race relations the liveliest." Percy noted that though the physical reminders of that house and garden were gone, he still has what Will Percy left him, "and I don't mean things" (SSL, pp. 65–66). Walker Percy was left with meaningful memories produced by what Casey calls "implacement," where place, action, and thought come together in particularized settings through embodied interaction (1999, p. xiii).

Percy's protagonist Will Barrett depicts a similar phenomenon in the novel TS. Barrett visits his cousin Lucy Lipscomb at Pantherburn, the old family plantation. The home contains a smell "as wrenching as memory" of "a hundred winters." As Barrett stands by the dining room sideboard contemplating the sights, sounds, and smells of the room over a few drinks, he remembers standing in the exact same spot 20 years earlier. He recalls the particularities of his Uncle Rylan fixing a drink for his aunt and knows exactly where the same decanter containing the same cheap bourbon is located (TS, pp. 141, 158–159). Similar to Percy's recollection of his uncle's home, Pantherburn is a place not just because of the material and architectural features but due to the embodied, communal rhythms of human interaction manifested there.

Percy also illustrates the particularity of place through descriptions of the passage of time within those places. In the novel LR, Tom More stops by the Little Napoleon tavern, a downtown establishment in Paradise, Louisiana, with an older history than More's suburban neighborhood. The detailed description of the tavern's interior suggests an older legacy than "the lounges of the suburbs" more recently favored by its customers. The "mahogany piece" that stands behind the bar is like "a miniature cathedral, an altarpiece" whose intricacy is reflected in its shelving, cupboards and "stained-glass windows." A large mirror "whose silvering is blighted with an advancing pox, clusters of vacuoles, expanding noughts" conveys the passing of decades. Many of the Little Napoleon's regular customers "have sat here in the same peaceable gloom" since the days of Prohibition and Huey P. Long. Percy notes in a subtle nod to the transition from the Old to the New South that *Gone with the Wind* "had its final run at the Old Majestic Theater" next door to the tavern (LR, p. 151).

The passage of time in place is found in other Percy novels as well at moments when important truths about characters are revealed. One example from SC is when Will Barrett finds himself "in a certain place … a desert place … a real place." It is a place whose "exact location could be determined within inches by map coordinates" but also a place in terms of the memories it houses. Forty years prior, a young Barrett sat in that very place, a spot in a meadow by a stream where his cook and frequent caretaker D'Lo stored "crocks of milk and sweet butter." On one occasion, D'Lo finds Will there at dinner time and begins to reminisce about their shared meals and close bond. The reader learns important information about Barrett's character through this recollection of the losses and turbulence he has already experienced in life. As Barrett reflects back on that moment in place as an adult, he ponders how the very spot where he stands has changed over time. First it became part of a country club golf course bunker: "For twenty years winter and summer thousands of golf balls, cart tires, spike shoes crossed the spot." The country club subsequently became a subdivision, with the spot where Barrett now sits part of a corner lot with ranch-style house. Twenty-five years later, it became part of a shopping center, with the spot then located between an "Orange Julius stand and the entrances to H & R Block." Barrett now returns to a spot inhabited by a deserted mall with sprouted weeds, a cracked terrazzo, water leaks, and "old tax forms" blowing in the wind (SC, pp. 275–277). The scene communicates Percy's multidimensional understanding of place as sites with distinct character-istics, memories, and experiences of both change and continuity.

To capture this multidimensionality, Percy uses terms like "spirit-presence" or "genie-soul" in MG. The terms refer to that unique sense of place "which every place has or else is not a place." Binx Bolling recalls a visit to San Francisco where this sense of place was acute. He envisions the genie-soul of the city leading him through the hills of the city before end-ing at the sea and filling him with sadness at arriving at "the end of America." Southerners, he suggested, are especially attuned to haunted nature of places "like Shiloh and the Wilderness and Vicksburg and Atlanta" and thus to the spirit-presence of Northern cities as well. Binx is therefore able to discern and negotiate the spirit-presence of Chicago when visiting the city with cousin Kate Cutrer. The city is given its inimitable identity as a place by the lake, the wind, its spaciousness, its tall monument-like build-ings, and "the five million personal rays of Chicagoans and the peculiar smell of existence here" (MG, pp. 201–203). Binx defines Chicago as a place in terms of how nature and culture come together to shape the mate-rial and human architecture of the city. Percy's description of Chicago cor-responds with Casey's observation that cities possess the "capacity to demand and distract" by enticing us of our homes and into the streets of "a more precarious and sometimes hostile extra-domestic world." The failure to properly navigate that environment, Casey continues, can result in deso-lation or the "loss of an accustomed center" (Casey 1999, p. 195).

These examples of Percy's phenomenology of place emphasize how lived bodies experience time and space, how place becomes a reservoir of memory, and how places are dynamic and not static in nature. A second contribution Percy makes to the philosophy of place is his concept of "non-place," which he distinguishes from displacement. One of the more vivid renderings of this concept is found in his 1980 *Esquire* magazine essay "Why I Live Where I Live." Demonstrating a willingness to introduce philosophical ideas to popular audiences, Percy explained his decision to live in Covington, Louisiana. He observed that Covington was not "a pleasant place" but instead a "pleasant nonplace," free of "the horrors of total placement or total nonplacement or total misplacement." Covington allowed Percy to avoid the total placement of writers rooted in cities with haunted pasts and deep family ties such as Charleston or Mobile. It freed him from the misplacement of writers who self-consciously chose to live in an exotic location and who expected to be "informed by the exotic identity" of that place. Percy looked instead to examples of negotiated nonplacement such as René Descartes, who lived "anonymously among the burghers of Amsterdam," and Kierkegaard, who lived and interacted with others "in the business district of Copenhagen." One important feature of nonplacement was its connection to place. Covington's proximity to New Orleans allowed him to "insert oneself into the South" and its accompanying deep-rootedness without being overcome by either "the ghosts of the Old South or the happy hustlers of the New South." Percy embraced the paradox of experiencing the place of New Orleans while embracing the nonplace of Covington—dissimilar in terms of identity, history, and consciousness but interconnected locales nonetheless (SSL, pp. 3, 4, 6).

The decision to live in a nonplace influenced Percy's decision to place Binx Bolling in Gentilly, a suburban area of New Orleans. Binx desired to be free of "the old-world atmosphere of the French Quarter or the genteel charm of the Garden" (MG, p. 6). It was there that Binx began his journey through Kierkegaardian stages. Nonplaces contextualize resolution in later Percy novels as well, such as the generic and unhaunted Holiday Inn where Will Barrett and his love interest Allison Huger take refuge at the novel's end. Nonplacement was not without its existential challenges, however. Percy once observed that William Faulkner's character Quentin Compson in *The Sound and the Fury* committed suicide not in the place-haunted South but on "the back streets of a bland Boston suburb." Faulkner is well-known for his awareness of the burden of place, but Percy suggested that he also knew something was awry in the "new nowhere places as well." For even these nonplaces weren't immune to the malaise of everydayness, the downsides of anonymity, or the "strangely diminished and devalued" character of many ordinary experiences of place and time (SSL, p. 163).

The specter of despair and disorder in places and nonplaces alike recalls a third use of place in Percy's works, that of "locational pathology." Places are described and inhabited in a manner that conveys disorder, disaffection, or dislocation on an individual or societal level. Jay Tolson used the term in reference to the description of Will Barrett at Princeton in LG. Barrett experiences déjà vu and an overwhelming sense of melancholy while in the same dormitory room, 203 Lower Pyne, occupied by his grandfather two generations earlier. Despite an inviting setting and friendships with "fine fellows," Barrett finds himself wishing he were "lying in a ditch in Wyoming or sitting in a downtown park in Toledo." His Princeton dorm room, with the historical weight of the institution and his family, felt like "walking on Saturn, where the force of gravity is eight times that of earth." Barrett is left to conclude that "this is no place for me" and leaves two years prior to graduation (LG, pp. 14–15). Tolson suggests that place in this context is a tool for Barrett to wrestle "his troubled relationship with the old southern patrician society" of his origins (1992, p. 153).

Places also serve as contexts or metaphors for the working out of philosophical, religious, or psychological crises. The burdens of place felt at Princeton—and similar feelings of dislocation at sites such as Civil War battlefields—compel Barrett to consider his relation to place. Drawing on his own biography and within the confines of the novel's plot development, Percy leads Will to a natural setting in New Mexico. "This was the locus of pure possibility," Barrett surmised, a place with "no antecedents." It was a place of silence, free of the memories and people that burdened his sense of self. Though his journey is not complete—we learn how his story develops further in SC—Barrett is mesmerized by the prospect of liberation, where "what a man can be the next minute bears no relation to what he is or what he was the minute before" (LG, p. 356).

SC provides more evidence of placement as an indicator of philosophical, religious, or psychological states for Percy's characters. SC finds Barrett in an imagined conversation with his father, who tells him, "there is no other place for you" while tempting Barrett to commit suicide. Barrett names numerous places—Atlanta, San Francisco, New Orleans, Santa Fe, for example—only to be met with a "No" from his father. "There must be a place," Barrett replies. He then begins a journey that draws on place imagery to escape the despair to which his father succumbs. Barrett crawls through tight quarters in a dark cave prior to falling into a greenhouse, a scene that suggests both Plato's allegory of the cave and a metaphor for being born anew. Barrett later decides not to return to the scene of a traumatic childhood Georgia hunting trip with his father that foreshadowed his father's suicide. Finally, the imagined voice of his father tempts Barrett to commit suicide by the Holiday Inn where he finds himself at the novel's end by suggesting that the son is "a placeless person in a placeless place." (SC, pp. 215–216, 337). Barrett rejects the despair of placelessness and embraces the hope of implacement with Allison.

There are other examples of individuals whose placement indicates a philosophical, religious, or psychological state. For example, Binx Bolling's journey upward through Kierkegaard's stages of existence begins, fittingly, in a basement apartment. Tom More finds himself in a Dantean dark wood, in a wooded area near an interstate, in the opening pages of LR. Lancelot Lamar of L resides in a cell-like space in a mental institution after killing several people, including his wife Margot, and burning down Belle Isle—the historic home that she helped renovate. He tells a priest hearing his confession that the South and the nation are "full of demonic women, who, driven by as yet unnamed furies, are desperately restoring and preserving *places, buildings.*" Among Margot's restorations is a pigeonnier for Lancelot to reside in. He recollects that she put in "a plantation desk and chair made by slave artisans" in the hopes that Lamar will write his memoirs "like Jeff Davis at Beauvoir." The problem, Lamar notes, is that he has no memoirs to write because "there was nothing to remember" (L, pp. 121, 18).

Examples of locational pathology also extend to society in general. Percy himself in interviews spoke of the negative effects of the homogenization of place. The sense of particularity that traditionally permeated Southern places and gave them such particularity was now being challenged by the New South phenomenon of "losangelization." While the rise of the sunbelt brought many economic benefits to an impoverished region, Percy noted, it came at "a terrible price." Cultural, commercial, and architectural homogenization meant that one could "drive through the suburbs of New Orleans and Baton Rouge" and find it looking plausibly like Los Angeles. The challenge for Percy as a writer was "to humanize" that environment and "to figure out how a man can come to himself, living in a place like that." (CWP, p. 215). Percy's challenge was complicated not only by homogenization but by encounters with inauthentic re-creations of place. TS depicts Tom More's wife and mother transforming an indigo plantation's former slave quarters into a series of row houses for those seeking "authentic historical Louisiana quaintness." Authenticity does not extend to the memory of the enslaved who once implaced these renovated buildings, however, despite the development's amenable name of

"The Quarters." More's mother, in a comment that exemplifies the sense of societal displacement, tells prospective buyers that these homes combine "the utility of a New York townhouse with the charm of a French Quarter cottage" (TS, p. 37).

His fictional portrayals of homogenization in the suburbs explore more than cookie-cutter layouts. In MG, Binx Bolling's morning walks in the suburbs reveal that homes handsome in sunlight and enhanced by perfectly manicured lawns were "forlorn" at dawn. Binx finds "the sadness of these glimmering dawns" to be "the mystery of the suburbs" and a phenomenon not evident in more rooted places, where everything looks the same day or night. Suburban homes, by contrast, "look haunted" at dawn and project societal malaise despite evidence of material comfort prosperity (MG, p. 84).

Evidence of things gone wrong is also apparent in LG's descriptions of Central Park, which is presumably an oasis in an urban landscape. But the opening sentences of the book refer to it as "a bear garden" with a "zoo smell," grass that is "course and yellow," and polished trees with "bits of hair" clinging to the bark (LG, p. 4). Allen Pridgen argues that Central Park is depicted as "a postlapsarian garden created by violent and foul-smelling exiles from Eden" who, despite efforts "to create a place of beauty and safety," end up producing "an oppressive zoo-like enclosure." These images of a fallen Eden, Pridgen concludes, reflect humankind as "seriously and universally diminished" due to the self being alienated from its original state (Pridgen 2000, p. 61).

This loss of self and need for recovery speaks to a fourth use of place by Percy. Places become sites where active and passive selfhood are contextualized and negotiated, often on a continuum between implacement and dislocation. In Percy's "last self-help book," LC, he imagines a scene on *The Johnny Carson Show* in which the host or a guest mentions an American city, followed by audience applause. Percy observes that the applause does not just happen for smaller, less acclaimed towns ("like Abita Springs, Louisiana"), but also for larger cities like New York or Chicago. He wonders if the audience member sitting in a Burbank, California, studio is applauding due to civic pride or perhaps because they are boosters driven by economic interest. But then he proposes that this "passive audience member" may feel "so dislocated, so detached from a particular coordinate in space and time, so ghostly," that the mere mention of a place compels applause (LC, p. 27).

Percy invokes several strategies in dealing with selfhood through the experience of place. His 1958 essay "The Loss of the Creature" examines this theme through a series of travelers visiting the Grand Canyon. Percy notes the sense of wonder experienced by Garciá López Cárdenas, the first European to see the Grand Canyon, and the federal government's effort to transmit that experience to generations of tourists through the creation of a national park. He suggests that these subsequent experiences of the Grand Canyon have been compromised by the "symbolic complex" mediated by postcards, geography books, tourist materials, and even "the words *Grand Canyon*." Strategies for recovering a more authentic experience of place include what Percy describes as "the Inside Track, the Familiar Revisited, the Accidental Encounter." The Inside Track refers to the idea of getting off the beaten track, but even that aspiration to spontaneity may be compromised through arrogation by tourism planners. The Familiar Revisited entails visiting a place again in a common fashion, such as a Greyhound bus tour. By appropriating the experience and "predicament" of other tourists, the place is "recovered from familiarity" by the visitor through an "exercise in familiarity." The Accidental Encounter involves a "breakdown of the symbolic machinery," such as a typhus outbreak that closes the park shortly after one's entry, that creates an opening for enhanced experience and "the recovery of sovereignty" (MB, pp. 47–50).

Place is central to the traveler's recovery of sovereignty. Percy gives another example of a tourist who decides to carve his initials in a public place. The tourist is not simply defacing public property but is responding to being reduced to a consumer of experience who is "deprived of his title over his being." Moving "like a ghost" through public places, the traveler's carving of initials becomes an act of defiance: "I am not a ghost after all; I am a sovereign person" (MB, p. 62). Ghostliness is a symptom of dislocation, or misplacement, that Binx Bolling in MG describes as the "danger of slipping clean out of space and time." Binx also feels compelled to make his mark, literally, in order to escape ghostliness. While watching *Red River* in a movie theater where he "first discovered place and time," Binx marks the arm of his seat with his thumbnail and wonders where that "particular piece of wood would be twenty year [sic] from now, 543 years from now" (MG, p. 75). These small but vital acts of reclaiming sovereignty reflect Percy's assumption that human beings can choose active participation over passive resignation when it comes to place. As Ari N. Schulman observes (in an essay drawing on both Percy and Casey), "a place is a realm of affairs for Nature and for humans." The decision to involve ourselves in those affairs requires deliberate attentiveness to how we "facilitate the experience of a place" in the hopes of eluding alienation and embracing authentic, sovereign selfhood (Shulman 2014, pp. 34, 37).

The strategies for eluding alienation and ghostliness may only bring temporary relief for Percy's characters. One example is the process of certification. Binx and Kate are in New Orleans watching a movie, *Panic in the Streets*, that was filmed in New Orleans. A scene reveals the very neighborhood in which they are watching the film. Kate's comment that the neighborhood is now "certified" leads Binx to observe that an uncertified place leads a person to live "sadly" and with "emptiness" in the neighborhood. But seeing one's neighborhood in a film allows one to live, at least temporarily, "as a person who is Somewhere and not Anywhere" (MG, p. 63). Percy explained that the concept of certification is a strategy for escaping "what Heidegger would call *alltäglichkeit*," or, "everydayness" (MCWP, p. 165). It is a symptom of the exhaustion of place that Binx Bolling perceives as first apparent in cities and now evident in "the countryside, even the swamps" (MG, p. 145). The experience of everydayness in places is part of the fabric of alienation and ghostliness that Percy wants to resist.

Places and the travel between them also factor into strategies for dealing with alienation and ghostliness. Two examples from Percy's writings are the Kierkegaardian notions of rotation and repetition. In his 1956 essay "The Man on the Train," Percy defines rotation as "the quest for the new as the new," or, "the reposing of all hope in what may lie around the bend." One example he gives is the curious "existential placement" of a commuter on a train who experiences "an absolute partitioning of reality" by being both in and not in the world through which he travels. The commuter also experiences a partition between himself and fellow commuters as well as one between himself and his own body. Percy imagines a rotation in which the commuter's train breaks down and he gets off the train only to converse with a man whose house the commuter passes by daily. The man offers to drive him the rest of the way and the commuter enters his home. Percy sees much more going on here than an inconsequential encounter. "A zone crossing has taken place," he concludes, an event "of considerable significance aesthetically-existentially." Stepping from a New York rail station onto a train, stepping off the train and into the yellow house, and entering into conversation with the owner becomes a way for the commuter to realize, albeit briefly, his own being through implacement (MB, pp. 87–88).

Repetition is a strategy, introduced in the same essay but evident throughout Percy's novels, that differs from rotation by involving a return to a place. Will Barrett travels through the South in LG and at one point returns to his father's home in Mississippi. Wrestling with the memories that place holds, Barrett feels "the tiny horsehead of the hitching post" at the house. He reflects on what drove his father to suicide—not just depression but the code of honor that his father lived by in the context of "the worst of times, a time of fake beauty and fake victory." Barrett then experiences an epiphany. The answer to alienation is not found through affirming his father's solitude, fondness for Brahms, reading of sad poetry, or commitment to abstract ideals. It is instead found "here, under your nose, here in the very curiousness and drollness and extraness of the iron and the bark" (LG, p. 332). Gary M. Ciuba describes this revelation as an "astonishing reappropriation of the immanent realm" in which Barrett embraces the tangible, particularized presence of a place and testifies "to its gratifying proximity" (Ciuba 1991, p. 117). Percy later describes Barrett's visit to his father's home as a repetition after a rotation road trip through the South. "I think Kierkegaard says," Percy continues, "'Every man has to stand in front of the house of his childhood in order to recover himself'" (CWP, p. 67).

Most of Percy's major protagonists and many of his minor characters employ literal and symbolic places in the recovery of selfhood. Mickey LaFaye, Tom More's former patient in TS, has "a recurring dream" in which she finds herself in her grandmother's farmhouse cellar. Vividly recalling the smell of "winter apples" and other sights and sounds of the place, LaFaye begins to sense that she is waiting there for a reason. She awaits a visitor who will arrive with a secret and ponders the implications: "What was she, her visitor-self, trying to tell her solitary cellar-bound self? What part of herself was the deep winter-apple bound self?" LaFaye recognizes that "the stranger is part of myself" and uses the symbolism of place to begin escaping a ghostly existence. Even her paintings of egrets were starting to look like the "elegant dead birds" of Audubon rather than "ghosts in the swamp" (TS, pp. 6, 372).

The recovery of selfhood often involves for Percy's characters the experience of re-placement, which is a fifth use of place in his works. Casey argues that when "concerted actions of re-placement" occur, what happens is nothing short of "a re-creation of the self who inhabits (or will re-inhabit) the place in question" (Casey 1999, p. 311). For Percy, places are consumed, departed, reentered, and returned to through the process of travel, exile, or pilgrimage. Binx Bolling, Will Barrett, and Tom More all embark upon pilgrimages or odysseys that connect the restored self to the process of re-placement. Percy describes the process of the self's travel and return in LC. The self leaves a home that has been "emptied out by the self itself." The trajectory of this movement frequently goes from the North to the South, "from a Protestant or post-Protestant place" to a Catholic place. Percy makes clear that while Catholicism is "absolutely the last thing the autonomous self wants," the "decor and artifact of Catholic belief" still hold appeal. One may also return home to a place whose abandonment has led it ironically to acquire "a certain solidity and integrity of its own." Travel—whether to old places, new places, exotic places, or mundane places—becomes the source of "quasi-religious hope" for the autonomous self: "if I can only get out of this old place and into the right new place, I can become a new person" (LC, pp. 148–49, 151, 183). Percy's comment recalls a scene from MG where Kate explains the restoration and order of her garden to Binx, who is struck by her enthusiasm about bricks, partitions, vines, and a fountain. He attributes Kate's seriousness and meticulousness to the assumption that "if she can just hit upon the right *place*," she can live her life (MG, p. 57).

Percy's use of travel between places illustrates his affirmation of Gabriel Marcel's concept of *homo viator*, or man the pilgrim or wayfarer. It is an insight at the heart of his Catholic existentialism that frames re-placement: "I am speaking of the mystery of human life, its sense of predicament, of something having gone wrong, of life as a wayfaring and a pilgrimage, of the density and linearity of time and the sacramental reality of things" (SSL, p. 178). The sacramental reality of things explains why Percy can envision a priest who identifies as "pilgrim and wayfarer" but still shares a sense of placement with a radio repairman. The priest is "home in his homelessness" and enjoys good cooking, "three Bushmills before supper," baseball, and conversations with friends (LC, p. 139).

Embracing the sacramental reality of things, however, is not easy. Percy acknowledges that people have trouble achieving "reentry into ordinary life, into concrete place and time" partly due to historical developments that have rendered it more difficult. The past several centuries witnessed a change in perception of humankind's place in the Cosmos. "The dethronement of man," as Percy calls it, rejects the centrality of the human experience in the universe, the uniqueness of humans being created in the image of God, and the assumption that human beings are sovereign over their "own consciousness." Humans are left with the desire to comprehend their "place in the Cosmos." This broad configuration of place does not negate the importance of specific places, however. For Percy, finding one's place in the Cosmos can be worked out through the wayfarer's navigation of particular environments and the opportunities they present for reorientation and re-placement.

"Man knows," Walker Percy asserted in a 1975 essay, "he is something more than an organism in an environment" (MB, p. 9). His writings are dedicated to exploring how the claim of human distinction and dignity affects how we live as implaced creatures. Percy's late-career Jefferson Lecture concludes with a distillation of his thinking on what he termed a "new anthropology." Drawing on Charles Sanders Peirce, Martin Heidegger, and Gabriel Marcel, it mirrors the "Judeo-Christian" concepts of creation, fall, and redemption. Peirce's "triadic creature with its named world" deals with the uniquely human qualities of language with its focus on object, sign, and interpretant. Heidegger's *Dasein* refers a being who "inhabits" both an environment and a world, has undergone a "fall" into "inauthentic existence," and yet has the capacity to recover. Marcel's *homo viator* defines humans as pilgrims and wayfarers (SSL, pp. 290–291). These concepts do not remain abstract or disembodied for Percy. He instead offers a rich oeuvre of place-thinking that gives shape to the embodied experiences, memories, and conversations of pilgrims and wayfarers. Places—and even nonplaces as Percy defines them—gather evidence of our predicament and flesh out our individual and societal pathologies. The reorientation and recovery of selfhood corresponds to the possibility of re-placement. Walker Percy's creative place-thinking restores the prominence of place in our experience and understanding of the world.

REFERENCES

Abádi-Nagy, Zoltán. 1987. The Art of Fiction XCVII: Walker Percy. *The Paris Review* 103 (Summer): 63–64.

Bachelard, Gaston. [1958] 1994. *The Poetics of Space*. Trans. Maria Jolas. Boston: Beacon Press.

Casey, Edward S. 1999. *Getting Back into Place: Toward a Renewed Understanding of the Place-World*. 2nd ed. Bloomington: University of Indiana Press.

Ciuba, Gary M. 1991. *Walker Percy: Books of Revelations*. Athens: University of Georgia Press.

Lawson, Lewis A and Victor A. Kramer, eds. 1985. *Conversations with Walker Percy*. Jackson: University Press of Mississippi.

Hartshorne, Richard. 1939. The Nature of Geography: A Critical Survey of Current Thought in Light of the Past. *Annals of the Association of American Geographers* 29 (3): 173–412.

Harvey, David. 1969. *Explanation in Geography*. New York: St. Martin's Press.

Johnson, Mark. 1989. The Search for Place in Walker Percy's Novels. In: *Critical Essays on Walker Percy*, eds. J. Donald Crowley and Sue Mitchell Crowley. Boston: G. K. Hall & Co.

Lawson, Lewis A., and Victor Kramer, eds. 1985. *Conversations with Walker Percy*. Jackson: University Press of Mississippi.

———. 1993. *More Conversations with Walker Percy*. Jackson: University Press of Mississippi.

Lefebvre, Henri. 1991. *The Production of Space*. Trans. Donald Nicholson-Smith. Cambridge: Blackwell.

Malpas, Jeff. 1999. *Place and Experience: A Philosophical Topography*. Cambridge: Cambridge University Press.

Merleau-Ponty, Maurice. [1945] 2002. *Phenomenology of Perception*. Trans. Colin Smith. London: Routledge.

Percy, Walker. [1960] 1998. *The Moviegoer*. New York: Vintage.

———. 1971. *Love in the Ruins*. New York: Picador.

———. 1975. *Message in the Bottle: How Queer Man Is, How Queer Language Is, and What One Has to Do with the Other*. New York: Farrar, Straus, & Giroux.

———. 1977. *Lancelot*. New York: Farrar, Straus & Giroux.

———. 1980. *The Second Coming*. New York: Picador.

———. 1983. *Lost in the Cosmos: The Last Self-Help Book*. New York: Farrar, Straus, & Giroux.

———. 1987. *The Thanatos Syndrome*. New York: Farrar, Straus, & Giroux.

———. 1991. *Signposts in a Strange Land*. Ed. Patrick Samway. New York: Farrar, Straus, & Giroux.

Pridgen, Allen. 2000. *Walker Percy's Sacramental Landscapes: The Search in the Desert*. Cranbury: Associated University Presses.

Shulman, Ari N. 2014. GPS and the End of the Road. In: *Why Place Matters: Geography, Identity, and Civic Life in Modern America*, ed. Wilfred McClay and Ted V. McAllister. New York: Encounter Books.

Tolson, Jay. 1992. *Pilgrim in the Ruins: A Life of Walker Percy*. New York: Simon & Schuster.

CHAPTER 11

On Being Jaded: Walker Percy's Philosophical Contributions

Nathan P. Carson

INTRODUCTION

Familiarity, so the saying goes, breeds contempt. But, why *should* familiarity breed such a negative thing as contempt, or other negative orientations? There is something paradoxical about this little folk saying. For, if one is genuinely *familiar*—possessing the *goods* of having a high epistemic grade of cognitive or appreciative contact—with some piece of reality, then why should *contempt* follow on the heels of such genuine epistemic and existential intimacy? At first glance, this seems both bizarre and incongruous. And yet, as anyone who has relegated their most intimate beloved to the status of *persona non grata* knows, such appreciative failure is the common stock of human experience. This is a "commonplace" mystery I propose to examine, with a focus on another experiential state parasitic on or constitutive of familiarity: *jadedness.*

Walker Percy, it would seem, has a lot to say about human jadedness, sometimes through the very means by which we are meant to inhabit ontological intimacy. For example, he notes:

N. P. Carson (✉)
Fresno Pacific University, Fresno, CA, USA
e-mail: nathan.carson@fresno.edu

© The Author(s) 2018
L. Marsh (ed.), *Walker Percy, Philosopher,*
https://doi.org/10.1007/978-3-319-77968-3_11

[T]he selfsame symbol which discloses being may be the means by which being is concealed and lost. ... A sparrow becomes invisible in ordinary life because it disappears into its symbol. If one sees a movement in a tree and recognizes it and says it is "only a sparrow," one is disposing of the creature through its symbolic formulation (SSL, p. 135).

How is it that familiarity with the sparrow renders it *invisible* to one's meaningful experience? Percy's sparrow illustrates one aspect of his "malaise" of the modern self, issuing in a widespread absence of experienced meaningfulness. But when it comes to being jaded, Percy's disappearing sparrow raises some puzzling questions. Does the *happenstance* evaluative silencing of the sparrow even count as being jaded? Or, does jadedness require an explicit, reflective "*devaluation*," as Percy might suggest, perhaps bordering on prejudice, cynicism, or bitterness? (LC, p. 104). After all, we can't appreciate everything all the time.[1] Further, does being jaded about sparrows require that I *care* about them as deeply impinging on my practical identity? One may (justifiably) not care much about sparrows, but intuitively people seem jaded about something that *matters* (or once mattered) to them in a deeper way. Finally, what are the personal or social *sources* of jadedness? Is it an individual problem only, or caused by broader cultural factors?

In what follows, I will attempt to sketch an initial theory of jadedness, and then expand that theory by attending to Percy's unique philosophical contributions. Percy's contributions suggest, I will argue, that there are at least two types of jadedness—a narrow, domain-specific psychological type and a global, existential type—that share structural similarities such as *volitional and epistemic inertia, an unsettled loss of meaning, a faulty assumption of epistemic completion or superiority,* and *a foreclosure of ontological possibilities.* I will then show how Percy uniquely integrates these two types of jadedness within a broader framework of what it means to be human (as *homo viator,* a creature), offering a distinctive and philosophically integrated account of why being jaded involves a fundamental distortion of our humanity. Finally, insofar as some types of jadedness involve failures of humility, I will argue that Percy's philosophical and theological work on our "unsignifiable" uniqueness provides an important critical alternative to prevailing philosophical accounts of humility, and also a unique *solution* to the problem of being jaded.

A PROVISIONAL THEORY OF JADEDNESS

Given the absence of any significant philosophical work devoted to the concept of jadedness, it seems helpful, methodologically, to follow Aristotle's suggestion that one attend to the appearances (*ta phainomena*), and then critically refine them through dialectic (Aristotle, I.1095b2-13). So in what follows, I will not offer a strict set of necessary and sufficient conditions for what it is to be jaded. Rather, I simply want to *progress* in the manner of *theoria* (taking a look), in a way that offers the kind of "seeing" that Wittgenstein calls a "perspicuous representation" (*eine übersichtliche Darstellung*) (Wittgenstein 1962, p. 122).[2] This will provisionally position us to see how, if at all, Walker Percy's philosophical work could contribute to a more mature theory of jadedness and its therapies.

So what is it, exactly, to be jaded? If one glances at popular English uses of the concept, there are frequent equations or associations of jadedness with negative valuational states—such as *prejudice, cynicism,* and *bitterness*— or *weariness, disillusionment,* or apathetic *indifference* over things one could or should value. An examination of these apparent "close cousins" may reveal an initially intuitive representation of jadedness. First, what is it to be *prejudiced*? A prejudiced person holds on to his beliefs for inadequate reasons—whether aversions, appetites, preferences, or attachments—and characteristically fails or refuses to critically assess and revise his favored views, even (perhaps especially) in the face of evidence to the contrary. For example, Roberts and Wood describe prejudice as an intellectual vice—involving a "malformation of epistemic will"—opposed to love of knowledge as an intellectual virtue (Roberts and Wood 2007, p. 162).[3] Typically, it would seem, a prejudiced person will lack some moral or intellectual virtues involving humility, open-mindedness, love of knowledge, courage, or intellectual flexibility, among others (Roberts and Wood 2007, pp. 119, 123).

Cynicism is a second, closer cousin to jadedness that frequently involves a mild, ironic, or direct contempt for realities that in ordinary human experience invites a positive axiological response. The ancient Cynics (such as Antisthenes of Athens) were known for disdaining pleasure, and the pleasures associated with good social standing, possessions, and accumulated wealth, hence the "doglike" or "churlish" meaning of *cynic* (*kunikos*) (Diogenes Laertius 1925, Book VI, pp. 38–41, 86–88, 91). Thus, an apparent defining feature of cynicism is the ironic or sneering stance of *seeing through* the (allegedly) naive, plebian, or sanguine axiological commitments of ordinary folk, sometimes combined with a misanthropic disposition to deny the reality of human sincerity, goodness, or the possibility of change for the better. Notably, many cases of cynicism involve some presumption of a possessed privileged epistemic position, as well as a disdain of hope and explicit foreclosure of social or ontological possibilities, and so can involve (as in the case of prejudice) failures of existential or intellectual humility.

Third, sometimes *bitterness* is associated with being jaded. It is natural to speak of people "becoming bitter and jaded as they age," in light of systematic experiences of disappointment, of unmet expectations, or of meaningful hopes being ruined. Perhaps more straightforwardly negative than cynicism (and lacking the latter's quasi-comic ironic distance and presumed epistemic superiority), being bitter seems to involve pointed or smoldering resentment at a (perceived) unjust or disappointing state of affairs.[4] Unlike prejudice or cynicism, though, bitterness seems distinctively focused on the *past*—a past that involves the avoidable loss of some otherwise achievable good or set of goods, whose loss (combined with counter-factual achievability) directly undermines core desiderata of one's identity, circumstance, or concerns in the world.[5] One is bitter about what *could* have happened, *should* have been one's own, or *might* have transpired if things had been different. A child can harbor bitterness toward his father for the father's failure to appreciate the child's artistic gifts—an achievable appreciation that could and perhaps should have obtained—just as an unlucky athletic contest can involve "a bitter loss" to a fan, for victory was within the team's grasp and counterfactually achievable, but nonetheless foiled by non-blameworthy circumstances.

This examination of apparent close cousins helps produce an initially compelling representation of jadedness. For, being jaded seems to involve similar defining ingredients: *volitional and epistemic inertia* associated with prejudice, *a faulty assumption of epistemic completion or superiority* and *foreclosure of possibilities* associated with prejudice and cynicism, and the *disappointment* over lost goods associated with bitterness. However, jadedness may possess these in a distinct way. For, prejudice, cynicism, and bitterness are less defined by apparent *indifference* or *apathy* than jaded-ness is. For example, a woman who has experienced a continued cycle of abusive relationships may become jaded about the prospects of a genuinely healthy relationship. Repeatedly disappointed ideals may give way to a malaise-ridden indifference over, or writing off of, a new relational prospect; it will now *cease to matter*, precisely because it mattered so much.[6] By contrast, the bitter person *cares* about the good that was lost; the cynic *knows better* than the *hoi polloi* mindlessly committed to vacuous goods and *cares* about (and perhaps even enjoys) his privileged epistemic status, as does the prejudiced person attached to his cherished views.[7]

By contrast, being jaded seems subtler, more existentially pervasive, and less indexed to a purely negative psychic stance toward reality (than cynicism or bitterness), and less attached to cherished positions than prejudice. That is, the defining features of prejudice, cynicism, and bitterness may be too narrow to capture the apparent diffuseness, 'negative' apathy, or evaluative *indifference* that seem to mark jadedness as such. In fact, the primary etymological terms for "jaded" associate it with *satiety* and *sleepiness* or *fatigue*. The *Oxford English Dictionary* notes the primary meaning of "jaded" is to be "worn out or exhausted; fatigued." Early English uses refer to falling behind ("Their Jaded Muse is distanc'd in the Course"; 1693), falling asleep ("his jaded eyelids close"; 1798), spurring on a tired horse ("jaded Pegasus"; 1809), and "Charming away the weariness of the jaded mind" (1865). More tellingly still, a secondary meaning is to be "dull or sated by continual use or indulgence" (including being "jaded to fashions" [1631] and nature's difficulty to "stimulate the jaded palate" [1828]) (Murray et al. 1961, p. 543).

If we take this etymology seriously, we may think of being jaded as a kind of *weariness* (or indifference) brought on by *plenitude*; one is lulled by continual use or experiential exposure. However, this proposal only grasps what is necessary, but not sufficient for jadedness. People living in a neighborhood with frequent gunshot activity may become used to it; they may flinch or duck, and then go on with their day. Being *full* of continual gunshot experiences around the hood, indifference (or at least a failure to notice much) settles in; one is (arguably) not *jaded* by it, but pragmatically *acclimated* to it.[8] Similarly, a mother of four children may become fatigued over frequently adjudicating their arguments, shutting them down quickly and decisively. Relative to the value of a peaceful, conflict-free home, she might be indifferent to the apparent injustice of most provoking situations, simply because she doesn't want to deal with the adjudication required.[9] However, mere decision fatigue, like experiential acclimation, doesn't amount to jadedness either. So, jadedness involves some form of weariness, apathy, or indifference brought on by continual exposure—unlike the first three cousins—but it might also require some of the compositional elements of those three states to be something more than mere context acclimation or pragmatic fatigue.

With respect to prejudice, being jaded *can* often exhibit the entrenched epistemic or existential stance of the prejudiced person, but for very adequate and even compelling reasons, such as a prior cycle of abusive relationships. The person may have good *reasons* for being jaded, even if the inference from past experience to future possibilities, together with volitional inertia, retains the tinge of prejudice. So, while being jaded does share some features of prejudice, like malformation of epistemic will (regarding future possibilities), it is often produced by genuine moral and epistemological insight, and activated by (at times) healthy prudential self-concern. With respect to cynicism, if one is full of, and therefore fatigued by, a father's recognitional failures, one implicitly assumes that one *knows* how this is going to go, once again, and it's not worth bothering about after all. In the jaded person, the explicit assumption or judgment of epistemic superiority in cynicism is often reflectively effaced and existentially diffused: it can remain *present* in jadedness as an implicit background assumption contained in the weariness, together with the foreclosure of possibilities and volitional or epistemic inertia also shared by prejudice.[10] In relation to bitterness, the negative construal of disappointment and resentment over expected but unattained goods gives way in the case of jadedness, to a deeper and more diffuse malaise or disillusionment. The normative stance that fuels the sharper, negative bitterness construal—what could or *should* have happened regarding the unattained goods—is *surrendered* in the fatigue of jadedness, while the muted negative axiological valence of ruined normative ideals may remain residually present. Being jaded is a *diffusely* negative loss of meaning; it is a malaise-ridden existential habiliment. Moreover, in light of the above examples, jadedness may contain genuine moral, prudential, and epistemological value and insight; it is not as straightforwardly negative or expressive of moral or intellectual vice as its cousins may be.

So, what is it to be jaded? Being jaded may involve the residual epistemic superiority, foreclosure of possibilities, and volitional or epistemic inertia of cynicism and prejudice, and residual disappointment over apparently unachievable (and hence surrendered) normative ideals relevant to bitterness. And in these residual senses, being jaded is not a *strictly* neutral, indifferent, or apathetic state; it occupies the space between. But keeping this in mind, it is clear that in the weariness that follows satiety and repetition, things cease to be *meaningful* for the jaded person in a way that *does* present as apathy or indifference. The goods at which the cynic sneers, to which the prejudiced person is attached, and about which the bitter person seethes, may simply cease to *matter* at all to someone who is jaded with respect to those goods. Indeed, jadedness may sometimes *presuppose* a cynicism, prejudice, or bitterness, that upon situational or experiential repetition, may be neutralized—the meaningfulness of the father's recognition loses its evaluative purchase or importance, good or bad; it may cease to matter at all.[11] When one is jaded one ceases to vividly *appreciate* the goodness *or* badness of a given person, experience, or state of affairs.

This lack of meaningfulness and appreciation is also an important distinguishing mark between jadedness and its more negatively valenced conceptual cousins. Apt appreciation—in the sense of first-personally engaged evaluative understanding or attunement—involves *whatever* cognitive, hedonic, conative, or emotional evaluative response is called for by the bit of reality being appreciated.[12] Since reality is evaluatively complex—at least on a value realist metaphysics, a view Walker Percy shares—when one is jaded, it is simply too narrow to say that one lacks *positive valuation* of things that one should enjoy or value. A worker during a dire humanitarian crisis may well become jaded—sated or filled to the point of weariness by the magnitude of suffering around her—and become unable to appreciate its gravity or badness, perhaps as a psychological defense mechanism. The sated weariness of jadedness seems to nullify our sense of the *significance, importance,* or *meaningfulness* of a given domain of appreciable reality, whether the experience is positive *or* negative. The humanitarian example (and others above) suggest that being jaded may at times be developmentally normal or contextually healthy, sometimes even involving unique prudential, moral, or epistemic value, as noted above. However, it is also possible for jadedness to become a negative, settled state of experienced meaninglessness that has the power to distort our humanity and our capacities of apt evaluative appreciation. This pictures a state of affairs broadly similar to the one Binx Bolling identifies in MG, when he says: "Now the only sign is that all the signs in the world make no difference. Is this God's ironic revenge?" (MG, p. 146). Of course, Walker Percy has a great deal to say about such losses of meaning, and to that we now turn.

PERCY'S MALAISE AS EXISTENTIAL JADEDNESS?

In addressing the puzzling question of how pride can function as "the queen and root of all sins" when its unique moral psychology is incompatible with other sins, Thomas Aquinas distinguishes between narrow and general pride. He argues that general pride can be common to all sins by its diffusion of governance and also by its effects, "since it is an effect of pride that one refuses to be subject to the rule of a superior, which every sinner does insofar as the sinner does not subject himself or herself to the law of God" (Aquinas 2003, pp. 329–330). In a similar fashion, jadedness might be diffuse enough in its existential losses of meaning, and in its effects on human life, that it may be intelligible to distinguish two forms of jadedness. First, there is the narrow, domain-specific form as outlined in the above moral psychological analysis, whereby one might be individually jaded *about* this or that particular context, person, or state of affairs. Second, however, the diffusion and effects that the loss of meaning in jadedness involves may point toward something like *global* or existential jadedness with similar structural features of narrow jadedness, while placing it within a broader context than individualistic moral psychology.

Percy's "malaise" of the modern self awash in conscious or unconscious despair has many facets, but might be a good reflective starting point for the contours of existential jadedness. For, he seems to offer linguistic, social, philosophical, and theological conceptions of being jaded *qua* human being in the wasteland of modernity—rather than simply being jaded *qua* son, romantic partner, or birder. Of course, Percy does not use (to my knowledge) the term "jadedness," and yet his treatment of different aspects and sources of the modern malaise bears too many similarities to ignore. His treatment is full of potentially distinctive and illuminating contributions to a more comprehensive theory of jadedness than the sketch given above. Most importantly, perhaps, interpreting Percy's malaise through the lens of existential jadedness can demonstrate how he offers a unique, *teleologically integrated solution* to jadedness (both narrow and broad), situated within our task as creaturely wayfarers who must answer the challenge of becoming a self before God.

The aspects of Percy's malaise that intersect most directly with jadedness sometimes occur in the context of his semiotic claim that human beings distinctively and sovereignly occupy the intersection of naming and being, ideally in a way that reveals, uncovers, and co-celebrates being with wonderment and joy. The cases of jadedness (by another name, for Percy) occur when this native task is subverted or experienced as impotent. Consider Percy's invisible sparrow again. If a bird is known and named as a "sparrow," eventually the wonderment of that individual creature is emptied out; it is relegated to the domain of the commonplace and rendered "invisible" through the overuse of its symbolic indicator: that bird is *only* a "sparrow" (SSL, p. 135).[13] An initial problem, as noted above, is that the sparrow case does not seem like narrow jadedness at all. The invisibility certainly includes indifference or apathetic disregard, but this seems more like the gunshot case of context acclimation. One cannot appreciate everything in experience, but that doesn't make one jaded. Arguably, as a necessary condition of coherent meaningfulness, some things simply *must* (and in fact most things *do*) fall into the appreciative background. Further, one may not *care* about sparrows much, or inhabit indifference as a defense mechanism against disappointed hopes about the sparrow. If no antecedent concern, muted disappointment, or loss of hope is residually present, it is hard to see how this would psychologically count as being individually jaded about the value, uniqueness, or other meaningful contributions of this sparrow to one's life or practical identity.

However, if generalized beyond the specific case, the sparrow *can* defensibly bridge toward the problem of existential jadedness, or jadedness in general. In Percy's MG, Binx Bolling comments on "the strange fact" of his "invincible apathy," noting that "[i]f God himself had appeared to me, it would have changed nothing. In fact, I have only to hear the word God and a curtain comes down in my head" (MG, p. 145). From sparrows to God, Percy suggests that for the average denizen of late modernity, things no longer "signify" *across the board*, even things which *should* be meaningful to us (TS, p. 121). One is *full* of sparrow experiences and God-talk to the point of sated weariness, indifference, and diffusedly negative apathy, feeling "in the deepest sense possible that something has gone wrong with one's very self" (Percy 1986).[14] When it comes to knowing ourselves and inhabiting the world meaningfully, we are caught, says Percy, between two hopelessly reductive paradigms: the Skinnerian-Darwinian view of ourselves as *merely* "beasts" (organisms in an environment) on the one hand, and the Cartesian view of ourselves as "angels," best (or only) capable of appreciating being through general or theoretical abstractions.[15] In either case, we remain self-estranged in a way that produces smoldering dissatisfaction and experienced death-in-life across wide swaths of our experience, sparrows included.[16] For Percy, the malaise of the modern self *is* a kind of existential jadedness. For, it is marked by a pervasive absence of experienced meaningfulness, tinged by diffuse unease or anxiety, that covers over our human status as wayfaring "castaways" and our task of becoming a self before God.[17]

Language, Social Consciousness, and Social Jadedness

In order to open up Percy's unique contributions to a theory of existential jadedness, his views on language—on meaningfulness and its loss—are critical. For Percy, employment of "triadic" symbols—a conflux of signifying mind, the signifier, and the symbolized thing—is uniquely constitutive of our humanity. For, *Homo symbolificus* (man the symbol-mongerer) responds to the cosmic environment like other organisms—in the manner of a stimulus-response *Umwelt*—but remains irreducibly unique by inhabiting what Heidegger calls *Welt*, a *world* of symbolic meaning and value-laden hierarchies of importance (MB, pp. 283, 288–297). The human mind, for Percy, uniquely provides meanings at the intersection of names and being. In order for a bird to be "known and affirmed," a *"pairing* is required: the laying of *symbol* alongside *thing"* (e.g. *this* is a *sparrow*) (SSL, p. 134, emphasis original). In fact, Percy views this as a *transcendental* act of consciousness: the *as* structure of triadic consciousness is epistemically basic, in that symbolic representation is a strict necessary condition for any meaningful cognition[18]: "Once it dawns upon one, whether deaf-mute or not, that *this is water*, then the first question is *What is that*, and so on, toward the end that *everything is something*. There has come into existence an all-construing mode of cognition in which everything must be formulated symbolically and known intentionally *as* something" (MB, p. 281).

In Heidegger's terms, this means that human namers transcend a mere *ontic* orientation toward a biological environment; we fundamentally inhabit an *ontological* stance toward being, as naming opens us to and makes us participants in revealing the *meaning* of being. For Percy the Thomist, such naming and knowing activity belongs to our proper nature; it is a central, defining feature of our creatureliness that (ideally) is "a means of *knowing* ... not in the sense of possessing 'facts' but in the Thomistic and existential sense of connatural identification of the knower with the object known" (MB, pp. 296–297, emphasis original). Symbolic activity is a fulfillment, for Percy, of one aspect of our natural created *telos* as beings, for we are made for appreciative *communion* with reality.[19]

Moreover, we are for Percy uniquely fitted for communion with other symbol-making selves, since representational activity—indeed consciousness itself—is irreducibly social. Consciousness is a *con scio*, a "knowing with" relation that emerges in shared linguistic forms of life: I am conscious that "this is a sparrow" because it is a sparrow "for you and me."[20] Thus, Percy rejects a philosophical view of the self as an autonomous thinking or conscious subject, including the Cartesian *res cogitans*, the Kantian transcendental ego, and the Sartrean prereflective ego, since all of these approaches *presuppose* consciousness. Thus, Percy argues, "[t]he decisive stroke against the myth of the autonomous Kantian subject is the intersubjective constitution of consciousness. There is a mutuality between the I and the Thou and the object which is in itself prime and irreducible"; intersubjective symbolic co-designation *"is itself"* the constituent act of consciousness" (MB, pp. 282–83, emphasis original).[21] We are therefore deeply (and transcendentally) dependent on one another for the worlds of meaningfulness we inhabit, and for the naming activity that makes us distinctively human[22]: "You—Betty, Dick—are like other items in my world—cats, dogs, and apples. But you have a unique property. You are also a co-namer, co-discoverer, co-sustainer of my world—whether you are Kafka whom I read or Betty who reads this. Without you—Franz, Betty—I would have no world" (LC, p. 101).[23] Problematically, however, the social co-constitution of meaning also opens the prospect of inauthentic modes of being. "The Thou is at once the source of my consciousness, the companion and co-celebrant of my discovery of being," says Percy, and also "the sole threat to my inauthentic constitution of myself."[24]

Indeed, Percy's notion of social consciousness and social sources of self-world understanding are among his most distinctive contributions to a theory of jadedness, in contrast to the individualistic sketch given above. In Percy's economy, *social* sources or constitutions of my jaded experience (through symbolic media) will be far more prevalent, and problematic.[25] One ignores the sparrow because *we* have relegated it to the status of *entité non grata*.[26] The selfsame symbol that provides access to being for a *community* of knowers may also conceal and close being off in a way that can produce experiential numbness *en masse*, in part, because of the way we relate to unique individual realities through theoretical abstractions and social classifications.

For example, in "Loss of the Creature," Percy notes that if a tourist visits the Grand Canyon and experiences it through the predetermined "symbolic complex" constructed by the tourist industry, brochures, and tour guides—seeing it "under approved circumstances"—he will be unable to directly appreciate the Canyon itself in the way its first discoverer had (MB, p. 47). The pleasure he experiences will be a function not of appreciative absorption and non-comparative wonder at the unique thing itself, says Percy, but the pleasure of the *correspondence* between the thing and the preformed system of socially constructed meanings, outlined by "picture postcard, geography book, tourist folders, and the words *Grand Canyon*" (Ibid). Thus, Percy notes, "[t]he highest point, the term of the sightseer's satisfaction, is not the sovereign discovery of the thing before him; it is rather the measuring up of the thing to the criterion of the preformed complex."[27]

Percy generalizes this problem to our experience of other things—art in a museum, trees, a dogfish in botany class, a Shakespearean sonnet—and he argues that "the sightseer should be prepared to enter into a struggle to recover a sight" of such things, including a struggle to resist the *self* being *signified* as a passive experience consumer in such contexts.[28] Moreover, this is not an *individual* problem; for Percy it is the standard social human predicament in modern technological society.[29] In this, there is a "double deprivation" involving a loss of "title" for the sovereign knower—who no longer discovers unexpected, spontaneous, and particular meaning—and the loss of the thing known through its "packaging," and through its being an instance of a type or abstract principle (MB, pp. 62–63).[30]

Moreover, in "Loss of the Creature" and elsewhere, Percy argues that the status people accord to modern science uniquely exacerbates this problem, whereby individual things (or persons) are *"disposed of* by theory" (MB, p. 62). The methodological abstraction native to scientific inquiry together with the authoritative status accorded it in the modern age combine to produce an "abstract self" that is alienated from its own unique particularity, and from its native way of being in the world.[31] For Percy, scientists (as well as artists) are the new gods of post-religious modernity, through which we vicariously experience transcendence from particularity (LC, pp. 114–123). Our indefatigable (and for Percy, idolatrous) faith in the development, successes, and sociopolitical applications of scientific progress causes us to dispense with the uniqueness and value of particulars in favor of universals. Thus does Percy note, "[a]s a result of the science of botany, trees are not made available to every man. On the contrary. The tree loses its proper density and mystery as a concrete existent and, as merely another *specimen* of a species, becomes itself nugatory" (MB, p. 63).

We are now in a position to see why the invisible sparrow counts as a form of jadedness; it is a symbolic function of our sociohistorical *zeitgeist*, a broader existential form of being jaded by way of theory:

> The dogfish the tree, the seashell, the American negro, the dream, are rendered invisible by a shift of reality from concrete thing to theory which Whitehead has called the fallacy of misplaced concreteness. It is a mistaking of an idea, a principle, an abstraction, for the real. As a consequence of the shift, the "specimen" is seen as less real than the theory of the specimen. As Kierkegaard said, once a person is seen as a specimen of a race or a species, at that very moment he ceases to be an individual. Then there are no more individuals but only specimens (MB, p. 58).[32]

Since science trades in classificatory generalities, we *accept* its symbolic, predetermined general meanings as the meaning of any individual existents we encounter, including ourselves. We become cultural Platonists by proxy, while ignoring the deep existential implications of overlooking the limitations of scientific inquiry, which turn out to be the limitations of theory in general. Alluding to Kierkegaard's famous critique that Hegel's system had explained everything except Hegel himself, Percy notes that "[s]cience cannot utter a single word about an individual molecule, thing, or creature in so far as it is an individual but only in so far as it is like other individuals," including the individual person herself (MB, p. 22).

ABSTRACTION AS INTRINSICALLY ALIENATING? PERCIAN APPRECIATION OF PARTICULARS

These issues raise the prospect that Percy is, in Kierkegaardian fashion, criticizing the intrinsic value or existential limitations of objective knowledge, abstraction, or philosophical theory.[33] Is he saying—quite apart from socially mediated, predetermined complexes of meaning—that conceptual mediation of the world through universals is, *as such*, alienating and a source of existential jadedness? If so, this suggestion is problematic, for appreciation of particulars would commit Percy to an implausible Sartrean theory of naive realism, whereby we directly intuit being without mediation by universals. However, such direct intuitions appear theoretically incompatible with Percy's irreducibly social constitution of meaningful consciousness. So, if he is saying that abstraction is alienating *as such*, then—assuming his social consciousness—we are tragically alienated of *necessity* from direct appreciations of particular being(s). Since Percy clearly does not hold this tragic view, he should not be interpreted as questioning the intrinsic value of theoretical abstraction as such. What, then, is the real source of our jaded inability to appreciate particulars? Moreover, can Percy offer a compelling philosophical account of what it is to appreciate particulars *through* abstract concepts, in an unjaded way?[34]

I think that he can. Percy's socially mediated consciousness naturally fits the persuasive view that experience is conceptually mediated all the way down to the bare perceptual level, as Wittgensteinian *Gestalt* construals show. Whether one "sees" a duck-rabbit *Gestalt* image as a duck or as a rabbit, the *exact same* sensory input is present, so the "seeing as" construal in either case is a *conceptual perception*, rather than bare sensory perception as such.[35] On this view, universal-mediated *understanding* configures even the most basic of immediate perceptions.[36] If general concepts are perceptually unavoidable and therefore a necessary condition of meaningfulness, then—assuming that tragic, ontologically necessary alienation is false—there must be a way to appreciate particulars (a sparrow or canyon, say) without the jaded loss of self and meaning that can accompany an experiential veil of abstraction and its more cognitively laden systems of objective knowledge.

What might this look like? Percy's notion of potentially non-jaded appreciation of particulars might be similar to what I have elsewhere called "phenomenal-affective appreciations," as distinct from the more refined appreciations of experts in a given domain (Carson 2013c, pp. 28–36). The "expert" appreciators I have in mind may possess "objectual understanding" as some epistemologists currently construe it: an occurrent or nonoccurrent cognitive grasp of some coherent set of true (or mostly true) propositions, the relational and logical links between them, and an engaged grasp of the relative value or significance of these things with respect to one another.[37] The crucial point to which Percy is sensitive is that many appreciations seem, at best, only minimally or indirectly related to such understanding, and marked chiefly by non-comparative wonder and first-personal phenomenal vividness. This may involve the understanding (*qua Gestalt* sense-making ability) that is minimally necessary for any intelligible perception and propositional knowledge, without the kind that presupposes an acquired grasp of some coherent body of propositional knowledge (Roberts and Wood 2007, p. 48).[38]

Suppose a child encounters his first waterfall and says: "Wow! Look at *that!*" Lacking an adult vocabulary for its aesthetic properties like "powerful," "magnificent," or "majestic," the child still ostensively appreciates the waterfall as an amazing "*that*," in and through his own phenomenal or affective experience of pleasure, delight, or a vivid sense of wonder or awe. A developed reflective or comparative understanding of waterfalls isn't necessary for him to appreciate this particular falls, and yet understanding of a minimal sort *does* structure his perception: epistemically, the child has some direct phenomenal acquaintance knowledge (he knows "what it is like").[39] Moreover, the appreciation is still comparative; it is relative to other things experienced like water, tall objects, spatial dimensions, temporal successions, and falling things. However, the achieved discursive understanding required for the appreciation of the waterfall expert—which presupposes vast propositional knowledge, skilled perception, and comparative background experience—is only minimally in view. Nonetheless, the child's appreciation is not only adequate and unjaded, but positively inspiring. Would the child's appreciation be *better* if he engaged in scientific study of waterfalls? Not necessarily. For, as Percy perceptively notes, "expert" appreciations can often undermine both the epistemic value (of direct acquaintance knowledge) and the phenomenal-affective meaningfulness of these other appreciations.[40] Suppose I am appreciating the waterfall as luminous, dazzling, and pristine, and a water treatment expert tells me to stand back, since the falls are pumping largely raw sewage from a nearby treatment plant leak. I would immediately be unable to appreciate it the way that I had (I now construe it as menacing, tainted, nasty), even though my initial appreciation was experientially rich and *perceptually* truth-apt.[41]

If these cases are similar to what Percy has in mind, then he is right to problematize the elimination of first-personal appreciations of particulars in favor of reliance on expert appreciations, when the latter eliminate the first-personal agency so critical to our humanity and meaningful engagement with reality. However, even Percy would deny, I think, that the two are *necessarily* incompatible, for he frequently discusses the phenomenal-affective delight of scientists who are not merely hovering in an abstract "angelism" of alternative transcendence, but who can, as it were, recover the sparrow. Percy notes that "[s]cientists recover the inexhaustible mystery of the signified from the mundane closed-off simulacrum of the world-sign." A layperson, continues Percy, "sees a line of ants crossing a sidewalk and sees it as—*ants crossing a* sidewalk" while the naturalist "Fabre saw ants crossing the sidewalk and stopped to wonder where they came from, where they were going, and how they knew how to get there. Then, like von Frisch and his bees, he discovered there is no end to the mystery of ants" (LC, p. 105).[42] First-personally engaged, phenomenal-affective appreciations are apparently available to *both* the child and the expert. Percy therefore does not posit a naive false dichotomy between the sovereign individual (who uniquely appreciates particulars) and the "expert" (who can only appreciate through the veil of universality).

More critically, however, if Percy's view that universals are socially mediated and epistemically basic for consciousness is correct, then when it comes to inhabiting a meaningful *Welt, neither* the child nor the expert *can* appreciate particulars *as* bare particulars.[43] The transcendental necessity of *conceptual* perception would mean that, for Percy, abstraction *as such* may not be the fundamental source of alienation and jadedness with respect to self-world encounters. Nonetheless, he can advance a philosophically compelling account of the jadedness problem in Grand Canyon (and other similar) cases. With respect to the self-world relation, the problem may be the loss of a first-personal, *contemplative activity* relation in favor of a third-personal, *static correspondence* relation. Both the child and the expert need, for Percy, a relation of contemplative wonder, of openness to the "mystery" of reality that includes active, first-personal discovery, of heretofore undisclosed possibilities of being.[44]

EXISTENTIAL JADEDNESS: PERCY'S INITIAL CONTRIBUTIONS

We can now summarize some of Percy's key theoretical contributions to what I have called existential jadedness. The three problems Percy contributes include (1) *the social problem* of the consumer self who ingests prepackaged, settled systems of meaning, (2) *the scientific problem* of mistaken epistemic superiority and settled correspondence systems of third-personal meaning, and the related (3) *abstraction problem* whereby fixed theoretical knowledge eclipses the native human vocation of active appreciative encounter. If we take the social problem seriously (in relation to the other two), Percy illumines the fact that jadedness often involves *unconscious* adoption of socially crafted roles, meanings, or self-understandings, that have broad power to undermine our humanity. In the modern age, the passive consumer and abstract theoretical identities are often adopted by *default*. The volitional and epistemic inertia, assumption of epistemic completion, and foreclosure of possibilities that we treated earlier as *individually* constructed realities of the jaded person may be unconscious practical identities co-constituted by our cultural *zeitgeist*. A consumer, for example, is passive by default (volitional and epistemic inertia), and his existential assumption of epistemic completion (*via negativa*) for *himself*—there is nothing for me to discover because *they* have it all settled—mirrors a cultural lack of intellectual humility with respect to scientific, social, or technological progress.[45] With respect to jaded foreclosure of possibilities, the existentially jaded consumer imbibes finished systems of symbolic meanings—*actualities* to which experience must measure up (the Canyon looks like the postcard), and in virtue of which first-personal discovery of being and its possibilities is (largely) eliminated. If a muted, ambiguous unsettledness or disappointment over unachieved goods (*which* goods one mightn't know) settles into malaise-ridden, sated apathy, one might never be able to *point* to one's own individual narrative for the source of the jadedness (e.g. past romantic disappointments, or fatherly failures).

A second contribution Percy makes is that he offers a compelling solution to the question with which we began the chapter: How can familiarity breed jadedness? There is an important *psychological paradox of jadedness* here, whereby meaninglessness is a product of meaningfulness. How does overexposure to, or satiation by, meaningful experience issue in felt mean-inglessness, or apathetic indifference? If Percy is right, then one way of resolving the paradox is to situate jadedness within a normative, teleological framework of authentic creatureliness. The consumer self has sated, *experienced meaningfulness* of one sort—settled, third-personal, specimen-correspondence meanings—that eliminates meaningfulness of another sort, which is the essential meaningfulness normatively required for creatureli-ness. One loses the meaning of *the thing*, discovered in its uniqueness by way of first-personal discovery and engagement, and the meaningfulness of discovering and wondering for *oneself*. The problem only makes sense in light of a normative teleological account of what it is to be fully human, whereby one inhabits one's native vocation of naming and knowing through active contemplative discovery and direct appreciative engage-ment. Perhaps, then, it is not *familiarity* at all that breeds jadedness, but rather a deep *absence of familiarity*, in the sense of genuine intimacy, between self and world.

Finally, Percy's perspective offers an *integrated* perspective on narrow and broad jadedness. Take the case of the jaded romantic or son, men-tioned above. It is plausible to say that each is jaded about the real prospect of a healthy relationship (or of fatherly recognition) because of a crea-turely failure to actively, contemplatively appreciate either the uniqueness of past negative experiences, or the distinct particularity of the new expe-riential moment. Instance-type overgeneralizations or mistaken analogical assumptions about case similarities do induce volitional and epistemic inertia, a sense that things are settled in terms of one's knowledge and of future possible states of affairs. Percy's solution to this kind of jadedness is akin to Iris Murdoch's emphasis on the deep moral importance and diffi-culty of appreciative attention: One must attend to a complex and value-laden reality beyond the self in a way that challenges the forces of inertia pulling oneself inward (Murdoch 2001, pp. 16–17). After all, *this* sparrow *is not* just like other sparrows; neither is this new relational prospect or fatherly interaction, just like previous ones.

Homo Singularis: Jadedness as Loss of the Individual[46]

Thus far I have focused on the problems of existential jadedness, and Percy's contributions with respect to the intersection of self and world. However, Percy's most distinctive philosophical contribution to a teleo-logically integrated account of narrow and broad jadedness lies in his efforts to articulate the singular uniqueness and transcendence of the individual self as a wayfarer, ineradicably marked by metaphysical privation and not fully knowable through the meaning-giving as structures of consciousness. At first glance, this is obviously an extension of the social and scientific problems outlined above.

Percy is well known for his excoriating criticisms of the scientific treatment of the self as an organism in an environment, and for the uniqueness of the specimen problem as applied to the individual human self: "The layman thinks that only science can utter the true word about anything, individuals included. But the layman is an individual. So science cannot say a single word to him or about him except as he resembles others" (MB, p. 22).[47] Percy adds, when "we allow ourselves to perceive ourselves as a type of, example of, instance of, such and such a class" as science requires, "to this same degree do we come short of being ourselves" (Percy 1986). Again appropriating Kierkegaard's critique of Hegel, Percy extends this problem beyond science to the inability of theory or objective knowledge *in general* to tell me, *qua* individual, how to become a self in my future-directed orientation toward my own existentially finite possibilities. For, objective knowledge cannot tell one "what it means to be a man living in the world who must die."[48] Like Wittgenstein, at issue for Percy is that even with a finished objective theory of everything, something of the meaning of our own lives would be left out.[49]

Percy recovers the singular uniqueness of persons in a distinctive way. As noted above, human symbolic consciousness involves an "objectifying act" that renders things "formulable," semiotically stable, intelligible, and therefore *meaningful* (MB, p. 283). However, Percy's symbolizing self is the one exception; it can never stabilize its own meaning *as* something, as an object in its own world: "I, who symbolize the world in order to know it, am destined to remain forever unknown to myself."[50] For, says Percy, "[s]emiotically, the self is literally unspeakable to itself. … The self of the sign-user can never be grasped, because, once the self locates itself at the dead center of its world, there is no signified to which a signifier can be joined to make a sign" (LC, pp. 106–7).[51] As John Sykes notes, the self is the originating vantage from which any symbolic seeing or knowing proceeds, remaining thereby invisible and a perennial mystery to itself, the naught at its core ever unfilled. "Since the self is doomed never to 'find' or finalize itself," says Sykes, "it is caught in an inevitable state of anxiety" (Sykes 2016, p. 1027).

For Percy, however, the "doom" of the unfinished self and its anxiety is a gift, for, following Kierkegaard's treatment in *The Concept of Anxiety*,

anxiety over "nothing" is a divinely given revelatory emotion that discloses our transcendent orientation and the task of becoming a self before God.[52] In "The Coming Crisis in Psychiatry," for example, Percy discusses anxiety as a non-pathological emotion intrinsic to the human condition as such, which, in the experiential face of oneself as an unsignifiable nothing, "may be quite the reverse of a symptom. It may be the call of the self to the self, in Kierkegaard's words: the discovery of the possibility of freedom to become a self," and therefore "a summons to authentic existence, to be heeded at any cost" (SLL, pp. 255, 259).[53] Percy ultimately defends the general existentialist insight that such anxiety is "a condition necessarily entailed by man's freedom," and reveals a "transcendence" that is "the one distinguishing mark of human existence," a sign of our "incurable God-directedness" (SSL, pp. 260–261).

The reason why modes of immanent or transcendent objectification of the self—as consumer, organism, or as the theorist who *understands*—are so deadly and productive of existential jadedness, in Percy's view, is that they involve the loss of the self as creaturely *homo viator*, as a being *in medias res* marked by metaphysical privation, possibility-oriented freedom, and participated being in relation to God.[54] The unsignifiability of the self *in anxiety* is thus, for Percy, the metaphysically inescapable and nagging thorn in the side of either domain-specific or existential jadedness. For, it marks our status as unsettled, perennially unfinished, radically dependent creatures, who *sense* that there is something wrong when, interpersonally or culturally, we are sated and thereby *finished* with self, world, or others.

PERCIAN HUMILITY AS RADICAL DEPENDENCE

Percy's solution to narrow jadedness—situated within the broader framework of existential jadedness and the need to recover oneself as creature—involves a radical critique of our existential and epistemic aspirations of self (or world) closure. Notably, in Christian theological history, humility is the creaturely virtue *par excellence* (often the root of the tree of Christian virtues), (DeYoung 2014, p. 78)[55] and in this closing section, I will argue that Percy's articulation of our dependent, unsignifiable creatureliness is a distinctive philosophical and theological contribution to this tradition.[56] For, Percy recovers a notion of creaturely humility as radical dependence that is not only a partial cure for problematic cases of jadedness, but also a compelling theoretical alternative to prevailing accounts of humility in recent secular philosophical literature.

The universally assumed account of Christian humility in recent secular philosophical literature is that it requires, as Norvin Richards claims, a "low opinion of oneself" or a low self-assessment. For, our status is trivial compared to God's, we are sinful even in our finest moments, and our virtues or good qualities are gifts of grace.[57] The secular literature usually strips these theological assumptions: sin and trivial status become acknowledgment of human limitations or cosmic insignificance; grace is translated into communal dependence or luck. Such theories then motivate why a chastened view of human abilities, achievements, or significance is morally or prudentially important (Richards 1988, p. 259; Driver 1989, p. 381; Dunnington 2016, p. 21). This not only encounters the problem that God cannot be humble—and in Christian theology, Christology and Trinitarianism seem to entail divine humility—but it also threatens to reduce humility to a pseudo-virtue or vice, since it may involve an *inaccurate* assessment of one's significance or achievements (Dunnington 2016, pp. 23–24). Accordingly, other prevailing secular accounts of humility (specifically intellectual humility) revise this definition such that humility is either (1) an *accurate self-assessment* of strengths, accomplishments, and social status, (2) a *low concern* for status and recognitional entitlements due to an intrinsic concern for other epistemic goods, or (3) an *owning of one's intellectual limitations* with suitable awareness, acknowledgment, and corrective activity (Whitcomb et al. 2015).[58] Among other problems, (1) accurate self-assessment seems compatible with intellectual pride, leaving (2) and (3) as the most defensible options in the contemporary philosophical literature.

In (2), the *low concern* view, articulated by Roberts and Wood (and more recently, West), humility is defined by negation: humility is low concern for social status, entitlements, or recognition for accomplishments, cross-balanced by possession of proper pride involving secure agency, self-confidence, a healthy sense of his human dignity, and intellectual independence. The intellectually humble person, for Roberts and Wood, is intrinsically motivated by love of knowledge, and this motivation partly explains the absence of concern for intellectual status, recognition, or dominance over other intellectual peers (Roberts and Wood 2007, pp. 236–256). (3) The *limitations-owning* view of both humility and intellectual humility is another contender in the literature, with versions defended by Whitcomb et al. (2015), as well as (on humility as a moral virtue), Nancy Snow. In this view, the humble person is concerned about and pays attention to her limitations, both in an individual and existential sense. Says Snow, "narrow humility is occasioned by an acknowledgement of personal weakness," but to count as humility, one must acknowledge and care about one's flaws. One must take them seriously and "be disturbed by having them" while accepting them and yet seeking to minimize their effects when possible (Snow 2005, p. 78). For Snow, such "narrow humility" can occasion "existential humility," whereby one reflects on and accepts the broader limitations of the human condition. Our individual limitations are part of the human condition, and Snow contends that "a feature common to such humbling experiences is an appreciation of the value of the reality that extends beyond your circumstances or transcends the limitations imposed by the human condition" (Snow 2005, pp. 79–80).

With respect to Percy's account of creatureliness, there are obvious connections between the low concern and limitations-owning views of humility. A low concern for status, combined with an intrinsic love of knowledge, clearly parallels Percy's treatment of our properly native task as co-namers and co-knowers, meant for contemplative and appreciative encounter with being. Similarly, an owning of one's limitations, whether epistemic, moral, or social, seems critical to a Percian resolution of both narrow and existential jadedness, as does a vivid sense of one's finitude as one engages a reality beyond the self. However, an accommodationist approach here fails to do justice to the radical character of Percy's proposal about the privative, unsignifiable, and ultimately wayfaring status of the self.

As Kent Dunnington notes, the low concern and the limitations-owning views share two assumptions prevalent in modern virtue ethics, which in my view also put them deeply at odds with Percy's account of proper creatureliness. First, says Dunnington, these two theories assume that "the ideal human self is the healthy self of modern psychological theory" (Dunnington 2017a). Such a healthy self has, say Roberts and West, "the kind of reflection-dependent self-construal that object-relations dynamic psychologists theorize to be the basis of a healthy self-concept." (Roberts and West 2017, chapter 6, section 2.3). Second, these theories assume that the virtues promote (and should never inhibit) mundane earthly flourishing (Dunnington 2017a). By contrast, notes Dunnington, radical Christian humility—advanced by Augustine, and by the fourth-century Christian desert fathers and mothers—insists on the normative ideal not of *low* concern, but rather of *no* concern for one's status, dignity, or accomplishments. The call to become oneself paradoxically involves the *unselving* of the self, whose ultimate *telos* lies in friendship with God.[59] Second, such radical humility does not simply own moral, epistemic, or existential limitations. Rather, it *embraces* them, including Christologically modeled weakness and suffering, and the self-giving identity of a Triune God, whose selfhood is "constituted by what it gives away rather than what it lays claim to, by openness rather than enclosure, by receptivity and neediness rather than independence and self-sufficiency" (Dunnington 2016, pp. 37, 39). For Dunnington, this Augustinian picture of humility involves an "embrace of radical dependence" at an ontological, moral, and identity level (Dunnington 2016, p. 27).[60] The most telling convergence with Percy's view lies in Dunnington's articulation of Augustinian identity dependence. For Augustine, "our very identities are dependent upon God in such a way that the 'natural' drive to fashion, stabilize, or protect an intelligible, secure, and self-sufficient identity" is exposed as an unnatural chimera, for we cannot "truthfully tell the story of who we are—of our identities—abstracted from God" (Dunnington 2016, p. 28).

It should be clear that this version of humility as radical dependence is something very similar to what Percy would endorse, and yet he has vital and distinctive contributions to make here. First, Percy denies the two modernist assumptions outlined above, that (1) the ideal self is the healthy well-adjusted self of modern psychology, and that (2) virtues will always promote the flourishing of this immanent self. His distinctive philosophical contribution here is that he not only *denies* these assumptions, he also offers an *account* of why assuming their truth—that the healthy self is a complex, socially adjusted organism with virtues exclusively conducive to immanent flourishing—is a positive disaster that leaves us awash in existential jadedness. Percy offers, then, distinctive resources to *critique* the limitations of the two best contemporary philosophical accounts of humility, for their complicity in our malaise by merely fitting us for immanent selfhood.

Second, Percy clearly shares the stated Augustinian view that self-referential identity formation is futile, and that the self as *privation* is ultimately meant to reveal our ontological identity dependence on God. Of course, Percy is famous for his exhaustive (and comedic) treatment of the futile human quest of identity formation, and particularly for his critiques of the quest for oneself as a stable, autonomous subject. However, a second distinctive contribution is his attempt (however successful) to offer an *empirical*, linguistically grounded account of *why* the self-sufficient identity formation project founders, and indeed why it leads—individually, socially, and theoretically—to the problems of jadedness, malaise, and loss of the self.

Finally, a partial Percian *solution* to problematic versions of narrow and existential jadedness seems to require such radical dependence humility (with respect to others, but ultimately to God).[61] Again, Percy provides this solution in a unique and distinctive way. The nothingness of the self is precisely an inability to *know* oneself in a coherent or stable way, so long as one assumes existential or epistemological self-sufficiency. So, Percy's "unselving" here is an *epistemological stripping* of the self-referential self, of its native naming and knowing activities and credentials, in a way that *naturally* fits it for such radical humility and embraced identity dependence. When embraced, the effect of this kind of humility on the narrowly or existentially jaded person is substantial. For, the sated weariness or apathy of jadedness derives partly from continually failed efforts to protect, defend, or secure a self-sufficient identity. Being jaded involves a muted background assumption of epistemic superiority or completion, and this assumption (under ideal conditions) will also be eliminated. When the unsignifiable self—who is conscious of her radical dependence and self-referential epistemological poverty—*embraces* her status as such, she may find the resources to combat the volitional and epistemic inertia as well as assumptions of foreclosed possibilities that also mark the jaded person.[62]

In these and in many other ways, Walker Percy's work surely enriches and defensibly contextualizes our philosophical understanding of the nature, sources, and alleviations of being jaded. For, he not only delivers distinctive social, linguistic, and theoretical resources that situate individual psychological jadedness within a richer explanatory frame, he also integrates the problematics of jadedness within a broader, compelling teleological account of what it is to be fully human as unfinished, dependent creatures on the way. Moreover, while I have focused particularly on Percy's philosophical contributions to jadedness, appreciation, and humility, there yet remains fruitful insight to be gleaned from his treatment of other virtues and vices, notably (in my view) on intellectual joy, empathy, and (relevant to jadedness) the virtue of hope. At least in philosophical moral psychology and virtue ethics, then, Percy's work continues to be a prescient and unique source of philosophical reflection and insight.

Notes

1. Many things are, after all, constantly (and automatically) relegated to "the background" of our evaluative experience, as a fundamental condition of any meaningful (foreground) experience. This point is relevant to my treatment of jadedness unfolding in this chapter. I assume that being or becoming jaded is prudentially, morally, and epistemologically problematic, and at times perhaps even constitutive of moral or epistemic vice

(perhaps similar to the vice of *acedia*). However, it is important to note that not all cases of jadedness are so problematic or vicious, and may indeed be a normal and healthy part of human development. Jaded disillusionment over broken relationships, for example, can make a person aware that something is wrong, and provoke a search for new experiences or options. So, while this chapter is primarily concerned with cases of problematic jadedness, it is important to acknowledge that there may be valuable kinds as well, and that this may be a fruitful area of future exploration. I am grateful to the professors and students of the Clovis Community College Philosophy Club, for their many insights into the prospects of a 'good' type of jadedness (Clovis Community College, April 2018).

2. Wittgenstein famously notes that "[a] main source of our failure to understand is that we do not *command a clear* view of the use of our words.— Our grammar is lacking in this sort of perspicuity. A perspicuous representation produces just that understanding which consists in 'seeing connexions'." This is the sort of methodology I pursue here, in an attempt to illumine the grammatical structure of our concept of jadedness

3. The authors follow John Locke's treatment in *Of the Conduct of the Understanding*. Roberts and Wood aptly describe prejudice as an intellectual vice "A person who suffers from prejudice adheres to certain beliefs for inadequate reasons, such as that he likes believing them, that is would cause him anxiety to give them up, that this is what people in his tribe have always believed, and that the investigation leading to the revision of these beliefs would cost him more trouble than he wants to spend. ... The four examples of inappropriate reasons ... are all appetitive states—aversions, preferences, attachments—which may not always be bad, except as they override the good of knowing the truth."

4. Of course, there is a sense in which bitter people can be driven by an inner insistence that others *should* see the evaluative picture the way the bitter person does. If a talented executive is passed over for a coveted vice-president position, which is given to an inferior person, he may well be bitter in light of the fact that the chief executive officer (CEO) (and now others in the company) don't *recognize* or acknowledge his genuine excellence and superiority over the other candidate. The fact that they have the evaluative picture wrong can be a powerful source of bitterness. But, the prideful stance of the cynic, while it can operate in tandem with seething bitterness, seems to involve what bitterness does not: ironic distance and a *detachment* from the social canons of evaluation in the company.

5. Prejudice seems capable of having past, present, or future objects, while cynicism seems more typically focused only on present or future realities. Bitterness seems distinctive in this sense, in that one can be bitter *about* one's present state or future prospects, but always (or characteristically) *in*

light of a past injury or unattained good, on which the bitter person disappointedly dwells. Of course, these mental states can interact: bitterness can *consequently* cause one to inhabit cynicism, or vice versa. For example, if the aforementioned father habitually disappoints the child in failing to appreciate the child's artistic gifts, the child may be bitter over the unattained recognitional goods, and grow up to take a cynical stance on his father. Suppose the father *does* begin to recognize and appreciate, the child may cynically and systematically deny the reality of the father's sincerity. Simply put, the cynical refusal to acknowledge goodness—because one "knows" better—is quite distinct from bitter resentment or disappointment over past goods unattained.

6. I am grateful to Dr. Adam Ghali, a clinical psychologist and colleague, for this insight while discussing his treatment of clients who become jaded. While being jaded may clinically *present* as pure indifference or apathy, the presentation, in Ghali's clinical view, is typically driven by something that matters (or once mattered) a great deal to the person.

7. For a thorough treatment of emotions as care-laden, "concern-based construals," see Roberts 2003. While it is true that the prejudiced person may be apathetic about or indifferent to beliefs or concerns that are not his own—in the sense that their evaluative or epistemic force may be silenced by his inadequate reasons—apathy or indifference is not *what it is* to be biased or prejudiced. For, prejudice is an *attachment* to cherished positions; indifference is a causal byproduct. For a thorough philosophical analysis of practical "silencing" in the context of virtue ethical practical wisdom and situational appreciation, see McDowell 1998, pp. 50–71.

8. I am grateful to San Francisco community activist Teresa Goines for this example. Goines is founder and CEO of *Old Skool Café* in the traditionally gunshot-ridden, southeast San Francisco neighborhood of Bayview/Hunter's Point.

9. I am grateful to Rachel Schultz, the mother in question, for this excellent example.

10. Toward the end of this chapter, this will become a critical point of connection between jadedness and failures of moral or intellectual humility.

11. Of course, this is just one possibility. Other antecedent and consequent relations between cynicism, bitterness, and jadedness (as well as contempt) are quite possible. For example, jadedness can sometimes function as a middle term on the journey from familiarity to something like contempt (or any number of other negative axiological orientations). If one becomes familiar with a given *x* to the point of fullness or satiety, one may therefore tire of it as well. Cases of marital partners becoming tired of each other is a common example here. When fullness followed by jaded fatigue sets in, this can apparently cause *subsequent* negative axiological psychic states beginning with the subtly negative judgment or construal that "this *x* isn't

worth my time." Of course, it isn't difficult to see why this can lead to further intensified states of cynicism, bitterness (over deserving something better), or contempt.

12. As "appreciation" is interpreted in philosophical aesthetics (where it receives the most systematic treatment), some historical examples include Aristotle's tragic emotions of pity and fear, Aquinas's delight in contemplation as an account of the beautiful, Kant's disinterested pleasure attending the awareness of beauty, and Dewey's notion of a complex yet unified "consummatory" aesthetic experience. For a denial that appreciation necessarily involves enjoyment, see Godlovitch 1997, p. 53. For a helpful literature review in philosophical aesthetics, see Carroll 2002a, p. 146. See also Schusterman 1997, p. 34, citing Beardsley 1958, p. 527; 1982, pp. 287–289. For an argument that cognitive appreciation just *is* evaluative appreciation (or understanding), see Boylu 2010, pp. 591–610. On the integrated character of appreciation, see Ryle 2009, p. 385. For a view that appreciation requires that we take the object (or one of its properties) to be good, or good *in some way*, see Dickie 1971, p. 105; Iseminger 1981, pp. 389–397. For appreciations that involve *indignation*, see Carroll 2002b, p. 149.

13. In this passage, Percy goes on to say that "[o]nly under the condition of ordeal may I recover the sparrow. If I am lying wounded or in exile or in prison and a sparrow builds its nest at my window, then I may see the sparrow. This is why new names must be found for being, as Heidegger thinks, or the old ones given new meaning, as Marcel thinks." Elsewhere, of course, Percy lists other modes of recovery as well.

14. I am grateful to Elizabeth Corey (2016, p. 1002) for this reference.

15. Percy does accept some aspects of these two theories, but seems to reject (1) their incoherent combination and (2) their respective claims to capture the whole of what it is to be a unified self. Scientifically he "subscribes" to a "Darwinian naturalistic concept of man" (SSL, pp. 113–15). However (without adhering to Cartesian substance dualism), Percy theologically subscribes to a "soul," viewing consciousness as a nonphysical entity. For a recent treatment on Percy's non-materialism, see Sykes 2016, pp. 1023–1042. For more on these issues from Percy, see SSL, p. 228 and CWP, pp. 63–64. For a summary treatment of the primary literature, see Carson 2013a, pp. 87–117. Notably, it is *unclear* whether Percy's non-reductive view of consciousness could be a type of non reductive *physicalism*, according to which consciousness is a real, emergent nonphysical property of physical systems, but not reducible to such systems. This would be closer, in fact, to a Thomistic "minimalist" dualism that borders on Aristotelian hylomorphism, but with some special persistence conditions assigned to the rational soul (while the self and the rational soul are nonequivalent). In fact, Thomistic hylomorphic dualism (whereby the soul is the form of the

material body) with a dash of Kierkegaardian reflexive self-relation seems like the best theory for Percy, given his frequent penchant for seeing human beings as a self-reflexive organic *unity* of the "angel" and "beast" categories. See, for example, LR, p. 35.

16. Revealing his debt to Kierkegaardian anxiety and a relational achievement view of the self, Percy notes that a person's "death-in-life may be manifest by the symptom of anxiety—the glimpsing of his own desperate plight and of the possibility, unrealized, of becoming himself." Southern Historical Collection, "Which Way Existentialism?". (Alexander 2016, p. 1054). For all Southern Historical Collection citations, I am indebted to Alexander for his excellent on-site archival work. For the non-Heideggerian sources of Percy's notions of anxious "death-in-life," see Kierkegaard 1980, p. 17.

17. Percy claims that "[t]o be a castaway is to be in a grave predicament and this is not a happy state of affairs. But it is very much happier than being a castaway and pretending one is not. This is despair" (MB, p. 144). Percy borrows the notion of selfhood as task from Kierkegaard, in such passages (for example) as The Concept of Anxiety, pp. 41–49, 111. Compare SSL, pp. 136–137 and MB, p. 24.

18. As he says, a "symbol is the vehicle for the conception of an object ... the vehicle by which we are able to speak and perhaps to think about something" (MB, p. 280).

19. For passages demonstrating this as a creational, "Edenic" gift and task, see LC, pp. 96, 106, 124.

20. Discussing the intentional as-structure of consciousness, Percy notes: "I am not only conscious *of* something; I am conscious of it as being what it is for you and me" (SLL, p. 124).

21. This is Percy's "symbolic corrective" of any attempts—whether by Anglo-American empiricism or existentialism—to defeat both the Cartesian *cogito* and the Kantian transcendental *ego*. Of course, this is similar to Wittgenstein's view that meaning is used in a social form of life, and Percy explicitly uses George H. Mead's notion that consciousness is "a phenomenon arising from the social matrix through language." For this and more on Percy's interpretation of Mead, see MB, pp. 266, 268, 274. Of course, Percy affirms Mead's thesis on the social constitution of consciousness, but rejects Mead's "dyadic" treatment of human beings as organisms engaged (merely) in stimulus-response behaviors.

22. Percy even claims that "it is inconceivable that a human being raised apart from other humans should ever discover symbolization" (MB, pp. 270, 272). Using Mead's social co-constitution of meaningful consciousness, Percy employs an empirically grounded, linguistic version of Gabriel Marcel's intersubjective communion and Martin Buber's "I–Thou" relation in order to develop a normative notion of what it is to be fully human

as co-namers and co-knowers, co-celebrants of being with each other. The *triadic* conception of the individual knower—including the symbol-maker, symbol, and object of Charles Sanders Pierce—becomes for Percy a *tetradic* intersubjectivity of shared knowledge and meaning between symbolizing selves. For more on Percy's treatment of Marcel and Buber, see MB, pp. 282–287.

23. What brings Percy's view close to Wittgenstein's claim that "meaning is use" in social life forms is that Percy does not restrict his claim about the role of others *simply* to that of origins, say, during our language acquisition process. Meaning is *always* for others, even if we are on a deserted island. Says Percy: "The second person is required as an element not merely in the genetic event of learning language but as the *indispensable and enduring condition of all symbolic behavior.* The very act of symbolic formulation, whether it be language, logic, art, or even thinking, is of its very nature a formulation for a *someone else.* Even Robinson Crusoe, writing in his journal after twenty years on the island, is nevertheless performing a through-and-through social and intersubjective act" (MB, p. 200).

24. MB, p. 285. Cf. p. 282. For more on Percy's treatment of social consciousness, see LC, pp. 96, 100, 105, and MB, pp. 265–276 (especially 275–276).

25. This problem of jadedness through socially established meanings can be construed in terms of socially mediated "experience packages," as Corey (2016, p. 1003) puts it.

26. Thus, says Percy, "[t]he bird itself has disappeared into the sarcophagus of its sign. The unique living creature is assigned to its class of signs, a second-class mummy in the basement collection of mummy cases" (SSL, p. 135). This is why Percy claims that "new names must be found for being, as Heidegger thinks, or the old ones given new meaning, as Marcel thinks" (LC, pp. 104–105).

27. The context here is illuminating: "The sightseer measures his satisfaction *by the degree to which the canyon conforms to the preformed complex.* If it does, if it looks just like the postcard, he is pleased; he might even say, 'Why it is every bit as beautiful as a picture postcard!' He feels he has not been cheated. But if it does not conform, if the colors are somber, he will not be able to see it directly; he will only be conscious of the disparity between what it is and what it is supposed to be. He will say later that he was unlucky in not being there at the right time" (MB, p. 47).

28. Thus does Percy note that "the tourist who carves his initials in a public place ... has good reasons for doing so. ... He does so because in his role of consumer of an experience ... he knows he is disinherited. He is deprived of his title over being. He knows very well that he is in a very special sort of zone in which his only rights are the rights of a consumer. He moves like a ghost through schoolroom, city streets, trains, parks, movies. He carves

his initials as a last desperate measure to escape his ghostly role of consumer. He is saying in effect: I am not a ghost after all; I am a sovereign person" (MB, p. 62).

29. This is a society, he says, in which "[t]here is a division between expert and layman, planner and consumer, in which experts take special measures to teach and edify the consumer. ... The expert and the planner *know* and *plan*, but the consumer *needs* and *experiences*" (MB, p. 61).

30. Throughout his corpus, Percy proposes various strategies for combatting this situation in order to recover the sovereign encounter with the freshness of particular being, through catastrophic ordeal, symbolic reinvention, phenomenological or poetic indirection, or appreciative absorption (even through scientific inquiry). For more on this, see LC, p. 105.

31. For an excellent summary of existential and methodological abstraction as it applies to the sciences, see Marsh 2016, pp. 993–998.

32. I am grateful to Corey (2016, p. 1005) for again drawing my attention to this passage.

33. For a thorough treatment of Kierkegaard on this matter, including arguments that objective knowledge plays an important and central role in his epistemology, see Carson, 2013b, pp. 29–49.

34. To gain a more accurate grasp of Percy's position here, it may be worth examining the details of his allegiance to the poet Gerard Manley Hopkins, who is notable for his view that we have an intuitive ability to grasp the "inscape" of things as particulars. What precise philosophical view of intuition, perception, and understanding does Hopkins's view entail? An answer would be illuminating here, but lies well beyond the scope of this chapter.

35. Roberts 2013, pp. 40–46 notes that one may *construe* it as (or *see it as*) either a duck or a rabbit (but never both at once), through a shift of role assignments to the different parts of the sensory data. What perceptually counts as a pair of ears (the rabbit) is perceptually reassigned a new role of beak on the duck construal.

36. Roberts and Wood (2007, p. 48) give a nice example of this "low-end" understanding. For instance, "to see a red bird outside of one's window involves something like understanding: recognizing the situation as having the elements and structure that it has: namely, that it is a bird, sitting on a branch, outside your window." Gestalt drawings make this role of understanding in perception more clear. Until one *makes sense* of the gestalt drawing as a duck or a rabbit, or both, all one sees is a jumble of lines and patches. So, say Roberts and Wood, "you have to understand even to have perceptions that give rise to propositional knowledge by way of basic belief formation."

37. For example, see Elgin 2006, pp. 199–215. See also Kvanvig 2003.

38. One example of this kind of appreciation, notes Klein, is a "direct, full, uncensored, unmediated, and unqualified experience." Klein also mentions watching sunsets, listening to Rubenstein, having sex, killing a charging tiger, engaging in battlefield experiences, and going on LSD trips. As a psychologist, Klein points out the contrast I will suggest. He says that "as our mental capacities develop ... we come to use our Power of Appreciation less and less. We reserve it for those special occasions when our mind says, 'This is an experience ... that is appropriate. Go ahead and appreciate it.' In other words, the cerebral realm of ideas and judgments *precedes* and acts as a censor of a more direct, appreciative knowing" (Klein 1988, p. 309). However, Klein is wrong to claim that such phenomenal-affective appreciations are "always positive," because negative and fragmentary appreciations (like the overwhelmed humanitarian mentioned above) are possible.

39. For a description of acquaintance knowledge, and how it differs from propositional knowledge and objectual understanding, see Roberts and Wood 2007, pp. 50–55.

40. For more on the nature of acquaintance knowledge (as opposed to propositional knowledge or high-level understanding), see Roberts and Wood 2007, pp. 32–58.

41. That is, a centrally defining feature of phenomenal-affective appreciative experience seems to be *the phenomenal quality of the experience itself*, rather than the epistemic goods involved in it, though the partial epistemic value of many such experiences can hardly be denied.

42. So while at times Percy does seem to promote an even stronger oppositional relation, namely, that sometimes phenomenal-affective appreciations have deep experiential value that is *unavailable* to more epistemically oriented appreciations "higher up" a supposed scale, he is not committed to the view of necessary incompatibility. He seems to endorse the far more plausible view that a progressive movement from the former to the latter *does not invariably deepen* one's appreciation, making it better and more rich. It may in fact do quite the opposite, in producing alienation from being.

43. This is so, even if the metaphysical object *qua* particular exists, as Percy seems to assume. For a rigorous philosophical defense of this view, see Kierkegaard 1985, p. 36. See also Perkins 1973, pp. 197–217. Note that I am here discussing only self-world appreciations, and not the unique appreciation of *persons*. The one case in which we may appreciate the particular as particular, for Percy, may be during the mutual "look" of pure intersubjectivity, whereby a mutual gaze between persons, under the right normative conditions, can function to affirm the unnameability or singular transcendence of the other. In this sense, the authentic intersubjective gaze affirms the non-universality of the other; no abstract concept can capture or settle the unique particular being who is the other. See SSL, p. 127; MB, p. 285.

44. Wonder, of course, is one traditional starting point for the philosophical activity of contemplation, and Percy may share Heidegger's concern that in our post-Cartesian lust for complete systems and their social and technological applications, we may lose our sovereign human task as meditative beings, who name but also actively *wonder* and contemplate at the intersection of naming and being. See Aristotle 2016, p. 5 (982b10), and Heidegger 1966, p. 56 (the "Memorial Address").

45. Commenting on Percy's diagnosis of the modern malaise, for example, Marsh (2016, p. 991) aptly notes that "[e]pistemic humility is not seen as a cultural virtue: it is the *zeitgeist* of the modern age that we exist in a (misperceived) linear trajectory of progress, progress here taken to be coextensive with *improvement*—morally, socially, technologically, economically, and scientifically."

46. I am indebted to Sykes (2016, p. 1023) for the label "*Homo Singularis*" as applied to Percy.

47. Percy also offers a more detailed example: "Modern science is itself radically incoherent ... when it seeks to understand man, not man's physiology or neurology or his bloodstream, but man *qua* man" (SSL, p. 271).

48. Here is the full Kierkegaardian context: "After twelve years of a scientific education I felt somewhat like the Danish philosopher Søren Kierkegaard when he finished reading Hegel. Hegel, said Kierkegaard, explained everything under the sun, except one small detail: what it means to be a man living in the world who must die." Southern Historical Collection, "Reflections of a Late-Blooming First Novelist" (Alexander 2016, p. 1047).

49. For a discussion of this point, see Marsh 2016, p. 992.

50. In his article "Is a Theory of Man Possible?" Percy elaborates: "Semiotics would call attention to the strange position of the symbolizing self in the world which it discovers. In a word, the self can perceive, formulate, symbolize everything under the sun except itself. A self stands in the dead center of its universe, looking out. The paradox of consciousness is that the stranger we meet on the street and glance at for a second or two we see more clearly than we shall ever see ourselves" (SSL, p. 127).

51. Here Percy jumps directly from this unsignifiability into a description of fallen people in despair who are "lost in the cosmos." Given his other texts and comments on the reality of unsignifiability as a creational aspect of human constitution, we must not interpret this text in LC to mean that the unnameability of the self is *only* a fallen predicament. For Percy, the fact that "the being of the namer slips through the fingers of naming" is a creational reality, tied as it is to the very makeup of triadic consciousness and being. And it is this unsignifiability that forever binds human beings to the task of becoming themselves in the "flux of becoming." Cf. SSL, p. 136.

52. See also SSL, pp. 135–136 for further connections to Kierkegaard. For a detailed analysis of Kierkegaard's *The Concept of Anxiety* and its relevance to Percy's project, see Carson 2007.

53. Here, and elsewhere, there is plentiful evidence that Percy views the creational self as *necessarily* marked by anxiety in light of semiotic unsignifiability, and not merely anxious in virtue of an aberrant loss of self in the modern age (SSL, pp. 260–261). He says, for instance, that such anxiety may be an "*appropriate*" reaction "for the man who confronts himself and discovers—nothing" (SSL, pp. 252, 254; Cf. also LC, pp. 109–111). Here, Percy draws upon and re-theologizes Erich Fromm's treatment in *The Sane Society* (1955), of a "pathology of normalcy" people experience due to being commodified in a capitalist age. Regarding the self as a "nothing," Percy clarifies that he is not endorsing a Sartrean view of the self as literally a hypostatized nothing: "The being of the namer slips through the fingers of naming. If he tries to construe himself in the same mode by which he construes the rest of the world, he must necessarily construe himself as a nothing, as Sartre's characters do. But this is not to say that I am nothing; this is only to say that I am that which I cannot name. I am rather a person, a namer and a hearer of names" (SSL, pp. 136–37).

54. In "The Scandal of Judeo-Christianity," Percy presses home the point that there is more to being human than either immanent selfhood or theoretical completion: "The so-called existentialists ... all agree that the objective posture of the sciences is wholly inadequate as a means of knowing man, both in its avowed attempt to understand man as a specimen-object and in its hidden elite category of man as scientist-man. Man is neither. He is neither that which can be so understood [n]or that which so understands. He is both and more." Southern Historical Collection, "The Scandal of Judeo Christianity" (Alexander 2016, p. 1053).

55. DeYoung (2014, p. 78, note 6) says that for Aquinas, humility is the root of the tree of virtues (*Summa theologiae* II-II 23.8 ad 2–3), and St. Benedict famously outlines 12 steps of Christian humility in his *Rule*, chapter 7.

56. Dunnington (2016) helpfully mentions one such case of humility's centrality: "Aristotle does not include humility anywhere in his ethics, but for Augustine humility is the centerpiece of Christian virtue. So crucial is humility to authentic virtue that Augustine argues in *City of God* that pagans cannot be genuinely virtuous because they cannot be humble (5.12)."

57. See Richards 1988, p. 253. See also Statman 1992, p. 432; Schueler 1997, p. 470; 1999, pp. 835–841. Also, Dunnington (2016, pp. 19–20) summarizes all of the key problems in. My survey of the issues in the humility literature is greatly (and principally) indebted to Dunnington 2016 and 2017.

58. Roberts and Wood hold to the low concern view, while Richards (1988) and Flanagan (1990) defend the accurate self-assessment view.

59. See, for example, Dunnington's (2016, p. 33) account of Augustine's critique that the pagan heroic virtue tradition is infected with *superbia*: "Augustine … locates a quest for a secure and independent self-image at the heart of pagan virtue. This, he argues, is in fact the essence of *superbia*, the quest for a self-image that is secure even in the face of biological death—a kind of immortal identity—and a self-image that reflects selfsufficiency—a kind of identity that is free from any ultimate neediness. For Augustine, Christian *humilitas* as the antithesis of pagan *superbia* is the rejection of these two impulses of pagan virtue." For materials on the desert fathers and mothers, see Dunnington (2017a).

60. Explaining how such humility can also belong to God, Dunnington notes: "Radical dependence is the will to receive completely one's being from the generosity of another and the will to give of oneself completely for the being of another. As such, the archetype of humility is the Trinitarian life of God."

61. While I cannot give it full treatment here, Percy's emphasis on identitydependence with *human* others is substantial, and plays a role in pointing us toward God-dependence. One aspect of Percy's unique cure for jadedness surely involves our deep dependence on others not only for our native vocation of co-discovering, and co-celebrating the meaning of worlds we inhabit, but also for their ability to unmask our drive to be settled, autonomous, objectified things. For Percy, the "I–Thou" relation of intersubjectivity is normatively loaded, for under ideal circumstances, the "look" of the other *unsettles* one's inauthentic settledness as an autonomous something or world-object with finished stable predicates, for the look "discovers" and affirms the privative, creaturely status of the self. It affirms my literal "unspeakableness" (unsignifiability) and makes genuine love and community possible (SLL, p. 127; MB, p. 285). Where such intersubjective communion and love occurs, it functions as a gift and "sign" that opens the self outward, for Percy, toward a transcendent source of that love. See, for example, the closing passage of Percy's novel SC, where the protagonist Will Barrett realizes that the love he shares with Allison Huger is a gift, and therefore a sign of a Giver (SC, p. 360).

62. Among other things, this is why Percy emphasizes the role of catastrophe or *ordeal* as a mechanism for recovery of the self, for surprise at the unanticipated (good or bad) immediately makes one present, volitionally and epistemically engaged, and aware of a new, heretofore invisible, possible way of being.

REFERENCES

Alexander, Benjamin B. 2016. Confessions of a Late-Blooming, 'Miseducated' Philosopher of Science. *Zygon* 51 (4): 1054.

Aquinas, Thomas. 2003. *De Malo*. Trans. Richard Regan. Ed. Brian Davies. Oxford: Oxford University Press.

Aristotle. 1999. *Nicomachean Ethics*. Trans. Terence Irwin. Indianapolis: Hackett.

———. 2016. *Metaphysics*. Trans. C. D. C. Reeve. Indianapolis: Hackett Publishing.

Beardsley, Monroe. 1958. *Aesthetics: Problems in the Philosophy of Criticism*. New York: Harcourt Brace.

———. 1982. *The Aesthetic Point of View*. Ithaca: Cornell University Press.

Boylu, Ayca. 2010. How Understanding Makes Knowledge Valuable. *Canadian Journal of Philosophy* 40 (4): 591–610.

Carroll, Noël. 2002a. Aesthetic Experience Revisited. *British Journal of Aesthetics* 42 (2): 146.

———. 2002b. *Philosophy of Art: A Contemporary Introduction*. London: Routledge.

Carson, Nathan. 2007. At the Heart of Anthropology: Søren Kierkegaard and Walker Percy on the Nature and Shape of Creational Selfhood. Unpublished Th.M. thesis.

———. 2013a. Walker Percy's Theory of Man and the Elimination of Virtue. In: *A Political Companion to Walker Percy*, ed. Peter Augustine Lawler and Brian A. Smith. Lexington: University Press of Kentucky.

———. 2013b. Passionate Epistemology: Kierkegaard on Skepticism, Approximate Knowledge, and Higher Existential Truth. *Journal of Chinese Philosophy* 40 (1):29–49.

———. 2013c. *Appreciation: Its Nature and Role in Virtue Ethical Moral Psychology and Dialectical Moral Agency*. Waco: Baylor University. (unpublished dissertation).

Corey, Elizabeth. 2016. Life on the Island. *Zygon* 51 (4): 1002.

DeYoung, Rebecca. 2014. *Vainglory: The Forgotten Vice*. Grand Rapids: Eerdmans.

Dickie, George. 1971. *Aesthetics: An Introduction*. Indianapolis: Pegasus.

Diogenes Laertius. 1925. *The Lives of Eminent Philosophers*. Vol. II (Books VI–X). Trans. R. D. Hicks; Ed. E. Capps, T. E. Page, and W. H. D. Rouse. London: William Heinemann.

Driver, Julia. 1989. The Virtues of Ignorance. *The Journal of Philosophy* 86 (7): 381.

Dunnington, Kent. 2016. Humility, An Augustinian Perspective. *Pro Ecclesia* XXV (1): 23.

———. 2017a. Radical Christian Humility. *Philosophy Lecture Series: Vice, Vainglory, and Humility*. Conference presentation, Fresno Pacific University, March 23, 2017.

————. 2017b. Intellectual Humility and the Ends of the Virtues: Conflicting Aretaic Desiderata. *Political Theology* 18 (2): 95–114.

Elgin, Catherine. 2006. From Knowledge to Understanding. In *Epistemology Futures*, ed. Stephen Hetherington. Oxford: Clarendon Press.

Flanagan, Owen. 1990. Virtue and Ignorance. *The Journal of Philosophy* 87: 420–428.

Godlovitch, Stan. 1997. Carlson on Appreciation. *Journal of Aesthetics and Art Criticism* 55 (1): 53.

Heidegger, Martin. 1966. *Discourse on Thinking*. Trans. John M. Anderson and E. Hans Freund. New York: Harper & Row.

Iseminger, Gary. 1981. Aesthetic Appreciation. *The Journal of Aesthetics and Art Criticism* 39 (4): 389–397.

Klein Donald, C. 1988. The Power of Appreciation. *American Journal of Community Psychology* 16 (3): 305–324.

Kierkegaard, Søren. 1980. *The Concept of* Anxiety. Trans. and Ed. Reidar Thomte. Princeton: Princeton University Press.

————. 1985. *Philosophical Fragments*. Trans. and eds. Howard V. Hong and Edna H. Hong. Princeton: Princeton University Press.

Kvanvig, Jonathan. 2003. *The Value of Knowledge and the Pursuit of Understanding*. New York: Cambridge University Press.

Lawson, Lewis A., and Victor Kramer, eds. 1985. *Conversations with Walker Percy*. Jackson: University Press of Mississippi.

Marsh, Leslie. 2016. Philosopher of Precision and Soul: Introducing Walker Percy. *Zygon* 51 (4): 993–998.

McDowell, John. 1998. Virtue and Reason. In: *Mind, Value, and Reality*, 50–71. Cambridge, MA: Harvard University Press.

Murdoch, Iris. 2001. The Idea of Perfection. In *The Sovereignty of Good*. London: Routledge.

Murray, James A. H., Bradley Henry, W. A. Craigie, and C. T. Onions, eds. 1961. *The Oxford English Dictionary*. Vol. V (H-K). Amen House, London: Oxford University Press.

Percy, Walker. 1971. *Love in the Ruins*. New York: Farrar Straus and Giroux.

————. 1975. *Message in the Bottle: How Queer Man Is, How Queer Language Is, and What One Has to Do with the Other*. New York: Farrar, Straus, & Giroux.

————. 1980. *The Second Coming*. New York: Farrar, Straus, & Giroux.

————. 1983. *Lost in the Cosmos: The Last Self-Help Book*. New York: Farrar, Straus, & Giroux

————. 1986. The Diagnostic Novel: On the Uses of Modern Fiction. *Harper's Magazine* 272: 39–45.

————. 1987. *The Thanatos Syndrome*. New York: Farrar, Straus, & Giroux.

————. 1991. *Signposts in a Strange Land*. Ed. Patrick Samway. New York: Farrar, Straus, & Giroux.

Perkins, Robert L. 1973. Kierkegaard's Epistemological Preferences. *International Journal for Philosophy of Religion* 4 (4): 197–217.

Richards, Norvin. 1988. Is Humility a Virtue? *American Philosophical Quarterly* 25 (3): 253.

Roberts, Robert C. 2003. *Emotions: An Essay in Aid of Moral Psychology.* Cambridge: Cambridge University Press.

Roberts, Robert C., and Ryan West. 2017. Jesus and the Virtues of Pride. In: *The Moral Psychology of Pride,* ed. J. Adam Carter and Emma Gordon. Lanham: Rowman & Littlefield.

Roberts, Robert C., and W. Jay Wood. 2007. *Intellectual Virtues: An Essay in Regulative Epistemology.* Oxford: Oxford University Press.

Ryle, Gilbert. 2009. On Forgetting the Difference Between Right and Wrong. In: *Collected Essays 1929–1968: Collected Papers Volume 2.* London: Routledge.

Schueler, G. F. 1997. Why Modesty Is a Virtue. *Ethics* 107 (3): 470.

———. 1999. Why Is Modesty a Virtue? *Ethics* 109 (4): 835–841.

Schusterman, Richard. 1997. The End of Aesthetic Experience. *The Journal of Aesthetics and Art Criticism* 55 (1): 34.

Snow, Nancy. 2005. Humility. In *Personal Virtues: Introductory Essays,* ed. Clifford Williams. Basingstoke: Palgrave Macmillan.

Statman, Daniel. 1992. Modesty, Pride and Realistic Self-Assessment. *The Philosophical Quarterly* 42 (169): 432.

Sykes, John. 2016. Walker Percy, Language, and *Homo Singularis. Zygon* 51 (4): 1023–1042.

Whitcomb, Dennis, Heather Battaly, Jason Baehr, and Daniel Howard-Snyder. 2015. Intellectual Humility: Owning Our Limitations. *Philosophy and Phenomenological Research* 91 (1): 1–31.

Wittgenstein, Ludwig. 1962. *Philosophical Investigations.* Trans. Elizabeth Anscombe. New York: The Macmillan Company.

CHAPTER 12

Percy on the Allure of Violence and Destruction

Brian A. Smith

Anxiety concerning the decline and fall of civilization appears throughout Percy's body of work. What sets Percy's account of this issue apart from others rests in his preoccupation not only with depicting actual disaster for what it might tell us about human nature or our politics, but also his focus on mining our obsession with the end of our society as a clue that might help explain our predicament in modern times.

> The contingency "what if the Bomb should fall?" is not only not a cause of anxiety in the alienated man but is one of his few remaining refuges from it. When everything else fails, we may always turn to our good friend just back from Washington or Moscow, who obliges us with his sober second thoughts—"I can tell you this much, I am profoundly disturbed..."—and each of us has what he came for, the old authentic thrill of the Bomb and the Coming of the Last Days (MB, pp. 84–85)

As a novelist and essayist, Percy saw his role as reading the signs of our spiritual and social disorders, and rendering them intelligible to an audi-

B. A. Smith (✉)
Liberty Fund, Inc., Carmel, IN, USA
e-mail: bsmith@libertyfund.org

© The Author(s) 2018
L. Marsh (ed.), *Walker Percy, Philosopher*,
https://doi.org/10.1007/978-3-319-77968-3_12

251

ence that increasingly possessed a language inadequate to understanding the situation.

Percy's method here matches his understanding of the limitations of current language. He suggested that if you tell a contemporary American he or she suffers from alienation, he or she probably will not understand your point. Indeed, without recourse to therapeutic or medical terminology, it is unclear that he or she could comprehend the diagnosis. By contrast, Percy suspected that a writer who depicts alienation in a story that engages the reader's emotions, naming the situation in relatable terms, might have some ability to reveal the notion to his readers. Percy wrote:

> A serious novel about the destruction of the United States and the end of the world should perform the function of prophecy in reverse. The novelist writes about the coming end in order to warn about present ills and so avert the end (MB, p. 101)

When authors attempt this warning function, however, Percy insists that a direct approach cannot easily avail itself of success. But how can a person with a deeply impoverished language and, hence, a limited notion of how to think about her existence, see her spiritual predicament?

Percy argued that having a talent for seeing the "fault lines in the terrain, small clues that something strange is going on, a telltale sign here and there" becomes an increasingly important role in times like our own, in part because sketching the appearance of apocalyptic moments and images of decaying social order provide important contexts within which we might examine ourselves (SSL, p. 155). The technique of presenting such notions as real stories or thought problems

> not only makes for ordinary good adventure but for interesting theological experiments. What is good and bad about wiping out the whole crazy edifice of Western civilization? What realities, good and bad, does a survivor confront who finds himself alone in a rest stop off I-80 in Utah? (MCWP, p. 131).

When we dismiss patterns of thought like this as evidence of insanity, we miss the chance to understand the motives behind the longing and the social and political disturbances they might portend. Percy believed that to address these ideas head on, in a directly moral or theological key, is to end the possibility of conversation with most modern people. The best way to address the real crises of the present comes from *not* talking about them directly at all (SSL, p. 158).

Boredom, Alienation, and the Idea of Death-in-Life

One source of our alienation rests in the ways that the very material objects and goals modern people pursue rarely satisfy us for long (LC, pp. 80–82). Indeed, once we secure them, boredom sets in, and creates one of the conditions under which the desire for disaster might creep into our consciousness. In LC, Percy offered several possible explanations of this condition. He noted that the very word boredom did not exist prior to the eighteenth century and asked why this might be, suggesting this answer as a possibility:

> Is it because there is a special sense in which for the past two or three hundred years the self has perceived itself as a leftover which cannot be accounted for by its own objective view of the world and that in spite of an ever-heightened self-consciousness, increased leisure, ever more access to cultural and recreational facilities, ever more instruction on self-help, self-growth, self-enrichment, the self feels ever more imprisoned in itself—no, worse than imprisoned because a prisoner at least knows he is imprisoned and sets store by the freedom awaiting him and the world seems to be open when in fact the self is not and it is not—a state of affairs which has to be called something besides imprisonment—e.g., boredom. Boredom is the self being stuffed with itself (LC, pp. 70–71).

Two crucial elements emerge in this description. First, an objective, empirically-oriented, and materialistic theory of the person as want- and need-satisfier faces significant challenges if the various wants and needs the human person pursues have the unintended effect of increasing their alienation from others. Second, Percy suggested here that the "softening" elements of modern progress—the elimination of inequality, struggle, violence, and so on—might contribute to our distress. Comfort may not deliver the happiness we initially trust it might provide.

Percy contended that American writers usually suffer deep alienation. Paradoxically, they feel a kind of envy for persecuted writers. Speaking of the 1960s and 1970s American protest novelists in particular, Percy wrote: "My theory is that he secretly envies Aleksandr Solzhenitsyn, despite the terrible ordeal Solzhenitsyn suffered, despite his rightest [*sic*] sympathies. He envies the fact that a novelist can so irritate the state that the state will go to a great deal of trouble to get rid of him" (SSL, p. 171). We might further distinguish Percy's point from that of strict materialists: an obsession with material causes misses a critical dimension of this problem in that no one is totally reducible to their set of material circumstances. If they were, alienation would be subject to surer and more permanent remedy.

Because Percy defined alienation in relation to the objective-empirical mode of self-understanding that characterizes scientism and materialism, he believed that naming our alienation could reverse that anxious and out-of-place feeling (MB, p. 84). By naming the phenomenon, the human person momentarily restores their sovereignty and sense of agency—they are no longer totally subject to the nameless circumstances of the moment. Reversal is an appropriate description of Percy's concept of alienation in two senses: first, that it literally inverts the materialist assumption that a good environment breeds happy people; second, it focuses on the opposite concerns, beginning from the heart and soul of the person and only secondarily considers the environment in which the person lives.

In his novels, Percy shed considerable light on the strange features that come with living in boredom and alienation. In SC, one of the protagonists, Will Barrett, recounts a discussion with his father about alienation and the state of being within which modern Americans must live:

> "The trouble is," the man said, "there is no word for this. ... It's not war and it's not peace. It's not death and it's not life. What is it? What do you call it?"
>
> "I don't know."
>
> "There is life and there is death. Life is better than death but there are worse things than death."
>
> "What?"
>
> "There is no word for it. Maybe it never happened before and so there is no word for it. What is the word for a state which is not life and not death, a death in life?" (SC, p. 126).

The idea that we might be biologically alive and nevertheless emotionally dead to significant aspects of reality recurs throughout Percy's novels, but here Will's father articulates above all the pain of not being able to name his dilemma. What distinguishes this account is the insistence that we can be like ghosts still haunting the earth, ill at ease with our condition but incapable of escaping it, either. Will's father ultimately refuses to countenance this state of affairs and commits suicide.

In MG, Percy presented a similar account through Binx Bolling's observations about how he and others deal with ordinary conversations.

Binx does not know how to deal with small talk, and Percy's presentation of his disposition bears some examination:

> For some time now the impression has been growing upon me that everyone is dead.
>
> It happens when I speak to people. In the middle of a sentence it will come over me: yes, beyond a doubt this is death. There is little to do but groan and make an excuse and slip away as quickly as one can. At such times it seems that the conversation is spoken by automatons who have little choice in what they say (MG, pp. 99–100).

This is not just an introvert's protest against small talk. The death Binx describes is that which follows from philosophical materialism: an alienated people who do not see themselves as capable of choice and reflection are left with little more than idle observations about the weather or the market—that is, forces beyond their control. People pronounce their bland opinions, seek to avoid offense, and this for Binx is another sign of their inner death.

However, this does not reach the depth of Binx's confusion and irritation at this state of affairs. He has an easier time dealing with "negative" emotions such as anger and hate than the sort of bland kindness one often encounters in our world. He explains this curiosity:

> Whenever I feel bad, I go to a library and read controversial periodicals. Though I do not know whether I am a liberal or a conservative, I am nevertheless enlivened by the hatred which one bears the other. In fact, this hatred strikes me as one of the few signs of life remaining in the world. This is another thing about the world which is upside down: all the friendly and likeable people seem dead to me; only the haters seem alive (MG, p. 100).

Opposition is at least lively; hate reflects a certain presence of will that all too many alienated wanderers lack. Compared to this, the objective-empirical approach of the social sciences as much as the kindness of a New Age toleration may not measure up as antidotes to our era's spiritual malaise. If the standard remedies to our unhappiness—seeking comfort, pleasure, and wealth—only make alienation worse, where might a person turn for an alternative?

Percy argued that many of the possible paths of escape from alienation and boredom defy the bourgeois understanding of happiness. Despairing of one's condition may be the beginning of wisdom and a search for a better way to live, but without an adequate language or theory of the self to cope with this condition, the despair may naturally lead to suicide. The moral and political danger Percy identified here rests in the fact that the easiest forms of escape from alienation result from some of the darkest motivations in the human heart. Envy is the most prominent of these.

Envy as Response to Alienation

The persistence of alienation does not prevent people from attempting to live by weak theories of the self or by immersing themselves in acts of consumption that never quite satisfy their longings. Thankfully, most people do not throw themselves wholeheartedly into radically illiberal or anti-bourgeois ideas or political movements. But at the same time, people do not simply embrace the fact of alienation and attempt to cope. Instead, Percy argued that the most common response to this feeling takes the form of envy. Envy erodes the basis upon which human relations flourish, but it confers curious pleasures on those that embrace it as a way of relating to others.

Percy addressed the subject of envy most pointedly in his 1983 satire LC. His analysis of the subject began with a broad definition, as he reminds the reader of "the root sense of envy: *invidere*, to look at with malice" (LC, p. 57). Thus, as a phenomenon envy incorporates not just the comparisons people make between themselves and others, but also situations where we judge past and present circumstances against one another. Think here of the way Percy used all kinds of invidious comparison between circumstances in MG—Binx Bolling continually contrasted being mired in the everyday. By sketching this mode of envious experience, Percy suggested that a searcher like Binx might constantly undermine the dignity and worth of his present relationships and places by contrasting them against a fugitive standard of perfection.

Percy began his discussion of envy in LC with an example of how we might rethink the concept:

> Everyone remembers what he was and what he was doing when he heard the news of the Kennedy assassination – or, if he is old enough, Pearl Harbor.
>> Why?
> The self deceives itself by saying that it is natural that such terrible events be etched in the memory.
>> It is not so simple.

The fact is that the scene and circumstances of hearing such news become invested with a certain significance and density which they do not ordinarily possess and with which ordinary events and ordinary occasions contrast unfavorably (LC, p. 57).

Perhaps it is in the nature of such comparison that the present usually comes up short when we measure it against the exciting moments of our past. The density to which Percy referred here seems to center on pain: people compare their awful past to the boring present, and, strangely, the past seems better. This provokes myriad dissatisfactions: we remember exciting and exceptional moments with a kind of vividness denied to our recollections and experience of everyday life, so those humdrum occurrences naturally lose value. Binx Bolling's desire to "savor" the passage of time springs to mind here. If we constantly engage in rumination and comparison between the vivid experiences of our past, the ordinary present almost always suffers.

Percy argued that as a result of this way our memory tends to distort the past and color our view of the present, a kind of nostalgia for the horrible past creeps into our lives. Given Percy's descriptions of this phenomenon, it is easy to imagine individuals looking back at war or crisis and thinking "at least then I knew my place and purpose." Walker's guardian William Alexander Percy's sensibility concerning war fits this notion as well—it was misery but vital, mysterious, and offered charms that civilian life could not. Immersion in such purposeful circumstances offers a way out of our boredom. The memory of that past can cast a shadow on the present, devaluing it in a way that makes it difficult to partake in communities or friendships that might guard us against the worst elements of our alienation.

Our envy toward others follows a similar pattern as this nostalgic longing: we look to others and imagine we see something better or less everyday than our own circumstances and feel anger or disgust at our life—or we see misfortune befall others and feel delight. Neither variation makes it easy to treat one's neighbor as a full partner in conversation and community. To take one of Percy's examples, imagine that our neighbor Charlie has received multiple pieces of good news today, and relates them to us with joy. At best we can express sympathetic happiness for Charlie. Percy asked his readers to ponder: "how much good news about Charlie can you tolerate without compensatory catastrophes, heroic rescues, and such?" (LC, p. 65). Percy's account of misfortune and envy focused on the comparisons we make in part because he suspected that the average alienated, depressed, anxiety-ridden person of our age can always interpret other people's misfortune in at least two ways (LC, p. 60).

First, we can see such bad news as "unrelievedly bad." Percy offered the example of a UFO destroying Omaha, Nebraska. A person given to view the situation in this category would have to "see nothing good about the loss of several hundred thousand people" (Ibid.). Percy believed that this is sometimes a difficult attitude to maintain, and that our temptations toward envy of interesting circumstances run deep. Percy's second way to view an unfortunate event, that of the "putatively bad," poses a challenge to us in part because there is a species of news which "by all criteria should be bad but in which you nevertheless take a certain comfort." The value here springs from the excitement new and dangerous circumstances generate. This relates back to nostalgia for war: death and disaster restore our appreciation for life, but only because of our general malice and indifference. So, when the aliens attack, Omaha might be nothing more than a crater, but an individual might say to himself that "I don't know anybody in Omaha," and become excited that the world just became a more interesting place because aliens are real (Ibid.).

In the case of bad news, Percy believed that people face serious temptations to feel excitement at others' misfortune. They might also suffer from the equal and opposite temptation to want the other person to suffer some disaster. The malice in both circumstances allows for a kind of imaginative escape from everydayness. In the case of bad news, Percy thought that the value this creates for the envious person comes from the resulting experience of seeing the world in a new light. So, for example, if aliens are real and may come to destroy our city next, that may cause us terror, but also brings about great excitement. More importantly, it restores unalienated focus to our lives. This notion is important because it helps clarify what so many scholars strain to explain: why so many Europeans volunteered for World War I with such excitement, and remained wedded to a view of the war as liberating or transformative for so many years.[1]

We face the temptation to view destruction and chaos as a positive good simply because it offers us an escape from our alienation and boredom with ourselves and our environment. People might embrace at least the idea of that escape perhaps even if that event will bring unimagined horror. Percy suggested that the mildest and most likely outcome is that we retreat into exceptions from the everyday in more mundane ways: through our imaginations, in our conversations about news, and in our attitudes—overt and covert—toward disaster.

DAYDREAMS OF CATASTROPHE AND THE DESIRE FOR ESCAPE

In comparison with our bored, alienated lives, contemplating our society's destruction, the end of the world, and even suicide bears certain charms. Imagining these events in a healthy manner might have some salutary effects. Thinking seriously about the decline and fall of our society may not just prompt the hypothetical, "what if we could do this...?" that liberates our thinking from convention; it may also have the important effect of helping shape ideas that forestall catastrophes and reinvigorate politics and society. When Percy wrote about the nature of creating apocalypse in fiction and likened his role to that of a canary in a coal mine, he also claimed that his goal was to avert the end before it arrived (MB, p. 101). This view might allow us to genuinely appreciate the gifts that life can offer and restore the concept of wayfaring to dignity.

Seriously contemplating suicide can have a peculiarly enlivening effect on the mind. In his discussion of suicide, Percy asked the reader to invert the usual hypothesis about depression, and, instead, consider the possibility that any human being who is *not* depressed in our era deserves to be called deranged (LC, p. 76). Percy considered undertaking a mental experiment with deadly seriousness. The reality of the choice—one that Percy implied people seldom contemplate with any frankness—is fairly monstrous. Percy did not think suicide a noble act by any means. Yet, he argued that contemplating and ultimately rejecting suicide "dispenses" the contemplative soul: "Why not live, instead of dying? You are free to do so. You are like a prisoner released from the cell of his life. ... Where you might have been dead, you are alive" (LC, pp. 77–78). The act of contemplating this enlivens the mind and lets us reconsider our situation, perhaps awakening the possibility of a search for a place of actual rest rather than the usual American journey toward fugitive perfection.

Percy claimed an "ex-suicide" knows that he does not *have to* live and can grapple with his or her alienation on better terms than others might. The person who drifts through life in acts of theory and consumption actively flees from recognizing this. Indeed, if a man chooses to live with the theorist-consumer belief that he is merely the product of an environment, if he grows depressed, on what basis could he resist the lure of suicide if the tools of psychiatry and therapy do not help him? Such a man might seek fulfillment by being either an immanent body seeking pleasure, or a transcending mind searching for complete answers. Both paths ignore our embodied nature and the real needs of the soul. While the ex-suicide can potentially see this, most of Percy's characters initially do not—and fall into more destructive patterns.

Percy explored this need for ever-increasing danger at the beginning of SC, where Will Barrett, deeply depressed, alienated, and suffering from inexplicable fainting episodes, plays a dangerous game with his father's old Luger pistol. In earlier times, he tells the reader that simply firing the pistol into a gorge had previously shocked him out of his "spells," but by the outset of the novel, the effect had diminished. So, Will acted more dangerously still, and fired the pistol past his own face (SC, p. 14). Only the real contemplation of self-destruction gives Barrett a few moments of respite and clarity. He accepts the possibility of exit but has no way of comprehending what this might tell him about his life. This "remedy" promises no communion with others, only a slight escape from alienation and the tedium of an ordinary Tuesday afternoon. At best it provides a possibility; a moment for a person to reconsider their choices in life. An external threat, however, sometimes proves more fruitful.

Percy thought that people usually fear pain and often fear death, but violence itself serves as a catalyst for escaping our alienation and boredom in the world. One illustrative example from MG demonstrates this well. In it, Binx Bolling recounts how boredom and alienation beset his life, and only a serious combat injury in the Korean War freed him:

> Everydayness is the enemy. No search is possible. Perhaps there was a time when everydayness was not too strong and one could break its grip by brute strength. Now nothing breaks it—but disaster. Only once in my life was the grip of everydayness broken: when I lay bleeding in a ditch (MG, p. 145).

Binx's quest to escape the everyday fails repeatedly; he finds respite only through accident and the memory of becoming a war casualty.[2] Binx does not give voice to why this is the case. Being injured and surviving focuses one's attention on all the details of one's surroundings, because only there does a man "miss nothing." In Binx's case it enlivened his mind. But if this becomes the standard for what being "cured" of everydayness entails, ordinary life must always suffer. Accidents can serve a similar function. Percy explored this through an incident in Will Barrett's life in SC.

Returning home after experimenting with the Luger, Barrett comes under rifle fire in his garage, suffering a cut from the ricochet. He notices two things about his life in the moments around the shot. Before the shot, he had observed a cat and realized that the problem with human beings is that unlike the cat, "for whom one place was the same as any other place so long as it was sunny," human beings are constantly out of place. Moreover, unlike man's perception of his own personhood,

> the cat was exactly a hundred percent cat, no more no less. As for Will Barrett, as for people nowadays—they were never a hundred percent themselves. They occupied a place uneasily and or less successfully. More likely they were forty-seven percent themselves or rarely, as in the case of Einstein on the streetcar, three hundred percent. All too often these days they were two percent themselves, specters who hardly occupied a place at all (SC, p. 16).

Percy presented a fascinating analogy for alienation here, one that provides an explanation for how people float between immanent, embodied pleasure and transcendent mental states. The idea that our selves need to be rejoined with our bodies in order for us to truly feel at home in the world echoes his account of why people use drugs and alcohol to achieve a catlike effect. They anesthetize the feeling of being out of place and can simply abide as bodies free from the peril of consciousness. By contrast, one can transcend one's momentary existence by becoming immersed in a world of fantasy or ideas. But neither lasts, and neither allows us to actually live with the reality of human everydayness, with what Barrett calls living as "forty-seven percent themselves."

Returning to the shooting, Will notes that when the shot rings out, he noticed a paradoxical difference in response between him and the animal:

> Quicker than any drug, in the instant in fact of hearing and recognizing the gunshot, he was, as he expressed it, miraculously restored to himself. The cat of course had jumped four feet straight up and fled in terror, as any sensible animal would, reduced instantly to zero percentile of its well-being. But Barrett? The missing ninety-eight percent is magically restored! How? By the rifle shot! (SC, p. 17).

Animals respond with alarm and fear at bad environments, but the same circumstances can heighten human reality in some ways. Fear and violence can move us out of alienation and into a sense of liveliness that was lacking before, especially if the events are not random but purposive. Indeed, Barrett betrays his disappointment that the stray shot came from a poacher, and not from an enemy wishing him harm (SC, pp. 18–19).

Percy thought that people often find the retelling of more distant disaster diverting as well. Percy's most Nietzschean character, Lance Lamar, called the anticipation he felt on watching the nightly news "the sweet horrid dread we had been waiting for" (L, p. 72). Using Lance, Percy intimated that alienated, bored, and sentimental people may not easily admit this longing, but that they enjoy hearing of disaster. But this distant and vicarious experience does not suffice for some people: if news alone sufficed, people would not stare at accidents or rush to disasters to look upon them in person (MB, pp. 6–7). Even this, however, stands at a remove from experiencing a disaster, violence, or accident oneself. Actually feeling the thrill of danger may be even better. In a 1990 interview, Percy observed the following:

> In Louisiana we have hurricanes. My theory is that people enjoy hurricanes, whether they say so or not. In a hurricane terrible things are happening, but there is a certain exhilaration. It comes from a peculiar sense of self, the vividness. ... Louisianans enjoy hurricanes, if they're not too bad (MCWP, p. 240).

Percy posited a curious relationship here: the closer the danger and nearer the experience, the greater is the escape from the ordinary. Natural disasters will come and go. The political danger here rests with the desire to not just embrace the exceptional circumstances when they crash in upon ordinary life, but rather to pursue them in a way that makes danger or violence the norm. In this vein, consider the works of Carl Schmitt and Ernst Jünger, both of whom defended a form of social and political life ordered around a warlike mentality. Percy's point in drawing our attention to these feelings is that our seemingly innocent longings of the heart all too often spill over into politics.

One reason Percy argued people enjoy disaster more than they let on is that in moments of excitement and disaster, like the ex-suicide, they become dispensed from their old activities. In that moment, their relations to other people change; community becomes a possibility. Percy used the example of a commuter on a train to explore this. Consider an ordinary commuter's situation, riding on the eight-fifteen morning train through Metuchen, New Jersey. He is in the city, but not really there. As Percy put it, the fact of commuting erects a "partition" between those passing through and those that actually live there. The commuter takes this train every day with the same people, but no one speaks to the strangers beside them. Outside forces can change this, though:

It is only in the event of a disaster, the wreck of the eight-fifteen, that one is *enabled* to discover his fellow commuter as a comrade; thus, the favorite scene of novels of good will in the city: the folks who discover each other and help each other when disaster strikes (MB, p. 87).

The fact that this describes a cliché of film, television, and novel plots does nothing to diminish the reality of the change that occurs when something turns out wrong and strangers find themselves forced to work together to escape, survive, or, in less drastic situations, simply pass the time until help arrives. Being thrown into comradeship by circumstance is not usually the basis for genuine friendship, however. It may collapse the usual boundaries that stand between people in ordinary life, but almost always falters when the moment of need passes.

There is a paradox of choice here that requires some discussion. Percy emphasized that often people feel at a loss in relation to the very freedom and wide-ranging choice available in their surroundings. Middle-class life in the US allows for the consumption of a tremendous array of relatively inexpensive on-demand media; the ability to instantaneously communicate with friends, acquaintances, and even strangers; access to a wide range of educational and cultural opportunities; and the opportunity to pursue a decently paying and physically undemanding, if not always particularly engrossing, form of work. None of these possibilities for consumption or interaction alleviates our alienation. But the fact remains that day after day, our society forces us to choose which path to take. The necessity of making a living compels us to work, but no authoritative pattern in our society tells us what to do, or how to cope with this range of choice. In a world of near-endless possibilities, often the temporary *loss* of such endless options comes as a peculiar kind of relief from our everyday alienation.

The problem remains deeper, though. Communities born out of emergency or necessity all too often fade when either the crisis recedes or even when terrible circumstances become the new normal and our alienation creeps back in. Nowhere does he explore this more pointedly than in his many observations on the nature of war as a possible source of escape from boredom and alienation. We cannot exempt ourselves from this analysis: whether we consider nuclear terrorism or contemplate the eventuality of great power war, the specter of destruction remains, making it extremely important as a window into the political importance of catastrophe.

WAR AS AN ANTIDOTE TO ALIENATION

War is in some respects the ultimate "bad environment." Percy argued that even in our comfort-obsessed bourgeois world, war retains certain appeals for some people. Consider the usual assumptions bourgeois people of whatever political persuasion make about war today: most scholars who study war have little appreciation for Percy's idea of alienation, and seem to ignore the idea that people often feel good in materially bad environments. Normally, modern people conceive of war in various rational ways: as tragic, but necessary; the destructive product of miscalculation, but largely unavoidable; or perhaps as the foolish or inhumane acts of a few against the unenlightened majority's real interests. It seems no exaggeration to say that people who follow this reasoning would conclude that only the mentally ill would value war as a possible path out of whatever bothers them about their own society.

Understanding war's appeal in terms of alienation and boredom, the first and perhaps most obvious source of its allure must rest in the excitement it generates, an energy that defies the objective-material understanding of the human being. Consider first Binx Bolling's claim that the only time he ever felt lifted out of his everydayness was when he was shot in the Korean War, or Percy's recollection that his Uncle Will was happy on December 7, 1941, and sad again when he realized he was too old to fight (MG, p. 145; MB, p. 4). This theme recurs constantly in Percy's writings, perhaps most directly in a brief exchange between Tom More and an elderly World War II veteran in TS. After recounting some of the local history of the Civil War and waiting until his niece Lucy leaves the room,

> the uncle leans close and won't let me go.
> "You know what they're always saying about war being hell?" he asks.
> "Yes."
> He leans closer. "That's a lot of horseshit."
> "Is that right?"
> "Let me tell you something. I never had a better time in my life than in World War Two" (TS, p. 142).

In the context of the story, Percy implied something was disordered about this situation, but *not* with the characters that state their love of war; he seemed intent on forcing his readers to confront the love of war and man's reasons for embracing it as an escape from ordinary life. The fact is that those with no exposure to war disbelieve in the possibility that people might enjoy it.

Percy also emphasized the ways that war fills in the emptiness of ordinary life by granting the aimless a purpose and the alienated a concrete, relational role in which to live. Moving from a world of strangers to one of comradeship helps alleviate loneliness. Percy used the backdrop of the American Civil War to note these themes. That war, fought for the soul and direction of a nation, inspired unprecedented sacrifices (SSL, pp. 72–73). One of the attractions war holds is the meaning and self-understanding it brings to the participants' lives. In describing the enduring fascination related to the American Civil War, he wrote:

> Yet, with all the horror, or perhaps because of it, there was always the feeling then, and even now as we read about it, that the things a man lived through were somehow twice as real, twice as memorable as the peace that followed. … In the ordeal the man himself seemed to become more truly himself, revealing his character or the lack of it, than at any time before or after. If a man was secretly cowardly or secretly brave, stupid or shrewd, that was what he was shown to be. The War infallibly discovered his hidden weakness and his hidden strength (SSL, pp. 74–75).

Thus, in Percy's view, war can serve as a kind of testing ground for human virtue and vice, or a place of self-discovery or self-disclosure. In times of comfort and peace, the implication follows that we do not easily learn things about ourselves that struggle reveals. Small wonder, then, that alienation and boredom find such frequent expression in literature and drama centered in affluent suburbs.

In TS, Father Rinaldo Smith explained his attitudes as a young man from New Orleans visiting Germany. Smith bitterly criticized the phoniness of his home, the home of "let the good times roll, which masked a cold-blooded marriage of moneymaking and social climbing, rotten politics and self-indulgence" (TS, p. 243). Smith's account of his parents and home excoriates the weakness and ill-defined purposes of living in the inter-war years as an American in a good suburb. Smith marveled at his experience in Germany in part because, through his friendship with the officer cadet Helmut Jäger, he found something entirely new, what a life with warlike purpose might entail:

I was aware of a serious and absolute dedication in him which I had never encountered before. He showed me his SS officer's cap with its German eagle and death's-head. It dawned on me that he meant it. He was ready to die. I had never met anyone ready to die for a belief. ... He was planning for war even then. Who could I compare him to? An American Eagle Scout? No, because even a serious Eagle Scout is doing scouting on the side, planning a career in law, insurance, whatever. Certainly death is the farthest thing from his mind. (TS, pp. 247–48).

Smith confesses that if he were German (and implicitly, even if he knew the way World War II would unfold), he would still have joined Helmut and the SS to pursue that life filled with martial purpose (TS, pp. 248–49). Percy asked his readers to contemplate the uncomfortable possibility that some of us would make a similar choice, not so much out of racism or the desire for political glory, but rather as a means of escape from our everyday alienation.

We need not contemplate such extremes to see Percy's point: if alienation rests primarily in our sense of misplacement and purposeless in relation to other people and the places which we inhabit. Catastrophe lowers the barriers between individuals and strips away our abstracted awareness of ourselves as separate from our environment: at least for as long as it lasts, disaster dispenses us from carrying much of the emotional baggage with which the alienated self commonly lives (MB, pp. 83–84). As a kind of extended disaster, war shatters many of the barriers between individuals that exist in civilian life. Moreover, those people that find peacetime life unsatisfying because of their own needs for struggle and violence—the man like Will Barrett's father, who was "born with a love of death and death-dealing," but had "no enemies"—find release in war (SC, p. 146).

Percy's thinking on this point poses troubling questions for individuals who hope to eliminate war, but also for those who think of violence as an aberration. It is certainly possible for such theorists to attempt reductive explanations of why we wish for catastrophe and war, but all of those would point to the disorder of the individual caused by bad environmental or social inputs. Instead, by inverting the usual scientific hypothesis, the desire for violence will always be with us. Will Barrett's question about what individuals in a mild bourgeois society do when they have a love of death provides some insight as a starting point. Unless moderated by some other force, presumably this sort of person commits suicide (as Will Barrett's father did), or turns to a life of violence against others (SC, pp. 146–49).

Percy would probably suggest such thinking may help explain the prevalence of affluent children of the Western world joining radical or revolutionary causes, and perhaps give some insight into the prevalence of nihilistic terrorism of various kinds since the dawn of the Industrial Revolution.

Percy was more concerned with the latent psychological and moral dispositions prevalent in society that might encourage the love of war than he was with any high-level political explanation of why nations make war. Indeed, when discussing the causes of war, Percy regularly dealt with it through *reductio ad absurdum*. Consider the following question from LC:

> (a) Will World War III happen absurdly, by an accident in a purely technological, sexually liberated age, e.g., by computer malfunction, misinformation, misbehavior by a small-time Qaddafi madman?
>
> or (b) Will World War III erupt because of the suppressed fury of the autonomous self, disappointed now even in the erotic, that demoniac spirit which is overtly committed to peace and love but secretly desires war and apocalypse and nourishes hatred of all other selves and perhaps of its own self most of all? (CHECK ONE) (LC, p. 192).

Taking the satire with a grain of salt as we might, this line of reasoning might nevertheless lead us to question whether the objective-material hypotheses that drive most scholarship on war do not miss something about the underlying desires and motives that make war thinkable in the first place. War may be irrational or wasteful in some objective-material sense, but decrying it on those terms may miss the point. We ought to—like the depressed person—invert the normal hypotheses about what makes war so common in our world: it may or may not be that wars happen so often because nations fall into irreconcilable clashes over interest, but there may be some value in pondering whether the desire for escape from normal social order through the violence of war does not make the recourse to conflict more *likely*.

Yet, the central difficulty remains the fact that people are reticent to confront our tendencies directly. These arguments suggest at least part of the reason we choose not to confront the fact that our age "is the most scientifically advanced, savage, democratic, inhuman, sentimental, murderous century in human history" (SSL, p. 309). Or rather, we choose not to confront this in a clear-eyed manner: indeed, perhaps because of how difficult it is to portray this easily in the present, Percy resorted to a science fiction fable in LC to explore this point most clearly. In it, he argued our sentimental, alienated, potentially murderous nature would be the first and most alarming thing an alien species might notice about us (LC, pp. 206–217). We need not agree with the extremity of this claim, but failing to acknowledge the persistent appeals of war does real damage to our ability to understand political life.

POLITICS AND THE ESCAPE FROM THE NORMAL

Percy's observations about the attraction of catastrophe may sometimes seem hyperbolic, but they make an important point. The fact we cannot forego the allure of enviously dreaming about and even hoping for disaster bears political importance. To some degree, the permanence of these desires provides justification for our own tendencies to detach and flee the real, fragile, and all-too-flawed communities within which we actually must live. Percy's characters often exhibit a detachment from their family, neighbors, friends, and colleagues that seems to flow naturally from their unease with the world as it is and their anticipation that things might fall apart.

Percy's works offer many examples where individuals attempt to satisfy their longings with theory or affiliation to different ideals or new communities and how the love of apocalypse plays a part in them. For the apostle of scientism, like Aristarchus Jones in LC, who proposed that the survivors of Earth's final war form a colony on Jupiter's moon Europa, the possibility of renewing the existing society holds no appeal. Instead, Jones emphasizes the possibility of departure from the old way of things:

> With a bit of luck, we can colonize Europa in much the same way as Europe colonized the New World, *except that*—and here is the exciting part!—there is no reason why we cannot develop a society ... based on reason and science, and do so without repeating the mistakes of the past, for example, the Dark Ages, two thousand years of Plato and Judaism and Christianity—a sexually free and peace-loving society where the sciences and arts can flourish freed from the superstitions and repressions of religion (LC, p. 246).

Perhaps the appeal of disaster at its extreme rests in this hope for a new order, purged of the previous beliefs we have come to know.

Percy emphasized that the aspiration to change the world through or after apocalypse always glosses over the human cost of these endeavors. In the story given above, Aristarchus Jones planned to abandon all those damaged by the radiation to their fate on Earth. The abstract hope to redeem the world trumps such "petty" considerations. The pretention to being able to control people and events sufficiently well to transcend the old order dies hard: readers might be repulsed and amused by Percy's depiction of Lance Lamar's deranged, fascistic hope for revolution, but Percy implied that despite Lamar's insanity, it is almost certain that someone dreams in a similar manner. Any inquiry into politics must take these thoughts seriously because, sooner or later, people will act on these desires.[3]

Notes

1. On this, see Mosse 1990. Mosse strives to explain the way soldiers saw value in the war as a consciously constructed myth, but Percy might lead us to rethink this point.
2. Another example where Binx is dispensed from alienation through violent accident comes during Binx's drive with Sharon Kincaid, when they have an accident and Sharon cares for him (MG, pp. 124–128).
3. This is not an idle speculation. At the fringes of our politics today, the "alternative right" culture embodies virtually all of what Percy attributed to Lance Lamar. For one influential member of this subculture, see Donovan 2013; 2016.

References

Donovan, Jack. 2013. *The Way of Men*. Cascadia: Dissonant Hum.
———. 2016. *Becoming a Barbarian*. Cascadia: Dissonant Hum.
Mosse, George. 1990. *Fallen Soldiers*. Oxford: Oxford University Press.
Percy, Walker. 1998. *The Moviegoer*. New York: Vintage.
———. 1999. *The Last Gentleman*. New York: Picador.
———. 1999. *Love in the Ruins*. New York: Picador.
———. 2000. *The Message in the Bottle*. New York: Picador.
———. 1999. *Lancelot*. New York: Picador.
———. 1999. *The Second Coming*. New York: Picador.
———. 1983. *Lost in the Cosmos*. New York: Farar, Straus, & Giroux.
———. 1985. *Conversations with Walker Percy*. Ed. Lewis A. Lawson and Victor A. Kramer. Jackson: University Press of Mississippi.
———. 1999. *The Thanatos Syndrome*. New York: Picador.
———. 2000. *Signposts in a Strange Land*. Ed. Patrick Samway, S. J. New York: Picador.
———. 1993. *More Conversations with Walker Percy*. Ed. Lewis A. Lawson and Victor A. Kramer. Jackson: University Press of Mississippi.

Name Index[1]

[1] Note: Page numbers followed by 'n' refer to notes.

© The Author(s) 2018
L. Marsh (ed.), *Walker Percy, Philosopher*,
https://doi.org/10.1007/978-3-319-77968-3

271

Subject Index[1]

[1] Note: Page numbers followed by 'n' refer to notes.

© The Author(s) 2018
L. Marsh (ed.), *Walker Percy, Philosopher*,
https://doi.org/10.1007/978-3-319-77968-3

275

Printed in the United States
By Bookmasters